The Shearers

Evan McHugh is a journalist who has written for newspapers, television and radio. His previous books include *The Stockmen: The Making of an Australian Legend*, *Outback Stations*, *Bushrangers*, *The Drovers*, *Birdsville*, *Outback Pioneers*, *Outback Heroes* and *Shipwrecks: Australia's Greatest Maritime Disasters*. Evan's book about true crime in the outback, *Red Centre, Dark Heart*, won the Ned Kelly Award for best non-fiction in 2008. He lives with his wife at Lake Macquarie, New South Wales.

The Shearers

The story of Australia, told from the woolsheds

Evan McHugh

VIKING
an imprint of
PENGUIN BOOKS

VIKING

UK | USA | Canada | Ireland | Australia
India | New Zealand | South Africa | China

Penguin Books is part of the Penguin Random House group of companies whose addresses can be found at global.penguinrandomhouse.com.

Penguin Random House Australia

First published by Penguin Group (Australia), 2015

1 3 5 7 9 10 8 6 4 2

Text copyright © Evan McHugh, 2015

The moral right of the author has been asserted.

All rights reserved. Without limiting the rights under copyright reserved above, no part of this publication may be reproduced, stored in or introduced into a retrieval system, or transmitted, in any form or by any means (electronic, mechanical, photocopying, recording or otherwise), without the prior written permission of both the copyright owner and the above publisher of this book.

Cover and text design by John Canty © Penguin Group (Australia)
Photography copyright as acknowledged
Cover photograph by Scott Bridle
Back cover photograph by Chantel McAlister
Typeset in Caslon Pro by John Canty
Colour separation by Splitting Image Colour Studio, Clayton, Victoria
Printed and bound in Australia by Griffin Press, an accredited ISO AS/NZS 14001 Environmental Management Systems printer.

National Library of Australia
Cataloguing-in-Publication data:

McHugh, Evan, author.
The Shearers / Evan McHugh.
ISBN: 9780670078158 (paperback)
Subjects: Sheep-shearing–Australia.
Sheep shearers (Persons) –Australia.
Wool industry–Australia.
Country life–Australia.

636.31450994

penguin.com.au

MIX
Paper from responsible sources
FSC® C009448

TO ALL THE MEN AND WOMEN OF THE SHEDS

Contents

1	CLICK GO THE SHEARS	*1*
2	THE RISE OF THE MACHINES	*30*
3	SHEARERS UNITE!	*37*
4	THE YEAR OF LIVING DANGEROUSLY	*48*
5	THE RISE OF A LEGEND	*90*
6	FIRE AND BLOOD	*102*
7	RISE OF THE MIDDLEMEN	*118*
8	THE GOLDEN FLEECE	*137*
9	A MATTER OF SURVIVAL	*178*
10	SUNDAY TOO FAR AWAY	*194*
11	WHATEVER MAKES IT EASIER	*224*
12	WOOL IS DEAD. LONG LIVE WOOL.	*239*

Glossary	*256*
Shearing Hall of Fame Citations	*262*
Shearing Records	*285*
References	*288*

I

CLICK GO THE SHEARS

(1788–1885)

Every year, in late January, the eyes of the tennis world turn to Melbourne for the Australian Open. International tennis stars, past greats, eager spectators and the global media gather for one of the most glamorous events on the sporting calendar. It never fails to provide its fair share of drama and spectacular action. But it's a safe bet that not much thought is given to the tennis ball that is thrown into the air, ready to be served, at the beginning of each game, let alone what it's made of. At the top of its arc, ball meets racquet, and minute filaments burst into the air at the point of contact. They slowly settle to the ground, at the end of a 35 000-kilometre journey that has taken them from one side of the world to the other and back again, and has at times involved plenty of action and drama of its own.

Those tiny filaments are wool, used by the Winterbotham, Strachan and Playne textile company in Gloucestershire, England, to make the felt that is in turn used to make tennis balls. In this case, the company uses a coarse wool sourced from New Zealand. However, it also uses fine merino wool from an Australian sheep station to make billiard-table cloth that is regarded as some of the best in the world. The company closely guards the details of its source but it has been buying wool from Australia for well over a century.

The reality is that wool is never far from any of us. It clothes, insulates, carpets, fireproofs and more. It has inspired artists, writers and filmmakers. For more than 150 years it has been the backbone of the Australian economy. It has also been the foundation for much of the Australian way of life, be it financial, social or cultural.

Mention that you're writing a book about shearers and you'll be surprised how many people will tell you about their connections with wool. One friend of mine used to be a cocky farmer and shore thousands of his own sheep. Others grew up on sheep properties. Even the bloke at the local boat chandlery turned out to be an ex wool-classer. As it happens, some of my own earliest memories are of the smells and sounds of the woolshed on my great-uncle's property at Lake Bathurst, near Goulburn. My grandmother grew up on her parents' sheep property not far away.

Up until 1998, even the money people earned paid tribute to wool. The $2 note (now replaced by a coin) carried the image of a merino sheep and early wool pioneer John Macarthur. Before that, from 1938 until decimal currency was introduced in 1966, the Australian shilling bore the image of Hallmark, the grand champion ram at the Royal Sydney Show in 1932.

For much of its history Australia has been described as riding on the sheep's back. Leaving aside the difficulties implicit in such a mode of transport, this perspective also ignores the group of people, mostly unsung, who did much more of the heavy lifting than any of the sheep they shore. If Australia rode on anyone's back, it was on the aching, creaking, flexing spines of Australian shearers. Some people love them, others regard them as a necessary evil, and they've even been referred to as the scum of the earth, yet there's one thing about shearers that's undeniable: their capacity for sheer hard work. Without them, wool would not have achieved all that it has, both in Australia and around the world, and Australia wouldn't have become the nation it is today.

Along the way, shearers contributed to the events that led to the formation of both the Labor and National parties. Notions such as the basic wage, union membership and collective bargaining, and mandated working hours such as the 38-hour week sprang from the epic struggles between shearers and their employers. Their activities may even have inspired Australia's national song, 'Waltzing Matilda', which was written on a Queensland sheep station.

And while shearers embraced the concept of union solidarity and the sense of mateship that went with it, they also cultivated a work ethic that valued individual achievement. They were fiercely competitive and intensely proud of their status as the elite among rural workers. Australia is often characterised as a classless society but, in subtle ways, social distinctions abound. Shearers may not look down on other rural workers, but plenty of rural workers look up to them or aspire to be them.

When starting work on this book, I made the mistake of associating hard physical work with low intellectual capacity. It wasn't long before I had to reconsider. Shearers may not be the best-educated people you might meet, although record-breaker Dwayne Black (see 'Shearing Records' on page 285) put his law studies on hold because he could make more money shearing), but those I encountered were consistently intelligent, articulate and, once they realised you were genuinely interested in what they had to say, open and honest in describing their lives and experiences.

I eventually discovered that while brute force can achieve much, willpower can achieve even more. It comes down to a variation on the saying 'when the going gets tough, the tough get going'. For shearers, there's a point when the body says 'enough', after which it takes pure determination to keep working. If you're not up to it, there's nowhere to hide in a shearing shed.

Shearing is a rough-and-tumble life but it's one that inspires genuine respect. Anyone who can endure shearing anything like 100 sheep a day, day after day, deserves nothing less. For an idea of what complete exhaustion looks like, look no further than Andrew Chapman's image of shearers at the end of a run in the picture section.

However, gruelling physical labour is only part of it; the shearers' story is also mixed with drama and humour. When they dug in and fought for their rights, they showed just how tough they can be. But even then, when the pressure was on, they demonstrated a sense of humour that has come to epitomise what it means to be Australian. All of which has made telling their story fascinating, entertaining and surprising in more ways than one.

***

In the early years of the Australian colonies, shearing as an occupation didn't exist. The majority of the motley assortment of sheep accumulated by the First Fleet as it made its way to Sydney Cove died shortly after arrival in January 1788. Governor Phillip reported in July of that year that all of his sheep were dead, and most of those owned by the government as well. So the demand for shearers was limited at best.

Nevertheless, within a few short years, settlers with expertise in woolgrowing (among them John Macarthur and Reverend Samuel Marsden) were bringing Spanish merino sheep to Australia and establishing the foundations of the Australian wool industry.

Not that there wasn't considerable room for improvement. In 1802, sheep were yielding between 1.5 and 2.5 kilograms of wool. In modern times rams may yield as much as 20 kilograms, with top ewes producing from 7 to 10 kilograms.

As for shearers for the newly arrived flocks, if the owners of the sheep didn't do the shearing themselves (as evidence suggests some did), they were drawn from the ranks of convicts, transported for anywhere between seven years and life mostly for trivial offences (serious offences such as murder were punishable by death). On arrival the convicts were assigned to landowners who were required to feed, clothe and accommodate them according to rules laid out by the government. The standard weekly ration became infamous as eight, ten, two, and a quarter: 8 pounds or 3.6 kilograms of flour, 10 pounds or 4.5 kilograms of meat, 2 pounds or just under a kilogram of sugar and a quarter of a pound or 110 grams of tea.

The convicts were, in effect, slave labour. As the words of the convict folk song 'Van Diemen's Land' suggest, they were treated no better than animals:

> The first day that we landed here upon that fatal shore
> The squatters came around us, full forty score or more.
> They ranked us up like horses and they sold us out of hand
> And they yoked us up to ploughing frames to plough
>   Van Diemen's Land.

The shearing such unfortunate people were required to perform was done with blade shears, machine shearing not becoming a commercial reality until the 1890s. Blade shears were slightly less sophisticated than a modern pair of garden shears. Two opposed blades about 175 millimetres long clipped the wool as they were opened and closed by hand. A leather strap (the driver) held the blades onto the shearer's hand so that control was maintained as the blades were squeezed and released while being pushed through the fleece. A cork or wood knocker stopped the blades closing completely (which would cause the points to snag in the wool and remain closed). The blades were kept sharp with the aid of a grindstone and if sharp enough could slice through wool rather than clip it.

The technique for blade shearing has changed very little since the times when sheep were first bred for wool, probably in Iran around 6000 BC (they are thought to have been domesticated for meat and skins in Mesopotamia around 5000 years earlier, in 11 000 BC). As one modern blade shearer described it: 'You get your shears, you get your sheep, you make a hole in the wool and you go from there.' When a learner is wielding the blades, the more common term to describe the process is tomahawking, suggesting the wool is hacked off, rather than neatly shorn.

Most historic images of blade shearing in Australia and overseas reveal no uniform process or location for the activity. Sheep are shorn indoors and outdoors, with the shearers in a multitude of different positions, both standing and sitting. There's no structured work environment involving pens, chutes and the 'board', the designated shearing area. Sheep are shorn wherever the shearer chooses. In some images, more than one shearer works on the same sheep.

In the early days in the Australian colonies shearing wasn't a specialised occupation. Most sheep stations were labour intensive, given that much of the labour was essentially free, and many rural properties were inadequately fenced, which meant that shepherds were needed to keep watch over flocks and to protect them from attacks from escaped convicts, Aboriginal people displaced from their land and food resources, and wild dingoes. With so many workers on hand, shearing was simply part of the duties of the existing workforce. In 1817, for example, there was this advertisement in the *Sydney Gazette*:

> SHEPHERD WANTED. A sober steady man capable of undertaking the Care of an extensive Flock of Sheep, must be thoroughly acquainted with their various Diseases, and also understand Shearing, will meet with extremely liberal Encouragement by making immediate application to S. TERRY, Pitt Street.

In 1819, the *Hobart Town Gazette* also advertised for 'Two steady Men, as Shepherds, who understand Shearing, and are capable of the Care and Management of Sheep'.

In Tasmania, being a shepherd was not for the faint-hearted. As large tracts of land were granted to companies and individuals seeking to establish sheep runs, the Indigenous people of the region were displaced across large areas. In the north-west the Aboriginal population was able to retaliate from forests so thick it once took surveyor Henry Hellyer eight hours to travel just a kilometre.

Many shepherds became so fearful of attacks they abandoned their flocks. Settlers threatened to leave their land if the government didn't protect them. Some northern Tasmanian woolsheds were built in solid stone, to afford protection from spears. They were also equipped with slits in their walls through which guns could be fired upon attackers. In later years, similar arrangements were put in place at woolsheds on western Queensland stations, such as Carandotta, now on Alexandria Station on the Queensland–Northern Territory border.

Not all the woolgrowers were so daunted. Among the settlers in Tasmania in the 1820s was one of the most significant figures in the early development of the Australian wool industry, and one of the least known.

Born in Glasgow, Scotland, in 1784, Eliza Forlong was the wife of Glasgow wine merchant John Forlong. In the early years of their marriage, the couple lost four of their six children to tuberculosis. Heeding medical advice to seek a warmer climate for their family, Eliza and John decided to move to New South Wales and start a sheep operation.

While John ran the business, Eliza embarked on a tour of Saxony (now part of Germany), walking nearly 2500 kilometres purchasing Saxon merino sheep, reputedly even better than the Spanish merino. In Leipzig, Eliza and her sons, William and Andrew, studied all aspects of sheep and wool production. Eliza ranged far and wide buying sheep, often alone and on foot, paying for the sheep with gold sewn into the hems of her skirts. She attached her own ear tags to the sheep she bought so they could be collected later.

She and her sons then gathered up their flock and walked them to the port of Hamburg. In 1829 William boarded the ship *Clansman* with the sheep, bound for New South Wales, while Eliza and Andrew continued selecting sheep. As luck would have it, on its voyage the *Clansman* called at Hobart to resupply. There Governor Arthur took one look at the sheep and offered William 1100 hectares of land if he disembarked in Tasmania.

William accepted and soon settled at Kenilworth, just north of Campbell Town in the centre of the island. Eliza and the rest of the family joined him in 1831. In 1835, the property was sold and the family relocated to Victoria, where Eliza died near Euroa in 1859, at Seven Creek Station.

Most of the Saxon merinos stayed in Tasmania where, to quote from the plaque on the statue erected in Eliza's honour on the main road through Campbell Town: 'Direct descendants of Eliza's sheep still roam the pastures in the Campbell Town district. They produce some of the world's finest wool, for which the Midlands of Tasmania has become famous.'

The significance of Eliza's contribution is brought home by another inscription on the plaque:

> UNVEILED BY PAOLO ZEGNA DI MONTE RUBELLO
> CHAIRMAN
> ERMENEGILDO ZEGNA GROUP – ITALY
> 19 APRIL 2013

The head of one of the world's most famous suit manufacturers (counting such luminaries as former Australian prime minister Paul Keating among its patrons) felt it worth travelling to Campbell Town from the other side of the world to pay tribute to a woman who died over 160 years ago but whose wool has contributed in no small measure to his company's success.

Today, the region is still a major centre in the Australian wool industry, and has produced generations of renowned shearers who have ranged across Australia, as detailed in subsequent chapters.

At the time, the Forlongs were just part of a wave of settlement that swept over inland Australia. The inability of government to control the acquisition of land by simply taking possession of it was a property bonanza rarely seen anywhere in the world. In 1831, George Ranken, Commissioner of Crown Lands, described the rush: 'They were pouring across the frontiers in scores, north, south and west. The Governor could not have prevented this, all the police and military in Australia could not have guarded an open frontier of 500 miles [800 kilometres]. The trespassers had found a new name for themselves – squatters.'

The squatters brought with them a boom in sheep numbers and quickly established wool as the foundation of the Australian economy. Soon, however, there was a shortage of people able to shear. In 1837 some shearers were being paid 20 shillings (in the currency of the time there were 20 shillings to the pound and 12 pence to the shilling) to shear 100 sheep.

Even at that price, the quality of shearers was mixed. In 1840 woolgrower Phillip Russell wrote to his brother at Geelong:

> I was glad to learn the Sheep Shearing was progressing, tho' not quite so rapid as you could wish . . . I am sorry to find the men lately sent have turned out such blacquards, but a determination on your part to make them do their duty will I have no doubt shew them the necessity of complying with the terms of the agreement; it might certainly prove advantageous to hold out some inducement of an additional pecuniary nature to those who behave well, but the evil disposed I would by no means give into.

The boom years soon turned to bust, and in 1841, with a depression leaving many unemployed, shearers were being paid 10 shillings per 100 sheep, half what they'd been getting four years earlier.

In her diary of 1843, Anne Drysdale, a partner in Boronggoop Station, in the Port Phillip district of Victoria, described what shearing of the time entailed:

> Tuesday, 12 October 1843: All the shearers arrived in the morning, and were engaged the whole day making a washing place, which consists of logs or spars put out in the river between 2 trees; the spars form 2 pens, into the first of which the sheep are flung and allowed to swim awhile; they are then pushed by a forked stick under the middle spar, and men with flat sticks rub off the dirt, after which they swim out.

In early November she wrote: 'Yesterday the wool shed was finished. It looks very well: 30 feet [9 metres] in length, by 14 [4.2 metres] wide; a skilling or verandah along one side, under which some sheep are to be placed all night; that they may be ready to shear in the morning, otherwise they would be so wet.'

In mid-November:

> Yesterday our shearing was concluded: the number shorn was 2060. We had all along been afraid that Vere, Armstrong's wife, would be confined before the shearing was over, which would have been unfortunate, as she is cook for the whole establishment; but she continued quite well and active the whole time until yesterday afternoon, when she took ill. Armstrong rode to Corio and brought Dr. Shaw, who arrived at tea. At 5 o'clock this morning, a fine boy, the 6th boy and 7th child, was added to the family, and she (Vere) is doing nicely.

Drysdale's account touches on many of the aspects of shearing that influenced its conduct for decades after. The washing of sheep was desirable to remove dirt and grease and make them easier to shear. It also made the clip – the total amount shorn for the season – lighter and cheaper to transport and more valuable to sell. As for the question of whether sheep are wet or not, and whether they can therefore be shorn, that has exercised the debating skills of shearers and woolgrowers ever since. Drysdale recognises the importance of the cook to the operation – which holds true today – but the fact that the cook in question worked up to the day before she gave birth to her seventh child highlights the lack of reasonable conditions of employment at the time, particularly for a woman in the final stages of her pregnancy.

The description also reveals the emergence of workers whose profession was 'shearer', although that might include skills in washing sheep and possibly building shearing sheds. However, it's a shift away from the job title 'shepherd' that includes the ability to shear. The statement 'the shearers arrived in the morning' also makes clear that they were itinerant workers, rather than permanent employees.

Convict transportation having largely ceased by the 1840s, most of the shearers were either free labourers (in the sense that they weren't assigned convicts) or convicts working out the last years of their sentences. In some areas, Aboriginal people found accommodation with the Europeans who had usurped their title to the land, and were employed as both shepherds and shearers, a permanent workforce who retained connections to their traditional land and therefore were readily available when required.

In South Australia, to which many German families migrated to escape religious persecution in their homeland, doubtless bringing more Saxon merinos and sheep-handling skills with them, women were employed as shearers. Chinese people were also used on many properties.

In 1847, Victorian squatter Alexander Mollison described his shearing operation in a letter of 28 November:

> I returned about three days ago from my station called Pyalong, about thirty miles hence, my sheep being all stationed there now. I do not bring them to Coliban [from where he was writing] to shear as formerly, but have built a shearing shed at Pyalong. I began rather earlier in the season this year, and the weather being fine, I finished this somewhat heavy task in four weeks. About 500 or 550 sheep were shorn every day, and the wool packed in bales ready for shipment. It is classed by a wool sorter. That is, each fleece when shorn is carried by a lad to the sorter who removes any stained or inferior parts, rolls it up and sends it to a bin in which are other fleeces of the same quality only. Three men are employed at the press. Two men bring sheep to the shed, take away the shorn sheep, sweep, and water the yards in which they are kept.
>
> Ten shearers were employed. We began at six o'clock and generally worked until half past six, when the shearers were dismissed to their huts. After that a good deal remained to be done by the master and overseer, and I was glad to smoke a quiet pipe at nine and tumble into bed. Another party of eight men under an overseer were employed at the same time in washing the sheep. They begin [sic] about a week before the shearers. The shed at Pyalong holds 600 sheep in pens or enclosures, separated from the shearing floor, wool table, bins, et cetera. When the weather is unsettled the shed is filled at sunset, so that the men are employed, even if it should rain. In the fine weather a few sheep only are housed to preserve their fleece from dew, and these are shorn before breakfast.

* * *

With sheep numbers steadily growing, and with them an insatiable hunger for land, increasingly arid and marginal country was being taken up further and further from the established centres of successful wool production. The pioneers of the 1850s and beyond found to their cost that the arid inland could be merciless with its prolonged droughts, followed at times by floods of biblical proportions.

Most breeds of sheep were unable to endure long periods on poor feed and scarce water. Even the relatively robust merino breeds struggled. They died in their hundreds of thousands, ruining the fortunes of many who greatly overstocked and little understood the carrying capacity of their land. And yet the sunlit plains beckoned, particularly in the north-west of New South Wales, the north of South Australia and almost to the Gulf of Carpentaria in Queensland. If only there were sheep that could survive out there.

Down in what was to become one of the most famed sheep districts in Australia, the Riverina, such sheep were eventually bred. In 1858 George Peppin and his sons took over Wanganella Station, which had been established a few years earlier by mercurial pioneer William Brodribb.

Three years later, the Peppins established a merino stud and set about creating a strain of merino better suited to the rugged conditions of the Australian inland. In 1865, they bought Saxon and Rambouillet merino rams, including one, Emperor, who famously cut more than 11 kilograms of wool. The breeding strategy was relatively simple, as detailed by Fred Peppin:

> We were satisfied with the type of wool that the country would grow, instead of endeavoring to produce what the climate and soil continually fight against. Thus we developed all its good natural tendencies and after the flock had a character of its own, tried experiments on a small scale only, and in such a way that they could do no permanent injury, and abandoned them when they were found not to achieve the desired object.

The result was the mainland equivalent of the success achieved by Eliza Forlong in Tasmania. Accordingly, between Deniliquin and Hay, there's a memorial to the Peppins, just off the highway outside the entrance to Wanganella Station. Beneath a statue of a merino ram the plaque states: 'This memorial commemorates the great contribution this now famous Peppin strain has made to the Australian wool industry, and acknowledges the debt owed to the merino by every Australian.'

In fact, nearly all the merino sheep in mainland Australia have a connection to the Peppin bloodline. The stations around Wanganella are almost all merino studs. Some, such as the adjacent Boonoke, also trace their original ownership to the Peppin family.

The Wanganella memorial provides some statistics on the state of the Australian wool industry in 1861, when the Wanganella stud was established, and 1961, a century later, when Australia still prospered in large part because of wool.

	1861	1961
Sheep population	20 million	153 million
Wool production	30.5 million kg	740 million kg
Wool cut per head	1.5 kg	4.8 kg
Merino wool price average fleece	48 pence per kg	154 pence per kg
Value of wool clip	£6 million	£314 million

Just down the road from Wanganella, at the Conargo Hotel, the walls are covered with photos of champion merino rams that have been bred in the district and gone on to win every trophy in sight.

High on one wall there's a small portrait of George Peppin, full-bearded in middle age with a penetrating look in his eye. Yet not even he could have foreseen the spectacular growth in sheep numbers that took place between his death in 1876 and the 1890s, when the worst drought Australia has ever seen took a heavy toll on an already embattled sheep industry. Nor could he have conceived of the epic struggles that would embroil woolgrowers and shearers as they set about shearing such prodigious numbers of animals.

The same year the Peppin stud was established, there was another development that would profoundly influence the coming struggle between shearers and growers. In 1861, the New South Wales government passed the Masters and Servants Act, which aimed to regulate the relationship between employers and workers. Given that the convict era had effectively ceased, in essence it was an attempt to continue as much of the old system as possible while acknowledging that people had to be paid something (although the Act still didn't apply to Aboriginal workers). It established the rights of a master over his servants, and left the determination of wages and conditions largely to the master's discretion. Wages and conditions for women were even worse than they were for men. Children were paid and treated worst of all.

Rural workers were among the lowest paid of all employees, often because many were remunerated partly in cash and partly in accommodation and rations. As such, there were powerful echoes of the previous relationship between masters and convicts. In his memoir, shearer and union activist Julian Stuart recalled spending part of his childhood on a property that had been established with convict labour. When he went to work as a shearer, he found that 'The ration scale ... eight-ten-two-and-a-quarter ... which was in general use on the stations was identical with that drawn up in the chain-gang days by the British authorities for convicts, assigned servants and ticket-of-leave men.'

Given some shearers were drawn from the ranks of former convicts, or were the children of convicts raised on tales of mistreatment at the hands of callous masters, the continuation of the convict ration scale must have cut deeply.

Elsewhere, more positive developments continued. In 1862, prominent South Australian squatter Thomas Elder (whose land holdings were larger than Scotland, the place where he was born) introduced camels to Australia, bringing with them their 'Afghan' handlers (many were actually from Pakistan and India). Elder is thought to be responsible for the modern wool bale, originally shaped and sized so two could be carried on either side of a camel's hump.

In 1865 the Western Australian Squatting Company started introducing sheep to the north-west of Western Australia. Within three years there were forty-nine runs in WA's north-west. The area was as challenging for woolgrowers as it gets: scorching sun, cyclones and incredible remoteness from facilities and markets. The sheep also had to be particularly hardy. For example, it wasn't possible to shear at the height of summer because of the risk of sheep suffering sunburn. In severe conditions it could kill them.

In such remote locations finding workers was a constant challenge. There, as elsewhere, the benefits of nurturing good relationships with the dispossessed local Aboriginal people were abundant. They combined a ready supply of labour with an intimate knowledge of the land and climate and an ability to detect early signs of drought and flood.

Unfortunately, in Western Australia and elsewhere, Indigenous workers often found the new employment arrangements created new problems. In the late 1860s William Locke, of Victoria's Kotoopna Station (now spelled Kotupna), described the workers from the remaining 144 members of the once-1200-strong Bangerang language group: 'During the shearing season of 1869 about 100 aborigines were employed at the Wyuna station (near Tongala run). These shearers all worked well but drank very hard and had no difficulty in obtaining drink at the shanties and even at many of the public houses.'

John McKenzie, manager of Wyuna, employed ten Aboriginal people as shearers at a paltry rate of 1 shilling per hundred sheep plus rations. He paid others 10 shillings a week and rations for sheep washing. He noted: 'On Saturday, 23 October 1869 at 5pm paid them all off. They went direct to a shanty about three miles [four kilometres] off and on Sunday 24th one of them died drunk, he was one of the best shearers I've had in the shed in the last four years.'

The practice of shearers and farmhands drinking their pay cheques certainly wasn't restricted to Aboriginal people. In the same era James Bonwick noted that some stations organised payment through the nearest publican: 'Who of course never handed over a cent. A man was compelled to stay there and knock his cheque down. If the cheque was drawn on somebody in Sydney, how could a poor devil get away to Sydney – perhaps a four or five hundred mile trip, without a penny?'

Not that the arrangement was always successful for the publican. In one incident, a group of shearers were drinking their cheques but hadn't actually handed them over. They then fell into an argument about who was the fastest cyclist on a fully loaded bicycle. A race was organised, with the shearers' bicycles packed with all their swags and equipment. The publican officiated. He lined them up on their marks, got them set, and go! The shearers tore off at a furious pace, growing smaller and smaller in the distance . . . Eventually they disappeared, they and their cheques never to be seen again.

***

While sheep numbers in Australia were rising rapidly in the 1870s, another subtle but almost as significant agricultural development was also underway. In the 1860s, there was a paltry 30 000 kilometres of fencing in the whole of Australia. During the 1870s, that number rose to 1.2 million kilometres.

The change was in part due to the cessation of convict transportation in the 1860s. Now, instead of having a ready supply of free labourers to work as shepherds, landholders had to pay them. It was cheaper to fence their land.

The consequent fall in the number of people employed in the rural sector also changed the profile of shearers. Where shepherds and other farmhands had been available to handle much of the shearing, now there was a growing seasonal demand for shearers to make up the shortfall.

The combination of increasing sheep numbers and a shrinking permanent workforce gave added impetus to the rise of the professional shearer, either working locally during the shearing season, or ranging further afield to ply his increasingly specialised trade as different regions shore at different times of the year.

One of the signs of the changing times was the first attempt by shearers to organise themselves to negotiate for better pay and conditions. In 1874 a group of fifty-three shearers at Jondaryan woolshed on the Darling Downs in Queensland were organised by shearer Benjamin Graham. Their attempt at forming a union was short-lived as summonses were taken out against them. Under Queensland's Masters and Servants Act, going on strike was a breach of the servant's contract of employment. Workers had to resign first. If they didn't, they could face up to three months in prison if they were absent from work for as little as an hour.

***

The spread of sheep to every state in Australia is well documented, but it's generally believed that the Northern Territory was so unsuited to woolgrowing that it has no shearing history whatsoever. Not so. One of the most remarkable shearing episodes of the 1870s took place in the Top End when two enterprising brothers, Ralph and John Milner, droved between 4000 and 7000 sheep from South Australia up the track for the Overland Telegraph to feed its hungry construction crews. Their journey began in 1868 and took more than two years, during which all but 1000 sheep (merinos) perished and John Milner died after being speared by Aboriginal people at what is now called Attack Creek.

When the sheep arrived in the Top End, they were immediately divided between the telegraph construction camps. Stockman and adventurer Alfred Giles was allocated 300 to take to his camp. In his memoir, *Exploring in the Seventies*, he wrote:

> The sheep, mostly ewes, were small and poor, averaging not more than 30 pounds [13.6 kilograms] dressed weight. I did not attribute their low condition wholly to the distance they had travelled so much as to their being heavily woolled, carrying an 18-month's fleece. The wool was of good quality and staple; the outer, or surface, was frayed and somewhat perished, but considering the inevitable knocking about the sheep had had, this was not to be wondered at.

The problem for Giles was that he had to take his heavily woolled sheep and backtrack 250 kilometres south to Daly Waters, through the tail end of a wet season that was so bad nothing had been heard from his camp for five months. The decision was made to shear the sheep before the journey, and Giles can claim the distinction of describing the first shearing in the Territory. It started on 13 February 1872:

> Shearing in the Northern Territory was a novelty indeed, and among all the Government outfit no such article as sheep-shears was catalogued or thought of. Fortunately, Mr Milner was able to supply a few pairs. Another remarkable fact was that out of more than 50 men in camp only one knew how to shear, and he happened to be the cook. Under his tutelage, four or five men started shearing, or, perhaps, I should say 'tomahawking'. The main thing was to get the wool off. There was no sorting or preparing. It was just chucked over the fence to rot, and would have grieved the squatter's heart.

It took the four or five shearers two weeks to shear their 300, which at five men and twelve days (assuming they took Sundays off) gives an average daily tally of five. Not surprisingly, Giles didn't identify a ringer – the fastest shearer – among the men, but he did recognise that there were considerable delays due to wet weather. The question of wet sheep probably didn't arise, as more often than not the sheep were thoroughly sodden.

Meanwhile, Alfred Giles had high hopes about the potential of the Territory for sheep, and he and others subsequently droved in excess of 20 000 of them to the Top End. Eventually, the heat, high humidity, wild dogs and remoteness from markets defeated them. In 2011 there were estimated to be only 1855 head in the entire Northern Territory.

**

Over in New Zealand, shearers were getting an early start on industrial disputation. In 1873, the record books of a pair of stations recorded that 'Shearers struck for 25 shillings per 100 sheep'. Then, 'Three shearers sacked for refusing to shear.' The record books also carried descriptions for each shearer, such as 'good', 'fair', 'agitator', 'bad influence in shed', 'rough', 'N. G.' (for No Good) and 'N. B. G.' (for No Bloody Good).

The situation was similar in Australia. In 1881, two woolgrowers, Colin Mackenzie and Roscoe Doyle, went into partnership at Weilmoringle Station, in the northern New South Wales inland. Weilmoringle had been running cattle but the new partners turned the property over to sheep and by 1884 had a flock of 40 000 and had built a 48-stand shed. They shore for three months a year, from August to October, with forty shearers. They scoured their wool before having it carted to Bourke, 160 kilometres away.

In 1885 Doyle gave a description of his staffing difficulties to a royal commission on water conservation. 'We get the scum of the earth out in this direction in the wool season and have to pay them high wages,' he said.

This station also ended up employing local Muruwari people. The Aboriginal camp on the station became a permanent community and its people worked as stockmen, fencers, offsiders for bullockies and horse teamsters, shearers, domestics, rouseabouts and station hands.

In *Weilmoringle: A Unique Bi-cultural Community*, Merri Gill, who moved to the station in the 1960s, described the early days of this relationship, which continued until she and her husband sold the property: 'It was the heyday of the big sheep properties and the confluence of the two cultures produced a culture and lore of its own.' *[Reproduced by kind permission of Merri Gill]*

Over in Western Australia, the scene was similar. The northwest had been opened up even further with the exploration of the Kimberley region by John and Alexander Forrest in 1879. As if the West didn't have enough grazing lands, enormous areas tempted the likes of the Duracks and the McDonalds to cross the continent with cattle and sheep to settle the new country.

Once again, Indigenous people provided the labour force. The scene was described by 'Bucolic' in *The West Australian* in 1889:

> During my visit shearing was on and I had the good fortune to see the men at work, 315 able-bodied natives ... one white man, and two Chinamen shear sharpening ... Shearing is done quite as well as by average white men and the sheep get better treatment. The men whilst at work keep up a merry conversation and the utmost good humour prevails. About 1200 sheep are shorn daily, but if it were necessary to make a push a great many more could be got over. In addition to the shearers, a great many old men and boys are employed making up wool and pressing. The wool is all shipped in the grease, and is dumped on the place, ready for shipment.

It's almost as hard to believe that 315 shearers could only manage 1200 a day as it is to believe the cliché about happy smiling natives. Especially when it came to shearing. Among the many difficulties that assailed the shearers of those times were Barcoo rot (scurvy), yolk boils, cuts from burrs that could become infected and even typhoid from poor sanitation. First aid for many injuries was a dab of kerosene. The cure for scurvy was a better diet but the supply of fresh vegetables in remote locations like the Kimberley was practically non-existent.

As for medical attention, at some stations deductions were taken from shearers' pay for a donation to the local hospital. Often the donation was made in the name of the station, rather than the shearers. According to Julian Stuart, some hospitals didn't roll out the red carpet when a shearer needed assistance. He wrote: 'The aggregate of our offerings appeared on the hospital receipts as the station's donation, but if we, who found the money, fell sick, we had almost to crawl on our hands and knees to get hospital treatment.'

The medical treatment for shearers was little different to that given to the sheep. Smaller cuts to the animals could be left but serious cuts required the application of tar, a generic name for substances that ranged from a tar-like unguent to a disinfectant gel. A severe cut was sewn up, often by the shearer who caused it. Worse injuries meant the animal became a 'killer', paid for by the shearer and usually slaughtered for the shearers' mess.

Another difficulty was that different sheep required different shearing techniques. Care had to be taken with older sheep, rams and ewes in lamb. Old sheep have tender skin that tears or cuts easily. Rams can die if they're held in one position too long. Pregnant ewes become uncomfortable and restless or could lose their lamb if held in one position too long or if treated roughly.

Drought could also take its toll. Stuart recalled shearing in 1888:

> Eighty-eight was a bad time for the pastoral workers in Queensland. Daandine, on the Darling Downs, the only shed I got that year, we had to knock off because of the drought. The sheep were too weak to be mustered and the manager sent a lot of us to wire net the creeks and waterholes to keep them from being bogged. Sheep were dying everywhere. Although there were a few union men there, no attempt was made to improve conditions at the shed, which were bad almost beyond description.

Stuart's account highlights one of the key features of shearing in the late nineteenth century. An unpredictable roving workforce travelled far and wide in search of employment, while large stations couldn't be entirely sure if anyone was going to show up to shear their sheep. Some stations required applicants for stands in their sheds to send a £1 bond to ensure they would honour their commitment. If they didn't turn up, they lost their money. Sometimes, though, they arrived to find there was no place for them anyway.

Some station managers also tried to turn cutting costs into an art form. There was nothing they could do about interest rates and rent but they could find any number of ways to reduce the cost of shearing. Shearers' quarters were often notoriously bad. Sheds were dilapidated. Any excuse for raddling or not paying for work was seized upon.

Before work started, shearers were also required to sign a station agreement that generally consisted of an extensive list of rules they were expected to obey. Infringements from poor shearing and cutting sheep to swearing, drinking or even whistling could result in penalties. Illiterate shearers sometimes found that the agreement that was read to them and the one they signed weren't the same, especially when it came to what they were ultimately paid.

Some stations imposed limits on the number of sheep shorn to ensure the quality of the shearing. If a sheep was badly injured or had to be killed, the shearer had to bear the cost. Most stations operated their own store and for shearers it might be the only place where they could obtain basic supplies. Profiteering was rampant, with mark-ups of fifty to one hundred per cent.

These were just a few of the problems that shearers had to deal with, and which contributed to their increasing interest in achieving improvements in their working conditions. Already during the early 1880s, mining and transport unions had started to form, with mixed results as the law and the judiciary combined to crush collective negotiation as a restraint of trade under the old Masters and Servants Act.

In 1885, shearers at Midkin Station, near Moree, organised against a reduction in the shearing rate from 17 shillings and 6 pence to 16 shillings and 8 pence per hundred sheep.

William Spence, who was to become a union organiser and politician, recalled: 'So determined were they, that any man trying to get in on the squatter's rate was promptly dumped into the station water tank. From these men's endeavours a union was formed at Moree, NSW.'

Fortuitously, just a year later Queensland passed the Trade Unions Act. Other states soon followed. The Act was intended to legalise and regulate the financial arrangements of trade groups whose members had achieved a required level of ability in the relevant trade. The idea was that you could say to a shearer: 'Are you a member of the trade union?' If they said yes, you could expect that shearer to have met the union's minimum standards. If they said no, it might mean they weren't good enough for the job you wanted them to do.

However, the legislation failed to recognise what would become known as 'new unionism', or unionism as most people understand it today. This style of unionism embraced differing levels of skill and its main object was the formation of a united front against the real or perceived excesses of employers. In a century where socialism had been championed by the likes of Karl Marx (who died in 1883), new unions also looked beyond the immediate issues of pay and conditions to wider questions of social, cultural and financial justice.

The immediate issues weren't long in coming to the fore. In April 1886, in response to falling wool prices (a consequence of increasing production as sheep numbers continued to grow), woolgrowers in New South Wales advised that there would be a cut in the then shearing rate of 20 shillings per hundred. An advertisement in *The Australasian* broke the news:

> The owners and managers of the undermentioned stations hereby give notice that the price of shearing during the current year will be 17s 6d per 100 sheep, but if any shearer is discharged for wilful bad shearing or other misconduct he shall accept payment at 15s 0d per 100 for all sheep shorn to date of discharge.

Seventeen stations and owners identified themselves in what could be seen as the formation of a cartel whose object was to manipulate the price of labour.

In response, William Spence, who had already formed mining unions in the southern states, was approached to form a union for shearers. He recalled: 'I wrote a letter which was published in the *Ballarat Courier* on 29 May, 1886, urging combination and offering to assist.' Shortly after, Spence was elected chairman of the Amalgamated Shearers Union, which quickly grew to 9000 members in Australia's southern states and in New Zealand.

In January 1887, in Queensland, shearers at Isis Downs formed the Queensland Shearers Union. While the Queensland union wanted better wages and conditions, they also wanted to exclude Chinese and Indigenous workers and passed resolutions to that effect. Eight non-white unionists were exempted by the resolutions, which were renewed in 1890. At the time, Chinese workers were paid as little as 4 shillings and 6 pence per month. Small wonder some employers wanted to continue to employ people under 'freedom of contract' (one defined by the employer), rather than the newly formed union's rules and wage levels.

Down in New South Wales, the woolgrowers may have been surprised at the speed with which shearers organised in the face of a fifteen per cent pay cut. For most stations, the savings were soon outweighed by potentially disruptive strike action and the ill will that ensued. For a station with 100 000 sheep it was at best a saving of £125. When many woolgrowers relented and the shearing rate was returned to 20 shillings per hundred, peace was restored to the woolsheds. However, the battle was far from over.

***

By 1890, a sheep population of nearly 100 million (it peaked at 106 million in 1892) was spread across a third of the Australian continent, from central Queensland to Tasmania, across into South Australia and down the western side of Western Australia. The shearers who shore them travelled by every conceivable means of transport: horse, train, bicycle, paddle-steamer and on foot.

Many stations and shearing sheds were great distances from railway lines or even roads. In the more settled areas of the more populous states, many shearers could work locally and only travelled for more work when the urge took them. However, in the vast outback regions of Queensland, New South Wales, South Australia and Western Australia, even local work involved large distances. Consequently, even good shearers faced long weeks without work as they wandered from shed to shed. When the largely seasonal work came to an end, there was no work at all. The situation was, in short, a shambles for all involved.

Nevertheless, as wool emerged as the premier industry in Australia, the shearer emerged as the embodiment not just of the industry but of a sense of freedom few occupations could equal. Shearers were often more worldly than other rural workers. They were more skilled and physically fitter.

However, opinion was still divided over whether they were heroes or villains. When Charles Bean (journalist and, later, official war historian) interviewed an old-time steamboat captain, Captain Pickhill, about the shearers he had seen in his years plying his trade on the Darling River, Pickhill recalled:

> Lots of those shepherds and shearers near Bourke, were 'old hands' [meaning ex-convicts]. Some of them were decent good fellows; and the rest – well, they were horrible! Unmitigated rascals, fearing neither God nor the devil. The language I have heard in Bourke made a man wonder the heavens did not drop down and crush the fellow. They were great, coarse, horrible brutes of men.

Others took a different view. A German political sociologist, Dr Robert Schachner, went and lived among shearers, miners and factory hands in an attempt to ascertain which of them had the best life. He concluded that shearers had a better standard of living, were better read and were more intelligent. He wrote: 'If the spicy air of the bush gives the shearer new life and energy for thought and reading it is far different in the factory... Scarcely fit to leave school, the boy enters the horrid gloom of the machine rooms... What wonder if his brain dries up?'

In his memoirs Julian Stuart gave a nostalgic view of what it was like to be a shearer, describing a night in the quarters on Northampton Downs, where he and his colleagues were 'disrobing 150 000 jumbucks'. Whistling Dick played on his tin whistle, Bungeye Blake sang, and Piebald Moore and Cabbagetree Capstick told some tales, but it was when Dusty Bob took the floor that Julian paid more attention. He considered Dusty to be 'the most fluent liar that ever crossed the Darling':

> His anecdotes about 'Crooked Mick' began and ended nowhere and made C.M. appear a superman... with feet so big he had to go outside to turn round. It took a large-sized bullock's hide to make him a pair of moccasins [preferred footwear for shearers].

He worked at such a clip that his shears ran hot and sometimes he had half-a-dozen in the water-pot to cool. He had his fads and would not shear in sheds that faced North. When at his top it took three pressers to handle the wool from his blades and they had to work overtime to keep the bins clear. He ate two sheep each meal ... that is, if they were small merinos ... but only one and a half when the ration sheep were Leicester crossbred wethers. His main tally was generally cut out on the breakfast run. Anyone who tried to follow him usually spent the balance of the day in the hut. Between sheds he did fencing. When cutting brigalow posts he used an axe in each hand to save time, and when digging postholes a crowbar in one hand and a shovel in the other.

Stuart also described the different kinds of mateship that existed among shearers. A pen mate, for example, was hardly a mate at all. The shearers drew lots to see which stand they'd get and it was pure luck who they were paired with. However, the two had to cooperate as they went about catching sheep from the same pen.

Then there were grinding mates. As he explained:

In the old blade-shearing days, when the 'keeping' of shears was a large item for the shearer's consideration, it was necessary for each man to have a mate to turn the grindstone for him ... in fact, each pair turned for one another; they were grinding mates and very often it was Hobson's choice on both sides, if you could believe them when they started arguing ... they nearly always did.

Last came real mateship, which according to Stuart was a thing that could last a lifetime but was sometimes difficult to understand:

Two hard old cases, Peter and Fred, mates of long standing, were knocking down their cheques in the good old-fashioned way, and quarrelled about some trifle. It looked as if it would end in a fight to a finish and the fracture of a lifelong friendship, so a bystander tried to act as peacemaker and started to lead Peter away, but was straightaway woodened out by old Fred. The two old battlers, reconciled, went back to the bar to resume the main business of life, cutting out their cheques.

2

THE RISE OF THE MACHINES

(1886–1887)

'Tis early in the morning,
As daylight does appear,
A whistle from the engine
Tells another day is here.
The cook's been up an hour or more
To get the buckets boiled,
So rise my lads and get some scran,
Before you start to toil.

We've travelled o'er the lonely plains
To reach the shearing sheds;
We've camped upon the old bore-drains,
To rest our weary heads
Without a stick to boil a quart,
Without a sheltering tree,
We've started on the track again,
Yes, fearless, bold, and free.

– Robert Matthews, 1908

It's easy for artists and writers to characterise a shearer's life as something idyllic, especially if they lack firsthand experience of it. Right or wrong, at a pivotal point in the history of shearing there appeared a view of it that has become one of the most recognisable in the country. In 1890, Tom Roberts completed *Shearing the Rams*, a painting that romanticises shearing and gives it an almost iconic status. The men are shearing with blades, rouseabouts are rolling fleeces and sweeping locks from the floor, sunlight filters in through the open windows. The work appears to be carried out in a harmonious, healthy atmosphere, although 'utmost good humour' may be going too far.

One shearer is engaged in a nearly superhuman feat, carrying a full-grown ram to the board. In her book *The Shearers*, Patsy Adam-Smith cites a shearer in the 1970s who remarked that Tom Roberts knew nothing about shearing. He maintained that rams were dragged onto the board, rather than carried, and that the shearer pictured wouldn't have lasted long. Not so. In 1890 it was stipulated in many shearing agreements that sheep had to be carried to the board, not dragged.

Such requirements were soon to change. The entire world depicted in Tom Roberts' beloved painting was about to be transformed by machine shearing. Perhaps one of the keys to the artwork's success was the nostalgia that surrounded it only a few years after it was painted.

Yet there are elements that are timeless. One can almost hear and smell Roberts' shearing shed. Timbers well-oiled by thousands of passing sheep shine as though polished. There's an unmistakeable odour of greasy wool, manure, old wood and sweat that rather than being repellent has the earthiness of nature in the raw. There are shouts from youngsters driving in more sheep, the bark of dogs behind them, the complaining bleats of sheep pushing into the pens, the clattering of hoofs on wooden slats. There are sounds of men grunting and straining as they go about their work, shouts of 'sheep-o' when pens empty and 'tar' when a slip of the shears nicks a beast. There is a bellowing like a wounded bull as a shearer stands and gives expression to the pain of straightening his back.

The painting may have become a time capsule of a bygone era but it remains the quintessential image of all that is best in a shearer. Looking at the painting today, one has to remember that it was painted twenty-five years before the slaughter at Gallipoli gave us diggers as the most potent symbol of Australian heroism. Back then, the heroic Australian was often embodied by shearers – strong, independent and free. *Shearing the Rams* is the timeless image that celebrates that status at its greatest height.

Meanwhile, back in the real world, every year, on most properties where sheep are raised and need to be shorn, there is an interruption to the normal routine that is welcomed as a source of excitement and novelty by some and looked upon with trepidation by others. When the shearing teams arrive – shearers, rousies, cooks, pressers, classers and others – there is a shift in the balance of power and the normal daily routine of station life.

Usually, station owners or managers are the masters of all they survey (bank debt notwithstanding). When they make a decision, their orders are unquestioningly obeyed. Any rules they make about how things are to be done are considered law. Even work starts when they decide its starts, ends when they decide it ends.

Then everything changes. What work is done when, and how quickly, is no longer theirs to decide. Whatever equipment is used to process the clip must be fully maintained and ready to go. Even the owner or manager becomes subservient to a new demand: keep the supply of sheep flowing to the shearers' shears no matter what. Even then, if the sheep are wet, the shearers will down tools. And there's nothing the woolgrower can do about it.

One woolgrower's wife rhapsodised to me about the refreshing change that came about during the shearing. For her, it was the best time of the year. Not for her husband. He muttered to himself some words that I couldn't quite catch.

Little wonder that over the years considerable effort has been expended on finding ways to dispense with the services of shearers, or failing that, to greatly reduce the need for them. In the 1800s, industrialisation was transforming workplaces in many industries. Tireless, uncomplaining, submissive machines were replacing their human counterparts by the hundreds. Why not shearers too? Even if they couldn't be dispensed with, many woolgrowers would welcome anything that got the shearing done faster.

The idea had a long gestation. As early as 1846, woolgrower William Russell of Dennistoun, Tasmania, wrote to his brother offering him the use of a steam engine and a novel suggestion: 'Perhaps you might think of shearing your sheep by steam power, when labour is so very high. A plan for the erection can be sent along as a guide to those that may put it up.'

Nothing came of the suggestion and it wasn't until 1866, at Edgarley Station in Victoria, that an inventor named Millear demonstrated a shearing apparatus that resembled modern shearing machines, although the power source was a horse and the sheep was shorn while reclining in a chair. In 1868 the first patent on a shearing machine was taken out by James Higham, a Melbourne printer.

Around this time English mechanic John Howard was experimenting with shearing machines, financed by woolgrower Fred Wolseley. It took the pair until 1885 to come up with a machine that actually worked. It was similar to modern machines, powered by a steam engine with a drive wheel situated above the shearer. The drive wheel connected to a downtube containing rotating threads of animal gut (modern machines use rods) that in turn drove a handpiece that swept a three-pronged cutter back and forth past a row of teeth, thereby shearing the wool.

In April 1887, the Wolseley shearing machine was demonstrated at the Goldsborough and Co. wool store in Sydney. Egyptian shearer

Hassam Ali, an assistant of John Howard, operated the new machine. He was pitted against gun blade shearer Dave Brown. First of all, Brown shore three sheep. Then Ali started his machine and from each of the same three sheep, lo and behold, he removed another kilogram of wool.

The result was compelling, and it spelled the end of blade shearing as the dominant method of shearing sheep. However, the *Sydney Mail* may have gone overboard when it foresaw that 'The introduction of the machine may render the employment of expert shearers unnecessary as it would not require more than a few days to enable any man of ordinary intelligence to learn to shear the sheep properly with machines'.

It's worth noting that while it is generally accepted that machine shears, which operate against the skin of the sheep, usually shear sheep closer, removing around a quarter of a kilogram more wool than blade shears, a good blade shearer can do even better. In his book *Sheep-O!*, A. R. (Bob) Mills described a contest in the 1950s between a machine shearer and a blade shearer that proved it:

> One day, when shearing was in full swing, and knowing that Tommy [Reiher] had been a blade shearer, someone ignorantly and rashly remarked that there was no comparison in the two methods of shearing for cleanness of work. Tommy would not agree the machines were superior in this respect, and a wager was the outcome. From his war-bag he produced a pair of blades that were as bright and shiny as the chromium plating on a new car. Tommy shore a sheep with his blades while the sceptic (as we all were) shore one with his handpiece. Then they swapped and Tommy took more wool off that machine-shorn sheep with his blades than the machine could take off his. Actually he did not shear it: he shaved it. His blades were so finely drawn and keen-edged that they did not need to close to cut the wool. Using the 'running blow', he operated them after the style of the good

old-fashioned blade razor, and with equal effect. *[Sheep-O! quotes reproduced by kind permission of Penguin NZ]*

The early machine-shearing handpieces also had numerous drawbacks. They tended to overheat and become too hot to hold. The cutters had to be kept sharp, well shaped and properly adjusted to function effectively. Few shearers knew or were trained in how to do so. The handpieces were also considerably more expensive than a pair of blade shears. And despite the hopes of the *Sydney Mail*, and probably more than a few woolgrowers, good shearers were still required to operate them.

Regardless, in 1887 Toganmain Station in the New South Wales Riverina became the first to install shearing machines. Giant Dunlop Station, on the Darling River, also installed machines that year.

At Dunlop, the men at first refused to shear with the machines, although other clauses in their shearing contract may also have been at issue. It took three weeks for the machine's inventor, John Howard, who was the 'expert' involved in setting up the equipment, to convince the men to use the machines to shear the station's 184 000 sheep. When they did, tallies were as low as forty-three a day (the then record for blade shearing was 275 in a day). Gradually, though, tallies rose. When Howard had a moment of inspiration and introduced bonuses for anyone who shore more than 150 sheep a day there was a noticeable boost in effort. The average for the shed rose to 120 per man per day.

The introduction of machines changed the approach to shearing dramatically. Blade shearing could occur literally anywhere sheep and shears could be brought together but machine shearing tied the shearer to a position close to the drive mechanism. The sheep had to be held so that the handpiece could reach them and shear with as few blows (sweeps of the shears across the sheep's body) as possible. As the drive shaft ran in a straight line down the board, for the first time shearers had to work in orderly lines, giving a more 'industrial' look to the process of shearing than had been the case with blades.

Shearing sheds also had to change. Many were simple bough sheds (wooden frames covered in whatever suitable foliage was available) that kept the elements off the sheep and allowed the work to continue in all weather. Such sheds and many others had just enough headroom for the shearers but their roofs had to be raised to accommodate the headgear (drive shaft and wheels) for the shearing machines. Often it was easier to rebuild the shed from scratch, assuming the station could afford it.

Perhaps most significant of all, the silence of the shearing sheds disappeared. The noise of machines replaced the quiet click or snip of the shears. Curious, then, that the first known publication of the folk song 'Click Go the Shears' came four years after the introduction of machines. It may have shared a nostalgic appeal with Tom Roberts' *Shearing the Rams*, as by then the winds of change were blowing hard.

In 1888, for instance, despite the early reluctance of shearers to adopt the newfangled machine shears, Dunlop Station became the first to equip a shed entirely with machines. In other sheds it was possible to see one side of the shed shearing by machine while the other side shore with blades.

Some shearers were able to adapt to the new equipment while others struggled to make the transition. As time went on, it became apparent that, overall, machines made shearing faster and did result in a cleaner or closer cut. More wool shorn in less time meant the average cost of shearing was reduced, particularly since other shed workers, such as rouseabouts, were paid by the day or week, rather than at a piece rate like the shearers.

The situation, especially the 'speeding up' of shearing, created divisions among the shearers that grew ever wider until one shearer and union organiser, T.J. Lonsdale, referred to a feud fuelled by 'hatred engendered in the hearts of the old blade men [he referred to them as 'Knights of the Blades'] towards the machine men' and their refusal 'to even learn to shear with the machines'.

3

SHEARERS UNITE!
(1888–1890)

While machine shearing created divisions between those who adopted the new technology and those who shore with blades, other tensions were more prominent. Woolgrowers were still licking their wounds after their mid-1880s attempt to cut shearing rates was thwarted by the rapid organisation of unions. In 1888, some woolgrowers responded by refusing to employ anyone who was a member of a union, while the union had begun to insist that only union labour should be employed in sheds.

In states like Victoria, which had smaller sheds and generally closer community ties, there was some resistance to what was seen by many as outside union interference. Elsewhere, in particular in more sparsely populated areas, union activity was widespread.

Where a shed tried to shear non-union, the union formed a camp from which its members would attempt to persuade a station's shearers to join up. Some woolgrowers were shocked when camps were set up right on their properties. Unionists had found that some properties had reserves and rights of way that had fallen into disuse or been forgotten. Legally, there was nothing owners could do to stop unionists camping on them. In some cases union camps were pitched right next to woolsheds.

Matters came to a head in August 1888, in the Riverina, where efforts by Amalgamated Shearers Union members to ensure all shearers joined the union resulted in a confrontation that became known as the Brookong Riot. Brookong owner W. Halliday gave his impression of what had gone on in a telegram to his agents, subsequently published in the *Riverine Herald*:

> Please purchase 40 Colt revolvers, with 100 rounds of ammunition for each; send them to Hanging Rock railway station by tonight's mail. Brookong is in a state of siege. Situation intolerable. Will you kindly inform law authorities that police authorities here are powerless. My servants have been dragged out of their beds and terribly maltreated.

Halliday, it seemed, had been trying to use non-union labour to do his shearing. Union shearers had formed a strike camp near his property and then met with Halliday's shearers to persuade them of the benefits of union solidarity. Rather than being dragged from their beds, some of Halliday's 'servants' had signed up and left the station.

Despite Halliday's accusation of police inertia, fifteen officers were sent from Wagga, 80 kilometres away, and a police magistrate read the Riot Act to the unionists at their camp. Eight were arrested and put on trial. At the trial, union secretary W. E. Head was arrested when he was identified among those who were in court to observe proceedings. Eventually, two organisers were given three-year prison sentences and three union members went to jail for a year, while non-unionists who had gone on strike after signing employment agreements were fined under the Masters and Servants Act.

Up in Queensland, Julian Stuart was finding that management attitudes to unions varied from property to property. He discovered that there was a degree of sympathy at Alice Downs – but only after he encountered resistance from an old farmhand whose name, he reckoned, was Narky Ned.

'For what and for why should I have to pay 10 shillings into your union? I get 25 shillings a week,' Narky Ned had protested.

'What about when the union gets it raised to 30 shillings?' Stuart had argued, referring to the rate that the newly formed Queensland Labourers Union was trying to get for rouseabouts and other station workers.

'I'll be getting the same as they get,' the canny Ned responded.

The Queensland Labourers Union, which was closely allied to the Queensland Shearers Union, had signed up its first rouseabout at Maneroo Station on 6 October 1888 and established its headquarters at Barcaldine. One of its organisers, George Taylor, was considered to be so persuasive he could 'sell a union ticket to a squatter'.

The Labourers Union eventually won the pay rise, although pastoralists demanded more work for the extra money. Back on Alice Downs, the situation allowed the station's manager, Charley Gray, to put Narky Ned in his place. Narky lined up to get his pay and enjoy his little windfall but was shocked when he was only handed 25 shillings. As he wasn't in the union, he didn't get the pay rise. Narky got even narkier.

'Take it and get!' Gray told him.

According to Julian Stuart, Narky joined the union soon after.

It was a different story at Barcaldine Downs. Wrote Stuart: 'We travelled west to be in time for the early sheds on the Barcoo. The first to call the roll, Barcaldine Downs, was owned by Fairbairns, Victorian absentees – and when we talked unionism they got their backs up and postponed the shearing rather than depart from the old conditions.'

While the unions had been gaining ground, their formation also prompted unification among the woolgrowers. Within six months of the formation of the Queensland Labourers Union, the first Queensland pastoralists association was established. Julian may not have known it, but he was only half right about the Fairbairns. They were indeed from Victoria but they were seldom far from the troubles that were about to erupt across Queensland.

Early in 1889, Burenda Station on the Queensland side of the border with New South Wales refused to employ Queensland Shearers Union members at 20 shillings a hundred. They were, however, prepared to take Amalgamated Shearers Union members or non-unionists at the then ASU rate of 15 shillings per hundred.

Something of a turf war developed as the two unions poached members from each other and woolgrowers took advantage of the division to play one side off against the other. Attempts to make arrangements for shearers working on both sides of the border initially made little headway.

Amid ongoing skirmishes between shearers and woolgrowers that extended from the Riverina in the south to the sunlit plains of northern Queensland, on 15 April 1889, a group of twenty-one central-Queensland woolgrowers representing thirty-two sheep stations met at Barcaldine. The meeting may have been organised at the behest of Victorian banker and station owner George Fairbairn Senior. His son, George Fairbairn Junior, was in attendance. Nine of the attendees either managed Fairbairn properties or owned properties that owed the Fairbairns money.

Julian Stuart may have dismissed the Fairbairns as 'Victorian absentees', but according to Stuart Svensen, author of *The Shearers' War*, the definitive text on the shearers' strike of 1891, George Fairbairn Snr is one of the better-kept secrets of Queensland history. His family owned several Queensland sheep stations in their own right but, through two companies they controlled, the Trust and Agency Co.

and the Union Bank, they held sway over twenty-eight Queensland stations carrying three million sheep, roughly a fifth of the Queensland sheep west of the Great Dividing Range.

Such a situation had come about after a period of spectacular growth in sheep properties and sheep numbers. The 1880s were a boom time. With constantly rising land prices all you had to do was buy, wait and sell to make massive profits. If you borrowed to amplify your investment, you could make even more profits. That wasn't necessarily a problem as long as property values continued to rise. However, if the bubble burst, things could get very ugly.

The April 1889 meeting at Barcaldine formed the Central Queensland Employers Association. In June of that year, the newly formed association and the Queensland Shearers Union met to negotiate a mutual shearing agreement drawn up by the CQEA and based on the shearing agreements operating in many sheds in the region. Or at least they tried. Union organiser Bill Kewley advised that the union rules (including the rates of pay and conditions of employment) couldn't be changed until the QSU's general meeting in January 1890. All they could do was circulate any proposal for discussion until then. Glaciers move faster.

In the meantime the shearers suggested an agreement that met current union rules. The employers objected to it on fourteen points. They wanted the word minimum struck out of 'a minimum rate of one pound [20 shillings] per hundred'. They also wanted to decide when sheep were wet. Their major objection, however, was to clause 20: 'The said Sheepowners hereby agree to conform and adhere to the rules of the Queensland Shearers' Union.' It effectively meant they had to 'shear union' and give up control of their shearing to the shearers.

Meanwhile, in July 1889, the CQEA committee, meeting on its own, reached a decision to reduce the pay rate for station workers from 30 shillings back to 25 shillings, effective from 1 January 1890.

When the Queensland Labourers Union heard of the cut it requested a meeting with the CQEA. The employers wouldn't budge.

Early in 1890 the CQEA renamed itself the Queensland Pastoral Employers Association. In January, while the annual meeting of the Queensland Shearers Union pondered its rules, the newly named QPEA entered negotiations with the New South Wales-based Amalgamated Shearers Union. While the QSU was insisting sheds had to shear union, the ASU was more conciliatory, at least for now. Eventually, both unions would insist that all shed workers – indeed, everyone working on the station – had to belong to a union.

While sheds in southern states tended to shear in spring, sheds in Queensland started in January, continuing right through into the winter months, which weren't as harsh as they were further south. Throughout the first half of 1890 the QSU mobilised its thousands of members in strike action against sheds that shore non-union. These included Barcaldine Downs, Oakwood, Mount Margaret, Bullamon, Narine, Noondoo, Lorne, Saltern Creek, Meteor Downs, Fernlees, Peak Downs and Isis Downs. Strike camps were established, supported by union funds, but the effort tested the financial reserves of the recently formed organisation.

One of the most significant disputes was at Jondaryan shed, on the Darling Downs, just west of the Great Dividing Range. When Jondaryan Station (a member of the Sheep Owners Association of the Darling Downs) refused to pay the QSU rates, they found non-union labour that 'tommyhawked the wool off somehow', as one account put it. Whereupon the Carriers Union refused to touch a single bale. The station then organised its own teams to take the wool down to the Brisbane docks. It got to within 10 metres of the steamship *Jumna*, bound for England, when the unionised waterside workers, supported by the Australian Labor Federation, informed the owners of the *Jumna*: 'Any attempt to ship Kent and Weinholt's Jondaryan wool, shorn by non-union shearers, will cause us to take such steps as we deem necessary to stop such being shipped in your company's steamers.'

Or as Julian Stuart colourfully put it in *Part of the Glory*: 'It would stay there till the Day of Judgement and a day or two after, if the owners of Jondaryan did not give an undertaking to grant Queensland Shearers' Union rates and conditions "henceforth and for ever more".'

A conference was organised for 12 May 1890 to sort things out. Even Amalgamated Shearers Union leader William Spence was invited. The recalcitrance of the employers was such that the chairman of the meeting, member of the legislative council Edward Forrest, was moved to observe: 'The labor delegates had done all they could to settle this matter, and if no satisfactory conclusion was arrived at and a disturbance eventuated, the onus must certainly fall on the Darling Downs squatters.'

Eventually, a deal was struck. According to Stuart: 'In the meantime the *Jumna* sailed without the Jondaryan wool. Then the owners heard the London prices calling again, and climbed down ... and promised to be good.'

Not quite. While the Sheep Owners Association agreed to shear union, two days before publicly backing down it collected £100 000 from its members for a fighting fund with which to take the unions on in battles to come.

In August 1890, it was the turn of the maritime workers to appeal to the shearers for help. The maritime strike that began in that month revealed how far the big end of town was prepared to go to fight the growing power of the unions. The essence of the dispute was pay rises that many shipping companies agreed were long overdue. However, once again, attempts at negotiation broke down and the maritime workers struck. Other unions went out in support of them, and at the height of the dispute up to 50 000 people weren't working, a third of the country's total union membership at the time.

As the crisis deepened, and public order was threatened, the troops were called out. In Melbourne, the words of Colonel Tom Price to the Mounted Rifles were widely reported:

> To do your work faintly would be a grave mistake. If it has to be done effectively you will each be supplied with 40 rounds of ammunition, leaden bullets, and if the order is given to fire don't let me see any rifle pointed in the air; fire low and lay them out so that the duty will not have to be performed again.

Colonel Price later protested that he meant his men should aim for the strikers' legs, and thereby 'lay them out'. Whether he intended to kill his fellow Australians or just cripple them for life, the words weren't lost on unionists around the country. In the ensuing confrontations between shearers and woolgrowers, many shearers felt that they were facing forces that would shoot to kill if it came to it.

Also in August 1890, the newly formed Australian Labor Federation held its first annual conference. The meeting soon made headlines as it articulated its political aims: to nationalise all sources of wealth and means of producing and exchanging wealth; provide pensions for children, the aged and invalids; and reform the electoral system.

Nationalising businesses was the one that got everyone's attention. In the newspaper that was the mouthpiece of the federation, *The Worker*, founding editor William Lane explained that assets wouldn't be seized; the state would acquire them with just compensation. It wasn't much comfort. The eradication of capitalism and creation of a workers' paradise was straight out of the socialist handbook. Little wonder the established order recoiled in horror.

In September 1890 Queensland shearers went on strike for a week in support of their maritime brothers. That month the QPEA gathered to consider new shearing and rouseabout agreements, and it was decided to conclude discussions at a national meeting of woolgrowers in November.

By the time the meeting was held, in Melbourne, the home town of George Fairbairn Snr and Australian capital in general, the maritime strike had failed (Illawarra maritime workers held out until January) and the union movement as a whole was financially exhausted by the fight. Representatives from pastoral associations in New South Wales, Victoria, Queensland and South Australia attended.

They decided to set up a 'free labour' (meaning non-union) bureau and a bond arrangement to ensure all pastoralists adhered to the new shearing and rouseabout agreements. It was moved to form a federal council 'to secure unanimity of action on the part of all members of Pastoralists' Unions, and to maintain freedom of contract in respect of the employment of all labour'.

In fact, the action had already begun. Late in 1890 union organiser Mick Fanning was trying to get Queensland rousies paid the union's 30-shilling rate. When the shearers at Bullamon Station refused to go back to work until all labourers were allowed to join the union, they were summonsed and fined £5 each.

They were prosecuted by attorney Ted Unmack, who became known as Ten Bob Ted for suggesting that 10 bob a week and rations was fair pay ('bob' being slang for a shilling). At the time, Ten Bob valued his legal expertise at £156 a day, though he had to pay for his own meals. Summonses were also taken out against thirty-eight shearers for disobedience under the Masters and Servants Act, and for setting fire to the horse paddock after they finally left the property.

Also in December, Queensland's four regional pastoralist associations formed the United Pastoralists Association. Representatives of the UPA attended the meeting of the newly formed federal pastoralists' committee later that month, where new shearing and rouseabout agreements were finalised.

At that meeting, without any consultation with shearers or their representatives, the federal pastoralists' association cut Queensland shearing rates, which had risen to 30 shillings per hundred, back to 20 shillings. When it came to other decisions it didn't all go smoothly for the new organisation. The South Australians wanted nothing to do with the new arrangements. They didn't have any labour problems and didn't want to start any. The idea of requiring association members to lodge bonds to ensure they complied with association policy also went nowhere.

After the meeting, letters were sent to Queensland pastoralists explaining that it had been decided to make a stand there in order to focus resources in one place. As shearing commenced in Queensland before any other states except Western Australia, it was the logical starting point. It was also thought that Queensland workers were more radical (given the Australian Labor Federation's stated political aims, it was probably true) and a win in Queensland would be 'more effective and more glorious'.

Most commentators on the epic battle that was about to take place cite falling wool prices as the reason pastoralists cut the rate that shearers were paid. However, in *The Shearers' War*, Stuart Svensen details how the average price for clean and greasy wool was virtually static during the late 1880s and early 1890s. From 1888 to 1890 the prices of clean and greasy wool didn't move.

Looking elsewhere for explanations of the pastoralists' behaviour, especially in a confrontation that was to cost far more than it ever saved, the telling factor is the unification of labour and the subsequent unification of employers. Union solidarity was a challenge to the old order, as defined by the various Masters and Servants acts, and couldn't be ignored.

As for those employers who preferred negotiation to confrontation, the fact that many of the Queensland properties were controlled by banks effectively removed their control over their own destinies.

The Fairbairn family in particular and other financial interests in general had more at stake than most. Anything that compromised the ability of stations to meet their interest payments was a threat – to the banks, if not the whole debt-exposed economy. Union demands for increased wages were a clear and present danger. One thing became the priority: smash the unions.

4

THE YEAR OF LIVING DANGEROUSLY

(1891)

As shearers and woolgrowers, workers and employers, faced each other at the beginning of 1891, much had already changed since machine shearing had started taking over from blade shearing (the previous year, 30 million sheep were machine shorn). The entire relationship that had existed between the two sides for decades was under threat. For some, change couldn't come soon enough. Shearer William Gough described his memories of the times:

> In the 1890s the housing conditions was very crude, unlined iron huts, some with earth floors, two tiers of bunks and chaff bags to fill with dry grass or whatever was around the shed.
>
> It was very hard on a learner. I have seen a young chap with his hands bandaged and his back aching battling to try to make his tucker in his first shed and I have seen the old shearers take the hat around for a trier at his first shed to help him on his way to

his next shed. That was blade shearers. The shearers used to come to the rollcall – mostly riding and leading a packhorse; some on foot carrying Matilda [their swag] and some in sulkies and four-wheeled vehicles with a hood to keep the sun off them – some of those men would camp in their wagonette during the shearing.

The rouseabouts were expected to be on duty at 7am and could be allocated to any job that the boss might order them to do – wool rolling, piece picking or if shearing was held up by rain or any other cause the boss could use the shed hands to work outside the shed. I have seen them working in gangs cutting wood, cutting rushes and digging out rabbits – only a few miles from Hay.

There was nearly always an overflow of men at the rollcall at the big sheds and they came there somewhat like the shearers, some with horses and vehicles and some on foot with swags up. Some of them could shear but had missed out on getting a pen. No money, so they'd take a job as rouseabout. Of course, food and clothing was cheap then or a lot would have starved. The good old days – so-called by some.

Most shearing in western Queensland in 1891 was still performed with hand shears, although the new Wolseley shearing machines had been installed at Barcaldine Downs, Terrick Terrick, Milo and Wolfang stations during 1890. Owners were struggling with the cost of installing the new equipment, and many reasoned that since shearers could be more productive with machines, they shouldn't be paid as much.

In fact, in some regions shearers were looking at a thirty-three per cent rate cut under the new conditions imposed by the federal pastoralists' association. The first Queensland station to shear under what became known as the Pastoralists' Agreement was Logan Downs. It was owned by the Fairbairn family and was scheduled to begin shearing on 5 January 1891. Not surprisingly, the shearers refused to sign the agreement.

A week later, the Queensland Pastoral Employers Association held its annual meeting. It decided to give the shearers a fortnight to reconsider their position, after which the QPEA would act 'to get the shearing done in any manner they consider necessary'. A committee was formed to carry out the resolution. It was given full power to spend the QPEA's money and 'to act in enforcing the agreements and upholding the objects of the Federated Association'.

The new committee was called the Pastoralists Special Executive and comprised John Niall (who managed two Queensland stations owned by R. Goldsborough and Co.), Robert Oliver (manager and part owner of Isis Downs, which owed the Fairbairns £50 000) and Ernest Mackenzie (manager of Malvern Hills Pastoral Company).

Mackenzie was soon replaced by George Fairbairn Jnr, although how and why isn't clear. Stuart Svensen suggests Fairbairn may not have been elected to the committee because some of the pastoral association's members were starting to worry about his stand against the unions. Mackenzie may have stood aside or been pushed, but the end result was that Fairbairn became an integral part of the secretive but immensely powerful strikebreaking special executive.

The same meeting set up another committee to decide what would constitute rations for those station hands paid a weekly wage and their keep. The committee obviously decided to make a naked appeal to appetite as the ration list comprised 3.6 kilograms of flour, 9 kilograms of meat, 1.8 kilograms of sugar, nearly a quarter of a kilogram of salt and 170 grams of tea, per week. This wasn't the old convict ration of eight, ten, two, and a quarter; it was eight, twenty, four, and three-eighths. Plus there was rice, preserved potatoes, dried apples, spice, raisins, currants, hops, vinegar, mustard, coffee, curry and soap.

The increase in the ration cost far more than was saved by the pay cut, but curiously, as the strike progressed and 'free labour' was brought in from southern Australia, the strikebreakers were paid what the union was demanding, 30 shillings, not the 25 or 20 of the Pastoralists' Agreement (rates varied according to region).

Last, but not least, the woolgrowers also embarked on covert political activity with the formation of parliamentary committees in each of the eight central Queensland districts in which they operated. The committees were to 'supervise the Electoral Roll and recommend members to represent such districts, securing their election if opposed'.

What was meant by 'supervise' isn't clear. However, at the time there were 108 116 white adult males in Queensland who were eligible to vote, but only 75 000 on the rolls. Of course, one thing that worked against shearers being on the electoral rolls was that you had to be a Queensland resident with a fixed address. Many itinerant shearers therefore couldn't qualify to vote. Those who 'supervised' the rolls simply had to ensure the rules were adhered to.

In the early weeks of 1891, the Queensland Shearers Union and Queensland Labourers Union found themselves in an almost impossible position. They didn't have nearly enough money to support a strike by their members. After the maritime dispute, none of their affiliated unions had the money to help either. Yet to accept the Pastoralists' Agreement would be to lose everything won over the previous few years. Meanwhile, as more and more union shearers encountered the new agreements, they went on strike anyway. They then turned to the union to which they had paid their membership fees for help.

On 19 January 1891 the central-district committee of the Australian Labor Federation met to consider its options. It was suggested that the Pastoralists' Agreement could be signed under protest while the unions recovered financial strength. A strike in July, when shearing would be in full swing, would leave the pastoralists little time to find free labour. Then they'd have to negotiate.

However, a strike camp of workers from Logan Downs Station had already been established at Wolfang Creek, near Clermont.

Other sheds had also refused to sign the agreement. At Bowen Downs they walked off because five Chinese shearers worked there.

Late in January, Bungeworgorai became the first shed to shear non-union, with Aboriginal shearers and men from south-east Queensland. Seven of the free labourers who had been hired had never shorn before and between them only managed to shear fifty sheep on their first day, over an hour per sheep.

At the end of that month the Australian Labor Federation accepted the inevitable and established its first strike committee in the central district. On 1 February, it issued what was described as a stirring manifesto: 'The Queensland bush is to be a battleground whereupon is to be decided whether capitalism can crush Australian unionism altogether into the dust ... If they want conference, we will offer it to them, but if they want to fight, we offer that also.'

It was just what the Queensland shearers wanted to hear. Shearers' cook Henry Smith-Barry wrote of the reaction to the manifesto at Isisford:

> At the most 'moral suasion' [talking to non-union labour about joining the union] is but a poor weapon in our hands ... The only certain method for the working man to get justice is by his becoming all expert in the use of the Winchester rifle, or what is better still the Gifford gun, as it leaves behind no smoke and is noiseless.

South of the border, the Amalgamated Shearers Union found itself in the same predicament as the Queensland workers. Shearing hadn't started in New South Wales or Victoria but the pastoralists there adopted the same position as their Queensland colleagues. Talks broke down and the ASU faced the prospect of supporting a strike it couldn't afford.

Back in Queensland, Julian Stuart was involved in the establishment of the first union camp with the Logan Downs shearers at Clermont. Not surprisingly, the appearance of a large body of angry men, many of whom were armed, alarmed the authorities in the small Queensland town. When attempts were made to move them on, the shearers claimed that as itinerant rural workers they had to camp somewhere. Similarly, when it was suggested that they turn in their weapons, the strikers claimed they wouldn't be able to hunt for food as they had always done.

According to Stuart, travelling to non-union sheds to use moral suasion on 'deliberate offenders against the code that meant so much to us' didn't always go to plan. Fellow unionist Harry Casey was trying to recruit workers at one shed but a big bloke kept telling them to ignore him. Eventually, Casey decked him.

'Split me knuckle on jaw,' Casey said. 'I suppose I ought not to have done it. It'll cost me a quid or two if the police make a case out of it.'

Stuart worried it might cost Casey as much as three years in jail. On the way back to camp the pair sighted troopers checking people passing out of the gate of the property. Casey eluded them by tying his red silk handkerchief to the top strand of the station's fence at a place out of sight of the law. Now his horse could see the obstacle and Casey spurred his mount to jump it. On the other side, he retrieved his handkerchief and slipped into the bush. Stuart then rode up to the troopers, who had the assaulted worker with them.

'Is this him?' the troopers asked.

'No,' the bruised bloke replied, 'he had a silk handkerchief around his neck.'

In other areas, as the number of strikers grew, police and police magistrates (who in central Queensland tended to be leading citizens such as station owners or bankers) turned minor charges, in particular obscene language, into the basis for issuing harsh sentences. Men who gave a trooper generalised directions on where to go and/or how far faced prison for weeks and in some cases months.

On 3 February 1891, 200 strikebreakers boarded the steamship *Derwent* in Melbourne, bound for central Queensland. The men were called 'free labourers', although they had signed employment contracts that if not honoured would see them imprisoned for six months. It was later found that the contracts and threats were illegal.

Some of the free labourers were described as 'unemployed scum' while others were 'true bush workers'. Their Queensland destination was supposed to be a secret but when they arrived at Rockhampton on 10 February they were met by 700 jeering unionists and sympathisers. On the docks, none other than George Fairbairn Jnr of the Pastoralists Special Executive directed proceedings as police cleared a path through the heckling crowd.

The men eventually were delivered to stations around Clermont. Along the way, some of these blackleg workers were convinced by moral suasion to join the union camps. At some locations, half the blacklegs walked out. All of them then had to be supported by the cash-strapped unions.

At Meteor Downs, near Springsure, shearing started under union rules. The property was owned by Australia's first cattle king, James Tyson. Tyson wasn't a member of the Queensland Pastoral Employers Association (he was a member of pastoral associations in New South Wales). However, the self-made son of a convict was an astute businessman and one of the richest men in the country. He owed the banks very little and could well afford the union rate (he actually bailed out the bankrupt government of Queensland with a low-interest loan a few years later), but he may have calculated that it was cheaper in the long run to concede to reasonable demands on pay and conditions than it was to fight them. In this he may have been in accord with the similarly self-made pastoralist Sidney Kidman, who was based in South Australia. There the Pastoralists' Agreement had been rejected by all and sundry.

Tensions continued to rise in central Queensland. When Police Inspector Second Class John Ahern was at Emerald railway station, he noticed union men moving large kerosene tins. On closer inspection the tins were found to be packed with bullets and powder. Not long after, eighty Winchester rifles thought to be bound for union hands were also seized.

More strike camps were forming as more sheds presented shearers with the Pastoralists' Agreement. Over 500 unionists established two camps around Barcaldine in the middle of February 1891. Around that time there were reports of threats to import and release rabbits into Central Queensland, which had not yet felt the full weight of the scourge that was ravaging southern states. The media went into a frenzy, describing union 'tyranny' and its 'insane projects'.

On 15 February, ten stations were declared black (placed under union ban) in the Barcaldine area. Three were Fairbairn stations. Two other stations, Pinkilla and Retreat, shore union.

On 19 February Queensland premier Sir Samuel Griffith sent the Queensland Permanent Force and the Rockhampton Mounted Infantry to Clermont. In effect, 258 soldiers and police were protecting what remained of the 200 free labourers who'd gone there. Those who remained had also been sworn in and armed as special constables.

The *Brisbane Courier*, which maintained that the 'rights of free men and free citizenship must be maintained at whatever cost' said of the Mounted Infantry: 'The general impression among the crowd was that the Mounted Infantry would have a very poor show with well mounted bushmen and truth to say the infantry displayed very poor horsemanship, their manoeuvers being greeted with shouts of laughter.'

The deployment of the military added to an already tense situation. Memories of the maritime strike and Colonel Tom Price's 'lay them low' remark were still fresh. As Queensland Shearers Union delegates attended national union meetings in Sydney and Adelaide, they drafted a new manifesto that concluded: 'The workers asked for a conference, and the capitalists answered with Nordenfelt guns [a multiple-barrel machine gun that in some demonstrations had fired 1000 rounds per minute, and which was part of the military equipment at Clermont].'

The strike camp at Clermont, run by Julian Stuart, was starting to be considered as the 'most dangerous of all'. It was also proving effective in disrupting the region's shearing. According to unionists the strikebreakers in the area were 'tomahawking' the wool off a mere twenty-six sheep a day. Even the pastoralists were claiming no more than eighty. At Rainworth Station, the number was only fifty. No woolgrowers were crowing about the quality of the shearing.

For all the tension, there were moments of humour. Among the shearers was a former telegraph operator, Snob Tregeagle, who reckoned he only needed to be near a telegraph 'ticker' to be able to pick up the gist of the morse code messages being transmitted. So Stuart and another unionist distracted the station master at Clermont while Snob (shearers' slang for the last and roughest sheep in the pen) sidled up to the telegraph office and listened. Wrote Stuart:

> As a result of this eavesdropping he told us that 35 free labourers were to leave a train at Back Creek siding (about 15 miles [24 kilometres] away) during the night. We did that 15 miles in pretty slick time, and were at the siding, waiting to interview the undesirables and persuade them to join the camp and ride back with us. When the train arrived, though, the laugh was against us. There were no non-unionists for the shed, the '35' were fat bullocks for the shearer's mess.

On 28 February the union shearers at Barcaldine held a 'Monster Meeting'. An estimated 2000 assembled at Lagoon Creek Camp, where two flags flew at the entrance gate: a Southern Cross flag (first flown at the Eureka Stockade forty years before) and a flag proclaiming the word 'Freedom'. Barcaldine's Oddfellows band led the parade that made its way, mostly on foot, into the town. Bringing up the rear were sixty mounted horsemen. The marchers carried banners that read: 'Evil be to him who evil thinks. United we stand, divided we fall'; 'Sir. S.W. Griffith. Traitor! Meet thy doom'; and 'Barcoo Murphy, MLA. Weighed in the balance and found wanting'.

The whole town turned out. Barcaldine had never seen anything like it. Nor had anywhere else in central Queensland. Not surprisingly, the atmosphere was strongly suggestive of the possibility of change.

Some were excited by the situation. Others were deeply troubled. Apparently, staying calm wasn't an option, if the experience of Police Magistrate John Macarthur was anything to go by. With so many strikers swelling the Barcaldine camps, the unionists ensured order was maintained by appointing a vigilance committee that patrolled the camps and the town. When Macarthur was told by Colonial Secretary Horace Tozer to swear in special constables, he explained that the vigilance committee had everything under control and that he had ordered the pubs to be closed at night. If he had to swear in specials, he'd swear in union officials.

Tozer was far from impressed by such moderation. He promptly transferred Macarthur to Muttaburra. It may seem unfair to compare a nice little outback town like Muttaburra to Siberia, but it is a long way outback, the surrounding country is somewhat featureless, and if it ever snowed there . . .

It's also worth noting that the man from Muttaburra, Police Magistrate Charles Morris, happily accepted his transfer to Barky.

The other significant development in February 1891 was a move by the Australian Labor Federation to draw up a new political program that dropped all reference to the nationalisation of everything. The original manifesto had attracted universal criticism since it had been adopted just three months earlier. For an organisation aspiring to have representatives elected to parliament it may have become apparent that Queenslanders weren't going to vote for a socialist revolution.

It may even have dawned on the federation that a lot of their shearer members were working their guts out to make enough money to buy their own 'means of production', such as farms, where they could sit back, watch their sheep safely graze and sing the alternative lyrics to the workers' anthem 'The Red Flag':

> The working class can kiss my arse
> I've got the boss's job at last.

On 6 March 1891 the woolshed at Arrilalah burned. A strike camp had been formed there by men from Maneroo Station, which also had a shed burned down. The striking shearers were determined to confront the blacklegs at Maneroo. The strike committee in the area accused the owner of burning the shed himself, to get the insurance money. The situation certainly was a golden opportunity. The bush was crawling with people who could be blamed for a fire while there was a pressing need to replace old, termite-ridden sheds with new ones with enough room to accommodate the headgear of the new shearing machines. As it happened, no arrests were made in relation to the Arrilalah fire.

The following day the decision was made to make the strike action general. It was a bold move, one the Queensland unions couldn't really afford; however, directions were given that from mid-month (time enough to get the word out) union shearers should give a week's notice at all sheds in the state.

The same day, union organiser Bill Hamilton received a telegram purporting to be from an organiser in Capella: 'Look out for train at Langton and Clermont, some free labourers on it.'

It was a Saturday and in Clermont a cricket match was being played: the soldiers versus the shearers. While the game continued, 200 unionists went to Clermont railway station. There, instead of free labourers, George Fairbairn Jnr and the two other members of the Pastoralists Special Executive emerged when the train arrived, along with two other pastoralists. Senior Sergeant Michael Dillon and four foot police were on hand to maintain order.

All five woolgrowers boarded a buggy for the short journey to their hotel, accompanied by jostling, vociferous shearers. Their passage was unhindered until they were 200 metres down the road. One hundred mounted unionists blocked the way, and there was more jostling and heckling while Dillon and his men cleared a path. Some 50 metres on, the buggy was stopped again and stones were thrown. Sergeant Dillon received a small cut while Robert Oliver of the Pastoralists Special Executive claimed he was hit by a bottle. However, none of the sheep men were injured.

At this point union organiser Bill Hamilton arrived and with the assistance of other union leaders he cleared the way so the buggy could complete its journey.

Subsequent accounts of what became known as the Clermont Riot saw union sympathisers play down the events while supporters of the pastoralists played them up. For the men in the buggy, surrounded by a mob, it may well have been a frightening experience. However, there are some curious aspects to the affair. For starters, the union organisers in Clermont claimed they sent no telegram. If they had, they wouldn't have referred to 'free labourers' – they'd have referred to 'scabs'. In any event, no free labourers were on the train. And why did the Pastoralists Special Executive utilise a regular service when they usually travelled in secret aboard a special train permanently at their disposal?

The matter didn't end there. In his memoir, Julian Stuart recalled what happened next:

> No damage was done, the dignity of the 'pure merinos' may have been hurt, but they reached the club in safety and the bushmen, disgusted at being brought in on a wild goose chase, went back to Sandy Creek. I was in charge of the town arrangements and noticed that the police got busy. A mounted trooper was stationed

at every street corner. The Gatling gun and the Nordenfelt at the Town Hall were hauled out and the gun crews mustered for exercise and instruction. From the balcony room where I was working nearly all night, I could see the troopers mounting guard and keeping watch, and from various parts of the town I could hear sounds that indicated that something was being got ready for the morning. Late in the night I got news of a big batch of warrants having been issued. As they were watching the front of the building I slipped out the back way, borrowed a hack from the butcher's stable next door and streaked for the camp which I reached just before dawn, and got the men together and told them to keep cool . . . that the camp would be surrounded at daylight and that warrants had been issued for about a dozen of them. I advised those who had been on the bridge [confronting the pastoralists] to get away to another camp. They had hardly saddled up and cleared before the Government forces made their appearance at the Sandy Creek crossing. They were led by a major who, in the Boer War, a few years later, made himself famous by getting hung up in a barbed wire fence while engaged in farm burning operations. He came with a big crowd, some mounted, some on foot, and a mob of lorries. A cheap looking, nondescript lot they were, who, if there had been trouble, would most likely have done more damage to themselves, and one another, than to anyone else. A lot of the townspeople followed at a safe distance and a couple of the camp committee waited at the crossing. They called to the Falstaff in charge to halt his mob and 'remain on the town side of the creek or there would be bloodshed'.

The major was fat and uncomfortable in the saddle and said something about taking the responsibility but he consulted the Sub-inspector of Police who had the warrants and the magistrate who was getting ready to read the Riot Act before the shooting started. After a few tense moments we agreed that the Sub-inspector and a couple of his men could cross and arrest any man for whom he had a warrant but they could not find any. (They were well on the backtrack to Barcaldine by that time.) A barney arose because the Sub-inspector claimed the right to arrest men without warrants. We objected but the magistrate cited the case of The Queen versus Thunderbolt where the outlaw was killed first and the warrant produced afterwards.

Two men were singled out (others may have been hiding in a cornfield) and went quietly. Another man was arrested at Wolfang Creek and six others were subsequently charged.

The raid was authorised by the premier of Queensland, Samuel Griffith. Colonial Secretary Horace Tozer also requested copies of speeches made by organisers George Taylor and Julian Stuart on the previous Thursday in order to ascertain whether there were grounds for prosecuting them for incitement to riot.

When Magistrate Robert Ranking questioned whether being at the scene was enough to be convicted of riotous assembly, Colonial Secretary Tozer responded that the defendants should be sent to Rockhampton for trial anyway.

As for the 'riot' itself, the *Brisbane Courier* questioned how riotous the crowd really was. Five police versus several hundred, yet the pastoralists had 'escaped without serious injuries'?

By this stage, though, even journalists had to be careful. In a side incident, the young editor of the Charters Towers *Republican*, Frederick Vosper, was arrested for his admittedly inflammatory article titled 'Bread or Blood'. He wrote:

> If your oppressors will not listen to reason, let them feel cold lead and steel; as they have starved you, so do you shoot them; and allow them not to destroy your liberties and deprive you of your bread without a fight. Better to see the last squatter and the last

member of this hateful Government butchered than to see one jot or one title of the sacred rights of the people lost!

Ultimately, the rioting charges from Clermont failed. Senior Puisne Judge George Rogers Harding (sent from Brisbane to hear the case) summed up strongly against the seven accused in late April. All seven were found not guilty but not before those in the dock had languished in prison for weeks. Several of the men were promptly rearrested on other charges. When they were found guilty, they were sentenced to periods of up to one month, despite having been held for months on charges that weren't proven.

Meanwhile, the Clermont Riot served the purpose of justifying the existing use of the military and subsequently increasing troop numbers. During March, as more shearers responded to the general call-out, the strike camps grew larger and more threatening.

On 11 March, sixteen police reinforcements were expected at Barcaldine. There were 700 unionists waiting for them at the station. Before they arrived, Sub-inspector Durham and seven local police confronted the unionists with revolvers drawn. Then Durham did some maths. Each of the eight police weapons had six bullets. If they started shooting, the best they could do was kill forty-eight unionists. That would leave about 652 angry shearers facing eight police with blood on their hands and nothing but smoke in their guns. They held their fire.

When the train pulled in, the reinforcements took one look at the crowd, left their kit and fled to safety, leaving all the other passengers on the train to fend for themselves. Lagoon Creek Camp organiser George Ellis cleared a way for the passengers to go about their business unharmed.

On the following day, 12 March, more than a hundred more mounted infantry were dispatched to central Queensland, this time to Barcaldine. On Retro, Langton and Peak Downs stations, grassfires were reported, although March was often the time pastoralists set fire to long grass anyway. Attempts to sabotage train lines and telegraphs were also reported.

By mid-March, Barcaldine was like a town under siege. On 15 March, 113 infantry and five ambulance-men were met by 1000 unionists at the railway station. A week later, fifty-two infantry and artillery-men were sent from Mackay and fifty from Rockhampton. Over the next few days another 104 were despatched.

Not all of the soldiers were willing participants. When a volunteer corps in Rockhampton was asked for volunteers to preserve peace and order, only four out of twenty-nine stepped forward. When a commanding officer went to inspect the Irish Volunteer Corps, he found all thirty-four men from G Company had gone absent without leave.

The number of police and military in central Queensland was doubled despite the disapproval of the premier, who may have started looking at the big picture and noticed how much was being spent (financially and politically) to save the sheep men so little. He objected to the government becoming an ally of one class against another. What if they picked the wrong side?

Also in mid-March there was consternation in union ranks when three shearers in Blackall ignored the call-out. They had made a prior arrangement to shear sheep at the Blackall wool scour and insisted on honouring the agreement. One of the shearers was a Blackall local named Jack Howe. Jack was a staunch Labor man but he'd also given his word to do the shearing and he refused to break it. He would soon become the stuff of legend, as detailed in the following chapter.

Julian Stuart wrote of the emotion swirling around the strike:

> We lived at high tension for the next few months, almost every day being crowded with incidents, more or less exciting. As the Peak Downs shed would be the first to start, it seemed to me

too much like 'long range sparring' to sit in the strike room at Barcaldine giving orders, so I did a 'non-stop' ride to Clermont, about 250 miles (400 kilometres). On the way I called at a small cattle station on the Belyando and found the owner packing up to send his wife and children away 'for safety'. He told me there were 5000 shearers on their way from the West, robbing the stations and burning everything behind them. He said that was the news in the Brisbane papers and that he had received a warning from Rockhampton. I convinced them that the Press reports were exaggerated so the lady decided to stay home. They showed me one paper which said that the bushmen were armed with rifles and shearblades fastened on sticks.

On 19 March, the free labourers from Melbourne who had been shearing at Arcturus and Rainworth stations were transferred to the Fairbairn-owned Peak Downs. They took a train through Capella and disembarked just north of Ebor Creek. A fortnight later, it was found that some of the piles of the bridge over Ebor Creek had been sawn through, but the bridge had failed to collapse.

While the free labourers were loaded into drays and their escort of sixty police and soldiers mounted up, between forty and eighty unionists arrived on horseback. They offered the blacklegs free food and horses if they defected. One unionist offered £5 to the first man who changed sides. There were no takers. When the strikebreaking blacklegs and their escort moved off, the unionists followed.

At the boundary of Peak Downs, union shearers claimed that Charles Fairbairn, George Jr's brother, told the commander of the troops, Major Percy Ricardo: 'You are on private property now – order your men to fire.'

Ricardo refused.

The unionists milled about on the property, preventing the strikebreakers from going further. They were then joined by another forty to 100 mounted unionists. Charles Fairbairn claimed one of them had a revolver at his side. Other witnesses thought some unionists had rifles. The Riot Act was read and the soldiers fixed bayonets.

At that point a union representative named Ford arrived and called the men away for 'a meeting'. They left and the strikebreakers went on their way. What was a confrontation at best became known as the Peak Downs Riot.

In its wake thirteen men were eventually arrested. All were charged with molesting hired servants, seven were charged with rioting and six with unlawful assembly. Four got off the molesting charges, five were found guilty but escaped sentences, and the remainder were given sentences of one to three months. Eventually, the seven rioting and two of the unlawful assembly charges were brought up in Rockhampton at the end of April, Judge Harding presiding. Six of the rioters were found guilty and were sentenced to up to three years' hard labour. One rioter and the two charged with unlawful assembly were acquitted.

In his memoir, Julian Stuart was somewhat ambivalent about what had happened to the bridge at Ebor Creek:

> The newspapers had stated that the destruction of bridges and the derailment of trains were to be part of our campaign, and big Tom Cook, an engine driver, discussed matters with us. 'Of course, if you cannot get at the hybrids any other way, do not worry about us,' he said, and quoted Adam Lindsay Gordon:
> What does it matter for one soul lost?
> Millions of souls have been lost before.
> We assured the big engineman that the wrecking of trains and the taking of human life did not find a place in our propaganda in spite of the shrieking of the daily press very much to the contrary.

The fact remained, however, that someone had attempted to do just that, however inexpertly, at Ebor Creek.

While the shearers' strike swirled around them, the newly constituted Pastoralists Federal Council convened in Brisbane and decided not to meet with the union until it conceded freedom of contract. It also decided to hire more strikebreakers. Premier Griffith, with a growing interest in resolving the confrontation through negotiation, noted the pastoralists' position as 'a policy of exasperation calculated to alienate the sympathy of impartial observers'.

While union shearers were growing increasingly frustrated with 'moral suasion' as a means of recruiting strikebreakers to the union ranks, members of the government were perfecting the use of every available means to beat them.

In late March, members of the Queensland Railway Engineers Association's Rockhampton branch met to consider a request from the shearers' strike committee to refuse to carry strikebreakers on any Queensland trains. The meeting didn't back the move but it did express sympathy and the men pledged a day's pay per month to the shearers' strike fund.

On hearing this, the railway commissioner instantly dismissed every person who'd been present at the meeting. The commissioner then sent to a telegram to his underlings: 'Any railway employee who is found either directly or indirectly assisting those at present acting in opposition to the constituted authorities must be at once prepared to leave the service.'

Who was acting in opposition to the constituted authorities? The Queensland Shearers Union was acting under the 'constituted authority' of the Trade Unions Act in opposition to the Pastoralists' Agreement of the Queensland Pastoral Employers Association, a shadowy alliance with no legal recognition whatsoever. The wrongheadedness of the commissioner was only matched by his high-handedness. Others saw it the same way and a public meeting at Emerald censured the railway commissioner and pledged money to the strikers.

In the absence of Premier Griffith (at negotiations on the establishment of the Commonwealth of Australia), Colonial Secretary Horace Tozer and the Queensland cabinet decided the best course was to commence mass arrests throughout central Queensland.

When Griffith was consulted, he advised against it and suggested instead that the union's leaders could be arrested on conspiracy charges as outlined in an English Act originally intended to suppress a rebellion in Ireland. Then, as now, the main ingredients for a conspiracy are a large slice of paranoia wrapped around a tiny morsel of truth.

Only a day after the Peak Downs Riot, on 20 March, warrants for the arrests of union leaders for conspiracy started being issued. Sure enough, conspiracy soon proved to be the most elastic concept in the legal book. Simply leading a strike camp, it turned out, was tantamount to conspiracy.

On 21 March another protest meeting was held at Barcaldine. This one may not have been union sanctioned or organised by the unions. Among the speakers was a former boundary rider named James Martin. Exactly what he said to the meeting is disputed, but the essence of it was: 'There is only one way and that is to fight the squatters. Take up arms and fight. I have a petition in my swag for electoral reform but the only petition I believe in is 10 000 resolute bushmen with 10 000 shearblades. There are 10 000 bushmen on the plains for active service and I am one of them.'

Then someone called for three groans for the Queen. Martin was reported as saying, 'I presume you have been groaning for Old Mother Brown, John Brown's widow.' It was an open reference to the suspected affair between Queen Victoria and her devoted servant, John Brown. Four days after saying all that, Shearblade Martin, as he became known, was arrested for sedition. His big mouth ended up costing him two years' imprisonment.

On 23 March, there was a confrontation between the manager of Lorne Station (near Charleville), John Power, and seventy union shearers. Shortly after the unionists departed, Power noticed that his woolshed was on fire. It subsequently burned to the ground. A contingent of mounted infantry set off in pursuit of the unionists, commanded by Colonial Secretary Tozer's own son, Vivian. The soldiers never got near the union bushmen. When the unionists encountered a police patrol the next day, they surreptitiously dropped burning matches, igniting small grassfires as they passed.

It was suggested that men be arrested for such incidents, but some police thought they couldn't be arrested without a warrant. Horace Tozer quickly produced a booklet titled *Notes for Peace Officers* to set them straight. He contended that police could arrest without warrant anyone breaking the peace or whom they had reasonable cause to believe had committed a felony, and detailed the penalties for the various crimes union shearers might commit. Setting fire to grass could see them face prison for three to fourteen years. Tozer underlined the additional punishment: 'The convict is also liable to be whipped.'

Setting fire to grass was only one of the tricks the shearers played on the police. Julian Stuart, writing years after the event, from the relative safety of Western Australia, described some of the more colourful incidents:

> Denny Devine, the scalper, who did the shooting when the camp meat supply needed replenishing, came to me one night when I was chairman of the camp, and asked for his rifle.
>
> I had roused on the senior-constable for dogging our tracks and taunted him about his failure to get within a hundred miles of Ned Kelly. (He was a splendid bushman, all the same, one of the best ever I met.)
>
> 'He's been watching the camp for the past night or two, and I'll fox him,' said old Denny.
>
> During the night, the senior-constable, spying on the camp to gain knowledge of our comings and goings and to learn

things that might 'be used in evidence' against us, yielded to the temptation to have a smoke. He leaned against a gum tree and shaded the match with his hand but the faint flicker on the white bole of the gum tree was enough for Denny, whose Winchester flashed 300 yards [275 metres] in the rear and whose bullet zipped into the bark, about three inches [7.5 centimetres] above the policeman's head.

Denny wore a satisfied grin when he brought the rifle back.

'An old dog for a hard road,' was all he said.

The things the senior-constable said and threatened and promised do not matter now but they led us to think we had hurt his feelings somehow. But he kept away from the camp at night ever after.

Then there was the story of Police Constable Handlow's boots:

P.C. Handlow was the biggest man in the police and military forces then investing Clermont, and a noticeable figure when he paraded the street, which he was very fond of doing.

The Brisbane police were camped in tents on the reserve and at meal times marched down in squads, fully armed, to the hotels for their food. A few mornings after Sammy's outburst (provoked by the arrest of two of his mates, who were marched barefoot to the cells) we were surprised and amused to see P.C. Handlow shuffling awkwardly along with his detachment, on the way to breakfast, with his feet encased in makeshift moccasins. His size rendered him conspicuous and he was anything but an imposing figure as he hobbled painfully along the centre of the roadway, which was gravelly and covered with pebbles. Sammy was close by and a few words from him were illuminating.

'Some bloke stole the big John's boots last night while he was asleep. He was in one of them bell tents and left the side hooked up to catch the breeze. Must have been a soft snap for the chap that got away with them. Wonder who it was?' he added seriously.

Something made me look at him but his face was as expressionless as a piemelon and I recollected having heard that in the sheds he was reckoned a pretty good poker player.

Stuart's enjoyment of such diversions was short-lived. On 24 March he was at Clermont railway station with fellow union organiser George Taylor when a contingent of fifty-six police and mounted infantry arrested them for conspiracy. Taylor tried to throw a bundle of documents into the crowd. The police intercepted them. The documents ended up providing much of the case, such as it was, for the conspiracy charges.

Other union shearers were arrested for their part in the Peak Downs Riot. Union organiser Paddy Griffin was arrested at Capella. The following day, 25 March, Hugh Blackwell, Bill Bennett, Bill Fothergill and Tom Ryan were arrested at the union office in Barcaldine.

The arrests had no immediate effect on the continuing need to provide protection for strikebreakers. Down near the border with New South Wales, in the Maranoa district, the Australian Pastoral Company's properties had been without shearers since the union men had walked out in January. Only five men had so far signed the Pastoralists' Agreement but they needed fifty. The manager at Noondoo Station wired a New South Wales woolgrower to see if he could send some shearers. While they were being organised, the union attempted to compromise and do the shearing if the strikebreakers were left in New South Wales. The station turned the offer down.

Allegations were made that Queensland's union shearers threatened to strew the Mungindi Bridge with corpses if the strikebreakers tried to cross into Queensland. As events transpired, they didn't get the chance. New South Wales union shearers got to the fifty strikebreakers travelling towards the troubled Queensland districts first, and from most reports gave them a flogging.

While some of the battered strikebreakers reached Noondoo, the New South Wales men headed to the strike camp at St George to give their union colleagues some extra muscle. They were described as 'good for anything from pitch and toss to manslaughter'.

Amid suspicions that bridges might be dynamited, perhaps in the wake of the discovery of the attempted sabotage of the Ebor Creek Bridge, pilot engines were introduced to proceed ahead of trains carrying strikebreakers. Colonial Secretary Tozer suggested prominent unionists who had been arrested could be carried in prison carriages with the pilot engines, essentially using them as human shields.

This disgraceful strategy wasn't implemented as more arrests took place. On 26 March Ned Murphy was arrested for conspiracy at the Roma office of the Queensland Shearers Union. Isaac Fry was also arrested. More documents were seized at the Roma office that provided evidence for the subsequent trials, including one in which organiser Alec Forrester explained how 'union mice have been destructive'. Two days later, on 28 March, Alec was arrested on conspiracy charges in a pub in St George.

The same day, there was violence at Boombah Station. While union shearers were talking to some strikebreakers, they were rushed by a man named Wildin, armed with a knife. Wildin was disarmed and given a beating. While some reports maintain that Wildin was hospitalised, when the unionists insisted the shearers leave the station and come to their camp, Wildin refused to ride, and ended up walking 25 kilometres unaided.

As these events were unfolding, heavy rain set in across central Queensland. Rivers rose in flood, cutting some strike camps off from the towns where they had been obtaining supplies. Life in the camps, already hard, became more testing as conditions turned cold, wet and muddy. It was no picnic for the police and military either. Many of them were accommodated in tents as well.

By that time, the numbers on strike and on protection duty had swelled immensely. There were 2000 men in strike camps at Barcaldine with 538 police and military in camps guarding the town and surrounding stations. During quiet moments, some of the troops around Barcaldine amused themselves by shooting emus. They started using the plumes to decorate their hats, beginning the style that continues in the Australian Army to this day.

And while the great strikes of the 1890s have been identified with the genesis of the Australian Labor Party, it is worth noting that in March 1891 pastoralists also called for the formation of a 'powerful country party' to counter the labour movement. Eventually, this became the Country Party, now known as the National Party.

The arrests of union leaders continued. On 29 March, shearers' cook Henry Smith-Barry, who had been sent to Clermont to take over after George Taylor's arrest, was arrested for conspiracy. He was picked up while taking food to the men who were already prisoners.

On 30 March, the Nive Downs woolshed and 150 bales of wool went up in flames. The shed was insured for £3000.

Meanwhile, Rockhampton MLA John Murray asked to travel down the central line swearing in railwaymen as special constables. Colonial Secretary Tozer gave his assent and asked him to take note of anyone who refused or showed reluctance. Accordingly, 300 specials were sworn in and thirty railwaymen were sacked.

On 30 March, the St George camp was raided. Newly elected organisers, including Robert Prince, were arrested for conspiracy. Alf Brown, the union organiser in charge of the Warrego district, was arrested on 31 March.

At the beginning of April 1891, as the shearers' strike entered its fourth month, 9000 men were domiciled in forty camps from west of the Great Divide to far western Queensland. The police and military were also numerous. At Barcaldine there were thirty officers and 768 men; at Clermont, twelve officers and 218 men; at Winton, three officers and fifty-one men; at Hughenden, two officers and forty-four men; at autumnal Muttaburra, one officer and 14 men; and at Delta, one officer and ten men.

Throughout the 1891 strike, the union shearers' strategy was one of non-violent non-cooperation. Given the provocations of strike-breakers, employers and some government officials, there had been surprisingly little violence. Woolsheds had been burned, wool bales and grass set alight, railway bridges and lines sabotaged to stop troop and strikebreaker movements. There had been punches thrown, an attempted stabbing, and a few 'pure merinos' had been jostled, but little more.

Monster meetings held in many towns had drawn almost the entire population. Most towns supported the unionists. Their businesses relied more on the shearers' and shed-workers' money than that of the absentee landlords or managers of the stations.

In central Queensland, the people of Blackall showed where their sympathies lay after a coach containing two strikebreakers was stopped by 100 to 150 people. The proprietor of the Tattersalls Hotel refused to give the strikebreakers a bed for the night so they ended up sleeping in the police barracks.

Behind the scenes, attempts were being made to settle the dispute. A key stumbling block was the woolgrowers' insistence that shearers be employed under freedom of contract while the union insisted shearers had to operate under union rules. What exactly was meant by 'freedom of contract' wasn't entirely clear. Not even the woolgrowers could agree.

Meanwhile, the Queensland government was coming under fire. On 11 April, 300 people at a public meeting in Adavale sent Colonial Secretary Tozer a resolution condemning the government. On 13 April, a public meeting was held in Brisbane. The crowd couldn't fit into the town hall and it was estimated they could have filled the building twice. The meeting urged an open conference and conciliation.

In coastal towns and out in the bush, other protest meetings also drew large crowds, deeply concerned that the government was mismanaging the situation. And all the time, protest letters were flooding in.

Amid all this, on 12 April, the Peak Downs rioters were given three months' hard labour. The conspiracy prisoners, by then eleven in number, including Julian Stuart, were remanded to Barcaldine.

On 13 April, Blackall's union organiser, Bill Hamilton, was arrested for conspiracy. It's thought there was some hesitation in arresting Hamilton because he was highly respected in his community and regarded as a calming influence on the situation. In the end, though, not even that could save him.

The Queensland government may have been embattled but it still had plenty of fight. On 14 April, six unionists were arrested for stealing sheep but were charged under the Cattle Stealing Prevention Act. This allowed a magistrate to summarily sentence the defendants to six months' hard labour. If they'd been charged with stealing sheep, a judge and jury would have had to consider the case. Given the mood in most of the towns, the chances of getting a guilty verdict out of a jury were slim.

Despite the obvious manipulation of the justice system, each of the sheep thieves was fined £50 (nearly a year's income) plus costs. Alternatively, they could do six months' hard labour. The financially destitute men had no option but to go to jail.

Colonial Secretary Tozer ordered a further escalation of the military presence, sending an artillery unit and cannon to Charleville on 16 April. The local magistrate, however, suggested that the cannon wasn't going to get far in the boggy conditions that still prevailed in the area and that machine guns might be more useful.

By this time, plans were being drawn up to forcibly disperse the strike camps. The commander of the military, Colonel George French, was their author. The unionists heard of the plans and advised the men in the camps that in the event of an attack they were to lie down and offer no resistance. However, Premier Griffith weighed in and refused to approve French's plan, the details of which have not survived. He'd sent all available military to maintain order but they were still outnumbered by the shearers by nearly twenty to one. It was suggested to the pastoralists that if they wanted more protection, they could recruit it themselves.

Meanwhile, a wagon with seventy-seven bales of wool was burned. The bullocky could offer no information to the police regarding the perpetrators. Another wagon and harness was also burned. The bullocky again was no help. Down on the Warrego, a ram worth £500 was shot dead one night by one of the special constables.

On another station, a special constable managed to shoot himself, though not fatally. A writer named Canney, who was on the station at the time, expressed his disappointment that the shooting wasn't a union raid. He wrote: 'It would have been a satisfaction, considering the state of things, to have shot one or two of the shearers had there been occasion.' Not long after, a union shearer saved Canney's life when he was caught in floodwaters. The bedraggled scribbler doesn't appear to have seized a golden opportunity to fill his rescuer with lead.

Fires continued to be lit around central Queensland. Huts and wool were burned at Thurulgoona and 165 bales were torched at Pinkilla. On 19 April an attempt was made to set fire to the Clermont courthouse. Grassfires around Waroonga, near Mitchell, led to further arrests. A goods shed at Amby also burned.

On 22 April, a public meeting of 400 Blackall residents urged the formation of a board of conciliation. Some of the woolgrowers may have started thinking it was a good idea. On the same day, sixty strikebreakers arrived out at Hughenden. Reports described them as being 'composed of a very low class', a description that Hughenden Station manager R. Gray soon discovered was accurate. The men started shearing the station's 75 000 sheep but after two weeks of tomahawking, Gray got rid of the lot of them.

On 24 April, Horace Tozer advised the government agent at Clermont, Robert Ranking, that the United Pastoralists Association had indeed started recruiting a private army. They had six teams of ten special constables.

While the union strikers were generally close-knit, the same could certainly be said of the government and the woolgrowers. This was evident in a series of communications that eventually became public knowledge. In late April, the secretary of the Queensland Pastoralists Association, F. Ranson, wrote to the police magistrate and assistant government agent in Barcaldine, Charles Morris:

> The twenty specials were engaged yesterday, and will leave here tomorrow by steamer. They should arrive at Barcaldine on Wednesday next, where they have been told they will be met by you. They go up in civilians' clothes, and will require to be sworn in when they reach Muttaburra, or possibly at Barcaldine. See [government agent] Ranking as to what would be best.

This was part of the woolgrowers' private army. However, Ranson was instructing a government appointee on how to manage them. The existence of a relationship between government and woolgrowers may have been obvious to many but this was hard evidence of how close the cooperation had become.

On 1 May, the date that would become synonymous with labour and socialist movements around the world (to commemorate the shooting of unionists in Chicago in 1886), the conspiracy trials of fourteen Queensland Shearers Union organisers were rushed into the Rockhampton court with Judge George Harding presiding. In the dock were George Taylor, Bill Fothergill, Hugh Blackwell, Tom Ryan, Bill Bennett, Alf Brown, Isaac Fry, Bob Prince, Bill Hamilton, Julian Stuart, Paddy Griffin, Henry Smith-Barry, Edward Murphy and Alexander Forrester.

While the conspiracy trial of the unionists got underway, the conspiring between woolgrowers and government continued. The manager of Darr River Downs, George Bunning, wrote to Barcaldine police magistrate Charles Morris on 2 May 1891 regarding the special constables:

> I enclose a copy of wire received by me from Secretary, Pastoralists Union ... It is impossible for me to get down to see personally to these men. May I therefore ask you to take the matter in hand for me. I think it will be advisable to have them sworn in as specials immediately they arrive in Barcaldine; then, as there does not appear to be any boss man amongst them, kindly get police to put an official over them to conduct them up here with all speed consigned to care of P.M., Muttaburra. Upon arrival here I will hand them over to the authorities to guide their youthful minds in the way they should shoot.

At about the same time, Morris made the mistake of placing an advertisement in the *Western Champion* newspaper that read: 'The Government are prepared to provide free rations and protection in police or defence camps to all men, Union or otherwise, who are willing to return to their work at once.'

His motivation may have been the fact that the situation in some strike camps was getting desperate as money and food became increasingly scarce. Men whose cash reserves had long since evaporated were starting to starve. However, the advertisement looked like a bribe and exposed the government to the accusation that it was actively supporting the breaking of the strike, not to mention promising to feed potentially thousands of people.

When Ranking learned of the ad, he insisted it be withdrawn, and that Colonial Secretary Tozer be told of it. He wrote to Morris: 'If you do not see your way to do it, I must, in self-defence. I could not let the

Government go to Parliament to have such a bombshell burst on them unawares.'

As expected, the first two vigilante squads of the pastoralists arrived in Barcaldine on 2 May. They were paid 30 shillings a week, the bill met by the stations on which they were deployed. Equipping them cost £15 per man. By the end of the month the Pastoralists Special Executive would have 134 special constables deployed on forty stations. The stations were obliged to pay their wages.

Also in May, the Vagrant Act was used to arrest union leaders. Again, men were held for extended periods before charges were dropped, due to the likelihood they wouldn't be proved if they went to court. Horace Tozer also had police reporting on the sympathies of magistrates. Prisons by that time were filled with hundreds of unionists, most being held on dubious charges that were never going to go to trial.

Another of Blackall's highly respected citizens, Bill Kewley, was also targeted as one of the last of the original leaders still at large. However, attempts to find a charge against him that would stick kept failing. Eventually, he was charged as an accessory to the burning of the Lorne woolshed. He was held for several months despite businesspeople in Blackall trying to put up bonds in order to have him released. Eventually, the charge against him was dropped and the government set him free.

As the strike wore on into May and some wool was actually being removed from sheep, the problem of transporting it loomed large. Union carriers wouldn't touch it until the pastoralists threatened to employ non-union carriers, and pay them less. The unionists buckled but insisted on maintaining their old rates. The pastoralists responded by setting up a joint stock-carrying company.

At the same time, the Pastoralists Special Executive took control of when stations shore their sheep and the management of the free labour that did the shearing. With that, the woolgrowers had effectively given up control over whom they employed to shear their sheep, what they paid them and when they shore them. These were the very rights they'd been so determined to protect.

The internal struggles with what 'freedom of contract' meant still vexed the Queensland woolgrowers. No less a personage than Queensland premier Sir Samuel Griffith, a lawyer by trade, had supplied a definition, the details of which have not survived, but it wasn't considered suitable. Around mid-May the Queenslanders eventually settled on the definition used by the pastoral unions of New South Wales, Victoria and South Australia: 'An employer is to be free to employ whom he pleases and ... an employee is to be free to engage or refuse to engage to work as he pleases.'

Out in the strike camps some men had started planting vegetable patches. Others were shooting kangaroos and anything else they could find. Many camps were issuing promissory notes to get supplies. Even with belt-tightening, it was costing £1400 a week to keep the strike going. By then 200 unionists were in jail, less than half having been convicted of anything. In May the most common charges against unionists were for stealing food, vagrancy and trespass.

Back at the conspiracy trial, prosecutor Virgil Power spent days reading seized union communications that established the conspiracy:

> All along the coast the men are of the opinion that constitutional means are very little good and that other methods must be tried.
>
> Things are quiet at Clermont. The first shot fired there will, may be, cause the Australian Revolution.
>
> I feel as if I have given moral suasion a fair trial without the slightest success. In my opinion, the only certain method for the working man to get justice is by his becoming expert in the use of the Winchester rifle.
>
> If you want to make a grand coup at any time you could concentrate a force and force a rising by putting a little more devil

in the fight. What chance would police and the military have against bushmen in their own element?

Union mice very destructive in West country, several fires having been started through the agency of these destructive cusses.

Charles Fairbairn gave evidence regarding the reception non-union labour received at Clermont Station. He told the court the four police present had done nothing to stop 200 unionists jeering at the men.

Judge Harding responded, 'Do the police want to see a man's throat cut before they do anything? . . . They all had six shooters. Four sixes are twenty-four of them. There would not have been many who boo-hooed the second time if I had been one of them.'

While giving testimony Senior Sergeant Michael Dillon explained the restraint he had shown on an occasion when his force was severely outnumbered. When the fire-breathing Judge Harding took him to task he replied: 'I acted as I thought best.'

Julian Stuart, one of the defendants, recalled the atmosphere of the courtroom:

> Virgil Power, the eminent Queen's Counsel, showed no venom in the role of Crown Prosecutor. The task of trying to 'lag' bushmen did not seem a congenial one to him. I believe he would have fought better for our defence. At times he seemed to absolutely despise the police witnesses for the barefaced rawness of their methods, and made no pretence of hiding his contempt for some of the witnesses who were prepared to swear anything in order to convict us. The police, as usual, had some dirty tools.
>
> On the other hand, Judge Harding who was on the bench was venomous and vindictive and bloodthirsty to an almost incredible degree.

While the trial went on, Henry Lawson's 'Freedom on the Wallaby' appeared in *The Worker* of 16 May 1891. It concluded:

> Our parents toil'd to make a home
> Hard grubbin 'twas an' clearin'
> They wasn't crowded much with lords
> When they was pioneering.
> But now that we have made the land
> A garden full of promise,
> Old Greed must crook 'is dirty hand
> And come ter take it from us.
> So we must fly a rebel flag,
> As others did before us,
> And we must sing a rebel song
> And join in rebel chorus.
> We'll make the tyrants feel the sting
> O' those that they would throttle;
> They needn't say the fault is ours
> If blood should stain the wattle!

Judge Harding commenced his summing-up on 18 May. By then the conspiracy counts had been whittled down to twenty. After taking all day to sum up, decidedly against the defendants, he sent the jury away to consider its verdict. On the following morning the foreman reported that there wasn't the slightest chance of reaching a decision. Judge Harding insisted they try. At 4.45 p.m. the jury again told the judge they couldn't reach a verdict. Harding refused to discharge them. They were locked up again. At 9 p.m., still no agreement. Harding had them locked up until 10 the next morning.

It was 20 May when the jurors arrived at what appears to have been a compromise. Ryan and Fry were acquitted. The other twelve men were found guilty on all twenty counts of conspiracy. The foreman requested leniency in sentencing.

Little did anyone know that Robert Ranking, who was sitting in court, had more warrants for the arrest of all fourteen defendants in his pocket. Even if they'd been found not guilty, they wouldn't have got out of the courtroom. Harding sentenced the twelve men to three years' hard labour. They were then to be on good-behaviour bonds for another year after that. Despite Ranking's warrants, Ryan and Fry were allowed to walk free.

The editor of *The Worker*, William Lane, attended the conspiracy trial and wrote of it in the 30 May 1891 edition of his paper. He restrained his frequently overblown style to distil the essence of the shearers' fight:

> Foolish some of these prisoners may have been; not one of them but has sought to aid his mates against the oppressor, not one of them but is being victimised now on general principles for having given that aid. They to-day, us to-morrow, you some other day; under some pretence or other those who love the people are doomed to suffer. And when our time comes, as theirs has come, may we be as they are, patient, courageous, and fearless, ready for the worst that can be done to us, comforting ourselves with the sure and certain knowledge that we prepare the way for those who will triumph in the end.

After the trial, the members of the United Pastoralists Association began to consider the possibility that they, too, could be charged with conspiracy. It could be argued that they had fomented trouble. They had even recruited and armed a private army. The conspiracy extended to members of the government. There was sufficient concern for the UPA to seek a legal opinion on registering the organisation under the Trade Unions Act and on whether they could face criminal prosecution.

Who better to ask than eminent former barrister and current premier of Queensland Sir Samuel Griffith. His view was that little was to be gained by registering the association. As to conspiracy, it would be improper of a premier to answer such a question. Then he answered it anyway: 'Your association runs no risk of being brought up under the laws of conspiracy whether it is registered or not registered.'

By 11 June 1891, less than 1000 men were shearing in Queensland. However, for the striking shearers, it was the end of the road. They were out of food, money and credit. Across the Central Queensland districts, as winter set in, thousands faced starvation. That day, men started leaving strike camps at St George, Tambo and Thargomindah. The camp at Isisford broke up the next day.

Within a week, Blackall, Winton and Hughenden's strike camps had dispersed. At Barcaldine, they hung on until 20 June, when the strike committee issued its final manifesto, urging union shearers to register to vote.

Attention now turned to a relief effort for men who had no food, money or employment. With the strike broken, many of the unionists being held awaiting trial were gradually released, some as late as September.

In Queensland's parliament, Tom Glassey MLA put forward a motion calling for a commission of inquiry into the strike. He was a lone voice but as he spoke to the motion he highlighted the disparities between charges and sentences during the dispute, the repeal in England of the Act under which many strikers had been charged, and the instance of the justice of the peace who wrote in the *Brisbane Courier*, 'if a little blood were shed, a great deal of good would result' but was not charged with conspiracy or struck off the JP roll. He also pointed out Judge Harding's comments during the conspiracy trial about shooting striking shearers dead and the ad placed in the *Western Champion* by Charles Morris effectively putting the government in the position of being a strikebreaker.

Much of this was already a matter of public record. However, there was more to come. Tom Glassey then read the letter from Robert Ranking to Charles Morris requesting he withdraw the ad and tell Tozer what he'd done. He revealed the identity of a man who may have been a police informant, the collusion of the government, and the plan that had been drawn up by Colonel French to put down the strike by armed force. He produced telegrams from what turned out to be a box full of documents that Morris had lost. One from Tozer to French read: 'Don't dilly-dally. Exercise vigour even if it causes bloodshed.'

It was abundantly clear how thoroughly the government was in bed with the woolgrowers, and the lengths to which it was prepared to go to defeat the strike. The ensuing debate on Glassey's motion provided the perspectives of both sides on the strike, its causes and its conduct. However, the motion was inevitably defeated by the government's numbers. A royal commission into the strike, held in London, did take place at the end of 1891 but little additional light was cast on the tumultuous events in Queensland in the first half of the year.

***

With Queensland's shearers defeated, attention shifted to New South Wales. Most areas there started shearing going into spring but in the warmer north-western parts of New South Wales, it began not far behind Queensland. The area was also similar to Queensland's pastoral zone, with big stations and sheds shearing big numbers of sheep requiring huge teams of shearers.

Anticipating trouble, the Pastoralists Union of New South Wales had already arranged for 500 strikebreakers from New Zealand to be sent to the north-western districts. On 6 July, the first of them arrived in Bourke. The local shearers, some of whom had crossed the border to support their Queensland colleagues, set up strike camps.

The Bourke shearers soon showed they still had plenty of fight. On 14 July 1891, 278 strikebreakers, armed with batons, were involved in a wild brawl with the town's union shearers. Around 100 strikebreakers were persuaded to join the union cause.

The shearers of northern New South Wales may also have been buoyed by the success of candidates representing workers in elections for the New South Wales Legislative Assembly just a few days before. No fewer than thirty-six seats had been won in the New South Wales parliament.

Less successful were the negotiations between the Amalgamated Shearers Union and the Pastoralists Union of New South Wales. The PUNSW still refused to attend a conference unless the ASU conceded freedom of contract. The union tried to compromise and said it would concede but that the conference should define the meaning of freedom of contract.

In August, the two sides met. The unionists had precious little bargaining power, their resources having been drained by the almighty battle in Queensland, and the pastoralists were anything but gracious in defeat. There was no negotiation on the meaning of freedom of contract. The unionists wanted the definition to appear towards the end of the agreement. The pastoralists insisted it go at the beginning.

A few small concessions were made by the pastoralists, relating to provision of combs and cutters, and the mess deduction for sacked men. Other than that, the contract agreed to was the Pastoralists' Agreement in its entirety. Later in August 1891, the same agreement was adopted in Queensland.

Despite the immediate outcome, there were no big winners in the strike of 1891. Documented costs to the pastoralists were around £53 000, while the documented cost of the strike for the shearers' unions was around £22 000. Both sides, however, may have had other significant expenses. The costs of private armies for the pastoralists and legal bills for the unionists may mean that the true costs could have been triple the known amounts. The cost to the Queensland government exceeded £76 000 but was also probably much higher.

As for the human costs, prison sentences and time spent in custody amounted to approximately 100 years.

There were few tangible gains. The shearers had failed to win the right to shear under shearers' union rules. The pastoralists had failed to smash the unions, although they'd gone very close. Brute force and deep pockets had maintained their right to employ whoever they wanted on the basis of their choosing but there had been no meek acceptance on the side of the workers. As such, the good old days of the Masters and Servants Act were in serious jeopardy.

Some on the woolgrowers' side were alert to the danger. In the early 1890s a book that purported to be a novel was published in Brisbane under the pen-name Wulla Merrii. Vehemently anti-union, its content was as inflammatory as the title, *The Fire Stick*. The story centres on a young shearer, Will Goodleigh, who dies of his wounds after battling to do the right thing by his employer in defiance of the union. On his deathbed, he delivers a final harangue on the risks of empowering the labour movement:

> I die a victim to a vicious system. My father was a Unionist, and at his request I became one; but if I had my time to go over again, I would join no such association. In itself, the idea is a good one; but New Unionism, as carried out by unscrupulous scoundrels who force themselves to the front, is a GIGANTIC LIE. Instead of the foundation being built upon a rock, and the superstructure reared upon truth and honour and right, the whole thing is constructed of materials compounded of falsehood and fraud, trickery and corruption. No man who has a spark of manliness left in him should join New Unionism. One of the ideas of the leaders, or sundowners, is to get into Parliament. God help the working men if they ever get there and have power to influence legislation. Whatever the troubles of the working man may be now, they will be increased tenfold

then. Their ignorance and effrontery, inexperience and utter want of sound principle and judgement to guide even the simplest transaction of a business nature, would necessarily result in disaster to the working classes.

As Wulla Merrii was penning his diatribe, workers were already doing what he most feared. Even one of the conspiracy prisoners, Thomas Ryan, was eventually elected to the Queensland Legislative Assembly in a by-election for the seat of Barcoo. Within a year, however, the member for Barcoo refused to seek re-election to parliament, saying: 'The friends are too warm, the whisky too strong and the seats too soft for Tommy Ryan. His place is out among the shearers on the billabongs.'

And out there under the coolibahs, the great battle of 1891 had reinforced the place of shearers in defining Australian identity, especially at the crucial moment when the form of the Commonwealth of Australia was being debated.

It may be coincidental that the first known version of the song 'Click Go the Shears' appeared in the *Bacchus Marsh Express* on 5 December 1891, under the title 'The Bare Belled Ewe'. It was a strangely nostalgic folk song that may well have been in circulation for some time prior to 1891, but it served as a definitive expression of what it meant to be a shearer, and an Australian worker, at the culmination of an unprecedented year in Australian history:

> Oh, down at the catching pen an old shearer stands,
> Grasping his shears in his long bony hands;
> Fixed is his gaze on a bare belled ewe,
> Saying 'If I can only get her, won't I make the ringer go.'
>
> Click goes his shears; click, click, click.
> Wide are the blows, and his hand is moving quick,

The ringer looks round, for he lost it by a blow,
And he curses that old shearer with the bare belled ewe.

At the end of the board, in a cane-bottomed chair,
The boss remains seated with his eyes everywhere;
He marks well each fleece as it comes to the screen,
And he watches where it comes from if not taken off clean.

The 'colonial experience' is there of course.
With his silver-buckled leggings, he's just off his horse;
With the air of a connoisseur he walks up the floor;
And he whistles that sweet melody, 'I am a perfect cure.'

'So master new chum, you may now begin,
Muster number seven paddock, bring the sheep all in;
Leave none behind you, whatever you do,
And then we'll say you'r fit to be a Jackeroo.'

The tar boy is there, awaiting all demands,
With his black tarry stick, in his black tarry hands.
He sees an old ewe, with a cut upon the back,
He hears what he supposes is – 'Tar here, Jack.'

'Tar on the back, Jack; Tar, boy, tar.'
Tar from the middle to both ends of the board.
Jack jumps around, for he has no time to sleep,
And tars the shearer's backs as well as the sheep.

So now the shearing's over, each man has got his cheque,
The hut is as dull as the dullest old wreck;
Where was many a noise and bustle only a few hours before,
Now you can hear it plainly if a pin fall on the floor.

The shearers now are scattered many miles and far;
Some in other sheds perhaps, singing out for 'tar'.
Down at the bar, there the old shearer stands,
Grasping his glass in his long bony hands.

Saying 'Come on, landlord, come on, come!
I'm shouting for all hands, what's yours – mine's a rum;'
He chucks down his cheque, which is collared in a crack,
And the landlord with a pen writes no mercy on the back!

His eyes they were fixed on a green painted keg,
Saying 'I will lower your contents, before I move a peg.'
His eyes are on the keg, and are now lowering fast;
He works hard, he dies hard, and goes to heaven at last.

5

THE RISE OF
A LEGEND

(1892)

The early 1890s were a time of unprecedented change, with nation-defining confrontation grabbing the headlines, but the image of the shearer – nomadic, independent, hardworking, hard-living – managed to transcend it all. The click of blade shears may have been giving way to the buzz of machines but the idyllic portrayal of the shearer's life in Tom Roberts' paintings and songs like 'The Bare Belled Ewe' reinforced the status of shearers as the embodiment of the best of Australia's character.

Such portrayals may have been romanticised and based more on myth than reality; however, in 1892, a shearer rose to public attention who personified everything the myth-makers were talking about.

His name was Jack Howe, and in the course of just one day, 10 October 1892, he achieved a legendary status that has been unrivalled from that time to this.

Jack was born in 1861, in Killarney, south-east Queensland, the son of an acrobat, clown and 'Australian champion llama shearer',

Jack Senior. His father's champion ranking was somewhat tongue-in-cheek, as at the time he may have been Australia's only llama shearer. Nevertheless, the athleticism of the father was passed on to the son. Jack excelled as a runner in particular, but had an enthusiasm for physical activity that left him still full of energy at the end of a hard day's shearing.

In one story, a sprinter from Rockhampton who fancied his ability bet Jack £10 that he could beat him, even if Jack had a 10-yard (9.1 metre) head start. Jack took him on and beat him. So the sprinter bet Jack he couldn't win if they started even. Jack beat him. Whereupon Jack bet the sprinter all he had left that he still couldn't win if Jack gave him a 10-yard start. Jack won again.

While still in his teens, in the 1870s, Jack started shearing with blades, possibly taught by Chinese shearers. He learned quickly and as he put it, 'things just came naturally to me'. However, he wasn't particularly fast. In later years, his long-time pen mate, Harry Dunn, recalled:

> When Jack Howe first started shearing he did not put up big scores. He had been shearing on the Darling Downs, and at one place the boss always gave a bonus of £5 to the man who shore his sheep the cleanest and best. Jack Howe invariably got the fiver.
>
> It may not be generally known, but it is a fact that Jack Howe sacked himself at Alice Downs in 1882. The place was owned and managed by Mr. Davidson, who always insisted on the shearers carrying, not dragging their sheep from the pen to the shearing board. Jack Howe was shearing wethers, and big wethers they were too, and as he always did, was turning the sheep over in the pen and dragging them out on the board. Mr. Davidson saw this and remonstrated, telling Jack Howe it was in the agreement that sheep had to be carried out. Howe tried to explain that he was not hurting the sheep, but the boss insisted on carrying, so Howe told him to get someone else to take his (Howe's) pen. Mr. Davidson

refused to do this, but told Jack Howe that if he (Howe) got a man as good as himself to take the pen he would let him go, but otherwise Howe would have to stay and carry out his agreement. Howe eventually got a man named Dash to take the pen, and left.

After his experience at Alice Downs in 1882, Howe went across to Langlo and shore there. In those days the ringer of the shed had the privilege of dealing with the cook, and, if necessary, sacking him. Howe was shearing considerably less than 100 a day. The ringer was Billy Manton, and one day Manton sacked the cook. At the dinner hour Jack Howe asked someone, 'Who sacked the cook?' Manton heard him and replied, 'A shearer, not a schnapper like you.' This rankled in Jack Howe's mind all that evening and night, and next morning he went to work with the expressed intention of no longer deserving the name of 'schnapper'. He shore 211 that day, and thereafter always cut Manton out of a good many sheep per day. This was the commencement of Jack Howe's tallies, and from then on he ranked with the fastest shearers in Queensland.

Jack wasn't particularly tall, at 177.8 centimetres, but he was a solid block of muscle, 127 centimetres around his chest, with 45-centimetre biceps, 37-centimetre forearms and 70-centimetre thighs. His left calf, which took most of his weight while shearing, was 49 centimetres, while his right calf was 47 centimetres. Images of Jack, young and old, show him with a sweeping moustache. He also had hands the size of dinner plates.

As his reputation as a clean, fast shearer grew, he did a season in New Zealand in the early 1880s. At one station, he was one of six Australians in a team of twelve shearers when the boss said, 'If you finish the sheep by noon Saturday, I'll shout you a couple of gallons of rum.'

The team needed no further encouragement. They got stuck in and did even better. They finished the sheep by midday Friday! Jack was the ringer with 196 in just half a day. If he'd been able to maintain that pace, and had enough sheep, he might have set a record close to 400 for the day (bearing in mind that the sheep may have been easier-shearing New Zealand breeds).

Jack knocked around Australia for the next few years. It seems that he may have tried his hand at gold prospecting before settling in the Blackall district. During the mid-to-late 1880s, he appears to have been earning enough from shearing to work at it for only five months of the year. Shearing in the region of 8000 to 9000 sheep a year would easily have brought in sufficient income for a single man to live on comfortably.

At a time when most shearers walked or rode bicycles from shed to shed, Jack was said to travel on horseback, carrying his personal effects and equipment in pack saddles.

It also appears that he was involved in the union movement as early as 1887. On 12 January 1890, he seconded a motion for the amalgamation of the fledgling Blackall Shearers Union with the recently formed Queensland Shearers Union.

Jack's circumstances changed on 24 April 1890, when he married Victoria Short at St Patrick's Church, Blackall. Their marriage certificate gives her profession as dressmaker. And indeed, Victoria soon turned her skills to producing the specialised vests that Jack wore while shearing.

Made from a flannel material, the vests had a button-up collarless neck and short sleeves. They also had the advantage of being close-fitting so that a struggling sheep couldn't snag and tear the material, and they absorbed sweat and prevented Jack getting chills. (It's worth noting that Jack's vests weren't like the Jackie Howe singlet that has since become famous.)

Jack was on the 1891 committee that decided on amalgamation of the Queensland Shearers Union with the Queensland Labourers Union. He was also a member of the Australian Labor Party from its birth (as the Union Party in 1891).

In the midst of the shearers' strike, on 11 February 1891, Victoria gave birth to the first of the Howes' ten children, Louisa Victoria. Now with a family to support, in March 1891 Jack, along with Jack Power and pen mate Harry Dunn (a top shearer in his own right), honoured his contract to shear for W. H. Banks and Mick Ryan at their wool scour on the edge of Blackall.

There appear to have been no consequences of their actions. Despite this seeming betrayal, Jack was trusted with hiding the union funds by Bill Kewley, who by April was the only union leader not under arrest. And no one, it seems, was about to call one of the best shearers and one of the most physically fit men in the Blackall district a scab.

However, Jack's conduct reveals another aspect of the relationship between shearers and woolgrowers. While there may have been antagonism towards the big station owners (disparagingly and often incorrectly referred to as squatters), who had little personal contact with their workforce, especially their itinerant workers, on smaller stations employing workers from the local district, relationships could operate on a more personal level.

In a town like Blackall, which seems to have been less militant than other areas, and whose union representatives were well respected in the community, union solidarity could take second place to honouring a commitment sealed with a handshake. Such communities worked together to get the job done. Other great shearers, for example John Hutchinson (a Shearers' Hall of Fame inductee – see page 270), have identified properties where they were welcomed back every year for decade after decade. Such appears to have been the case with Jack at Blackall.

In 1892, at the age of thirty-one, Jack was at the peak of his shearing powers. In October, he was shearing at Alice Downs where he put up a tally of 1437 sheep in the first week – five eight-hour days and a Saturday morning: Monday, 249; Tuesday, 257; Wednesday, 258; Thursday, 262; Friday, 267; Saturday, 144.

It was the tally for Saturday morning that started the Blackall tongues wagging. Had he maintained the same pace all day, he'd have shorn 288, just a dozen sheep short of a massive 300 in a day: a shearing feat that had never been achieved.

Many of the pundits said 300 in a day couldn't be done, especially given the situation at Alice Downs. The station had barely enough sheep left for two more days of shearing and with a weekend intervening it would take Jack longer than a day to regain the suppleness and rhythm to get anywhere near such a high tally. Jack thought otherwise. He decided he would attempt to shear 300 sheep on his first day back after the weekend, when he was fresh and there were still enough sheep.

The Blackall punters got busy.

There was more than just the glory of the achievement at stake. A Cootamundra eucalyptus manufacturing company, Coleman and Sons, had a standing offer of a gold medal, valued at 10 pounds 10 shillings, for the highest tally of sheep shorn by hand each year. They also had a 5 pound 5 shilling award for the biggest tally shorn by machines. It was probably no accident that business interests of the time were actively encouraging faster shearing.

On Monday, 10 October 1892, it wasn't quite business as usual at the Alice Downs shearing shed. Gathering in the early dawn light, amid the bleating of sheep in the pens and dogs barking as stockmen brought in the last of the station's flocks, interested onlookers joined the shearers, rousies, pressers and classers at the shed, along with the station manager. Some, such as the owner of Bloomfield Station, were there in an official capacity. In his case, he was the official timekeeper.

As the bell rang to signal the start of shearing, Jack knew the simple mathematics of the pace he had to keep. He had four runs in the day, each of two-hour duration. He had to do better than seventy-five sheep per run, thirty-eight sheep per hour. Every sheep had to be caught in the pen, carried to the board and shorn in just over one minute and thirty seconds.

In the first run, he was either on the pace or slightly ahead of it. By the end of the second run, he was looking even better. There was the usual lunch break, after which Jack came out and really cracked on the pace. According to the timekeeper, the actual time Jack took to remove a fleece (apart from catching, carrying to the board and releasing each sheep) was just fifty-five seconds.

By mid-afternoon, at the end of his third run, Jack was well ahead of the pace he had to maintain to achieve an incredible tally of 300 sheep blade-shorn in a day. The tallies for each run aren't recorded, but he probably only needed forty-six sheep in the final two hours to reach the target.

With an hour still to go, Jack was almost there. In the excitement of the moment, and the realisation that he was easily going to achieve the seemingly impossible, according to Harry Dunn, some of those present started trying to throw Jack off. They tickled him and jumped on him; they tried to throw his sheep back into the pen. Jack took the practical joking in his stride and shore on past 300 with about fifty minutes still to go. Still the tally mounted.

'You've done enough, man. You've done enough,' some of the spectators cried.

After seven hours and forty minutes, and with 321 sheep shorn with blades, Jack decided to knock off for the day, twenty minutes early. The average time he'd taken to catch, carry, shear and release each sheep was one minute and twenty-six seconds.

Had he shorn through to the end of the run, based on his average time, he'd have shorn 334. Had his high-spirited supporters not been hindering his shearing, the tally might have been higher still.

The blade-shearing record Jack Howe set that day has never been matched, let alone exceeded. And while some circumstances of the shearing at Alice Downs made the achievement easier (for example, the sheep were all under twelve months of age, essentially making them lambs, and the fleece weights of the time were perhaps half what they are today), other aspects made the shearing harder (Jack was shearing merino sheep, in shed conditions, without any of the preparation and selection sometimes done with other record attempts). He also had to carry every sheep, rather than drag it to the board.

Some sense of what Jack Howe achieved can be gained by checking the tallies of the other gun shearers with him in the shed that day. The next highest was 219, over 100 sheep behind. Under the circumstances, Jack Howe has rightly earned the title of the Bradman of the Board.

The achievement is universally recognised. In his book *Sheep-O!* New Zealand writer Bob Mills reflected:

> This blade tally of Jackie Howe's has never been equalled in any country and establishes him as the greatest blade shearer of all time. If ever there was a legendary figure in the shearing world it is Jackie Howe. To this day if you walk into a clothing store of the right kind and asked for 'a couple of Jackie Howe's' you will be given the black or blue sleeveless woollen singlet so favoured by shearers and Bushmen in Australia and New Zealand.

What is perhaps even more remarkable is that, later in 1892, at Barcaldine Downs, Jack showed his versatility by setting a new record with machine shears of 237 sheep in a day. This meant he acquired both the blade-shearing and machine-shearing medals for that year.

It's also worth mentioning that while Jack's blade-shearing record has never been equalled with blades, it took sixty years for a machine shearer to equal it. In 1950, Australian Ted Reick shore 326 merinos in seven hours and forty-eight minutes.

Newspapers of the time carried an article about Jack's shearing tallies from 1886 to 1893. In it, Jack was described as 'the ringer of Queensland shearers'. The figures were: 1886, 7300; 1887, 8100; 1888, 15 600; 1889, 8400; 1890, 8000; 1891, 9100; 1892, 13 700; 1893, 12 200.

The report went on:

> This is a total of 82,400 for the eight years, which at £1 per hundred gives a total receipt of £824, or an average for the eight years of £103 per year. This seems a small average for such a first class shearer, but it is well-known that Mr. Howe, in his bachelor days at all events, would never take more than two sheds a year, and consequently worked for only five months out of twelve. His best year was 1888, when his tally was 15,600, which gave him £156. The small receipts in 1891 is of course accounted for by the strike, but taking the two years 1892 and 1893, Howe's average was 12,950, or £129 10s per year. If he chose to accept a stand in sheds open from March till December he might easily increase his earnings to £200 a year, and then have a holiday for three months during the hot weather. No other labour men are paid so well as these, except our representatives in the House, and Jack Howe, if he had chosen to let himself be nominated, might be the member for the Barcoo today.

It appears that Jack's marriage, in 1890, and starting a family, in 1891, was as strong a motivation to achieve big tallies as being called a 'schnapper' had been in the early 1880s.

Jack also appears to have preferred to make a living than lose time and money in a strike camp. He spoke strongly against the strike action of 1894, which all but destroyed the shearers' unions. It was badly organised and badly timed (many sheds had already finished), and the lessons of 1891 weren't learned. Jack believed parliamentary representation could achieve much more, although some elected officials failed to take the fight to the government once they found themselves in the comfort of office (as detailed in Chapter 4). Jack's view may have carried some weight but in 1894 Blackall voted 75 to 19 to strike.

In later years, Jack supported the parliamentary ambitions of Labor's T. J. Ryan (not to be confused with shearer Tom Ryan), who took the seat of Barcoo. They remained good friends for the rest of their lives, as Ryan went on to become premier of Queensland.

As Jack's fame grew, it doesn't appear to have changed his easy-going nature. Stories of his sense of humour sit alongside those of his prowess.

On one occasion, a woolgrower rushed up to him in a pub in an agitated state.

'Mr Howe! Mr Howe!' he said. 'Can you shear my sheep?'

'How many?' Jack asked.

'Sixty,' came the reply.

To which Jack responded, 'What are their names?'

Jack wasn't shearing well on a day when a group of station managers visited the shed to see the famous ringer in action. They asked if he was Jack Howe. Jack shook his head and pointed to a young bloke down the board who was ringing the shed.

'Are you Jack Howe?' the managers asked.

'Not me,' the youngster replied, 'I'm just any bloody how.'

In another shed, Jack was shearing away, doing modest tallies of 111 a day. A gun shearer thought he was doing pretty well against the great Jack Howe, with tallies up around 150. Then came Saturday morning, a half-day. The gun shore seventy-five. Jack did 111.

It shouldn't be surprising that Jack didn't put up huge tallies every time he shore. He may well have been able to put on impressive spurts, but shearing inevitably takes its toll. As a general guide, over the course of a shearer's career, their tallies start modestly, increase to a point where they are at the top of their game physically and in terms of skill, then gradually decline as the ravages of time and thousands of sheep shorn takes the edge off. Such a course may not be a smooth progression up and down, but more a series of steps, as something new is learned, an injury is overcome, or an injury is incurred. In Jack's case, being belittled lifted his tallies, as did marriage, but even for great shearers, for every highlight there's a twilight.

In 1900, aged thirty-nine, Jack retired from shearing and bought the Universal Hotel in Blackall. In 1902 he sold the Universal and bought the Barcoo Hotel, which became one of the town's shearers' hotels. He sold the Barcoo in 1907 and returned to the Universal, where he remained until 1919. He also became a car dealer for Ford.

In 1914 one of Jack's sons drew a 3500-hectare block near Tambo as part of the immense land distribution that started after the depression years of the 1890s. The newly named Shamrock Park satisfied the family's desire to own a grazing property but wasn't big enough to support them all. The need for improvements drained the family's resources instead. Tambo Park, from which the Shamrock Park block was taken, bought the land back in 1919.

In 1915, another of Jack's sons drew Ravensbourne, which was renamed Sumnervale. At 8000 hectares, it presented the family with the same problems as Shamrock Park. It was big enough to get them into trouble, but not big enough to get them out.

In time Jack became overweight, as many shearers do, and this may have contributed to ill health in later life. In 1919 he sold the Universal Hotel and retired to Sumnervale. Within a year, just short of fifty-nine, he died in Blackall Hospital from inflamed kidneys and heart failure. His grave is in the Blackall Cemetery.

Jack Howe's stature has grown ever since. Ask anyone to name a shearer, and the most likely answer will be 'Jack Howe'. Before Jack, men wore flannel shirts with rolled sleeves that could catch the hoofs and horns of struggling sheep. After Jack's record tally, many shearers tore off their shirt sleeves in imitation of the short-sleeved flannel garment Jack wore. Anything that might make a difference was worth a try. Eventually, when a company made a sleeveless singlet in a similar style, they named it a Jackie Howe. The singlets reputedly came out after Jack's death. His wife sought legal advice about being compensated for the use of his name but the matter wasn't considered worth pursuing.

The Model T Ford Jack owned and drove is still in existence and has been fully restored. It occasionally appears at Jack Howe commemorative events. In 1992, as part of celebrations to mark the centenary of Jack's blade-shearing record, it was used to convey then prime minister Paul Keating (a politician noted for his preference for Italian suits made from fine Australian wool) from the airport to the Blackall wool scour.

Sumnervale remained in the family until Jack's son Henry Howe's death in 1981. It was auctioned in 1988. That year, a sculpture was unveiled in Blackall to commemorate Jack's record-breaking feat. It depicts Jack carrying a ram and stands proudly in Blackall's main street to this day.

6

FIRE AND BLOOD

(1893)

After the shearers and woolgrowers had slugged it out in 1891, peace could be said to have returned to the woolsheds of eastern Australia. However, uneasy truce may be more accurate.

In May 1892, Queensland's United Pastoralists Association met to consider implementing new wage cuts for shearers and station hands. The woolgrowers had insisted that wasn't their aim during the battles of 1891 but it wasn't surprising that it came to the fore when they emerged victorious. . The cuts contemplated would have made wages for such work among the lowest in the British Empire.

The shearers were in no position to fight. Their union was crippled by the costs of the previous year. However, some of the woolgrowers may have had enough experience of the danger of going near an injured animal to be wary when it came to dealing with the cornered, wounded union shearers. Their fears were well grounded. Much of Queensland had gone into drought and the country was a tinderbox.

The incendiarism of 1891 would be as nothing if the firesticks came out in 1892. Not only that, a state election was due in early 1893. Retaliation could easily find expression in the ballot box. The idea of wage cuts was quietly dropped.

By then, though, the country was in the grip of an unprecedented economic downturn. During 1892, 14 000 people registered when the government opened a labour bureau in Sydney. In July, miners in Broken Hill struck when their pay deal was torn up, and non-union labour was employed. At one point a group of strikers' wives were confronted by police and troopers with fixed bayonets.

The next year, 1893, the perceived injustices of the political system prompted *The Worker*'s founding editor, William Lane, and others involved in strikes, the union movement and the fight for social justice to depart Australia aboard the ship *Royal Tar*. They set up what was hoped would be a Utopian society on land purchased in Paraguay, South America. *The Bulletin* described the undertaking as 'One of the most feather-headed expeditions since Sir Galahad pursued the Holy Grail'. And so it proved. The scheme failed but some descendants of the Utopians can still be found in South America.

It seems to have made no difference to Lane and his colleagues that many legislatures in the country were starting to see Labor representatives elected. In 1893, Queensland discovered the new strength of workers at the ballot box, many of whom had found good reasons to enrol to vote for the first time. Labor won 35.5 per cent of the vote and sixteen seats in the Queensland Legislative Assembly. It was a definitive win for the labour movement in general and shearers in particular.

By this time, the banks had problems of their own. Many that had been faltering since the 1892 economic downturn started to fail in 1893. At the beginning of April, the biggest bank in the country, the Commercial, suspended operations. Within days, twelve other banks had followed as people rushed to withdraw their savings. At the end of the month, the Victorian government closed all the banks in the state for a week while it tried to deal with the crisis. Small investors lost their savings. Land speculators went bankrupt. Businesses closed and the unemployment queues grew ever longer.

In Queensland, July 1893 saw the question of wage cuts revisited. Soon after, wages for farm labourers were reduced by twenty per cent. A proposal to cut the shearing rate to 17 shillings and 6 pence per hundred was put forward but again it met with resistance. Eventually, a rate of 20 shillings was retained for most districts, while the lower rate was applied to sheds in the Darling Downs. After the decision was made, the new rates were kept a closely guarded secret. The fight would be on again in 1894.

The dire economic situation also prompted action in New South Wales and Victoria. There the woolgrowers repudiated the 1891 Pastoralists' Agreement they themselves had formulated. Whiteley King of the Pastoralists Union of New South Wales wrote to the Australian Workers Union (the AWU was formed by the unification of the Amalgamated Workers Union and the General Labourers Union in 1892) on 14 April 1894: 'This Union hereby gives notice from this date its members will discontinue working under the said agreement.'

A new agreement was formulated that stripped away what little had been conceded in 1891. The shearing rate was reduced by 3 shillings per hundred. A new clause stated: 'It is hereby distinctly understood and agreed that the person in charge of the shed, on behalf of the employer, shall be the person to decide all questions arising under this agreement and that his decision upon all questions shall be final and conclusive.'

The reaction of the Australian Workers Union was predictable. According to William Spence in his *History of the AWU*, shearers faced 'a battle royal. It was a straight out contest in which there was no place for compromise and no quarter would be given'.

Some woolgrowers were unhappy about the breaking of the 1891 agreement but as the economic situation worsened, those banks that hadn't collapsed continued their strategy of trying to preserve their financial position while cutting the conditions of shearers and farmhands.

With another strike looming, Julian Stuart, recently released from jail and having to be careful that he was always on his best behaviour or face another year behind bars, soon discovered that times had changed. As the then secretary of the Bourke branch of the AWU, Donald Macdonell, told him: 'Labor militant is not the same as Labor triumphant.'

Stuart went to Sydney where he discovered Macdonell was right. He found the Labor parliamentarians:

> A bit lukewarm and disappointing. 'But,' I reminded them, 'these men the squatters are trying to crush are the men who sent you from the sheds and the coal pits to Parliament. You fought with them, and why can't you fight in the Assembly the same as you could on the creeks and billabongs? Must a man lose his punch just because he has a cushioned seat?'

Apparently, he must.

In May 1894, a month after the pastoralists of New South Wales had notified shearers of their new deal, the United Pastoralists Association in Queensland published details of the rates it had kept secret for months. The shearers' union, since 1892 the Amalgamated Workers Union of Queensland (which included the Queensland Labourers Union), sought a conference with the UPA. It was refused.

Not surprisingly, the savage cuts to wages revitalised unions. For the twelve men jailed for conspiracy in 1891 and released in 1894, it was as if nothing had changed. They went to jail during a shearers' strike. They came out of jail during a shearers' strike.

In June 1894, the Amalgamated Workers Union recommended members fight the new agreement. Although many sheds had already finished shearing in Queensland, the fight there was as bitter as it was in New South Wales. Soon eight sheds were set alight, seven within a 100-kilometre radius.

It turned out that this was the area Shearblade Martin had gone to after his release from prison. He was arrested and tried in 1896 with three others for the burning of Ayrshire Downs shed. One of the witnesses against him had been arrested in connection with the poisoning of more than fifty men, one of whom died, at Bowen Downs in 1895 (as detailed later in this chapter). Martin was found guilty and sentenced to fifteen years in prison.

Given the economic situation, the shearers' hopes of achieving any kind of victory were extremely slim. It was suspected that pastoralists may have been contributing to unemployment ranks by laying off as many workers as possible, in an attempt to force wages down even further. As one description put it: 'There are three men anxious to obtain the work offering for one.' And yet, as woolgrower George Mair admitted at the time: 'A shilling or two per 100 sheep would make no great difference in the annual balance sheet.'

The fight soon got ugly. On 16 July 1894 a leaflet was discovered advocating murder. At the same time, a unionist was shot in the leg while watching strikebreakers sign a shearing agreement. A policeman, a Sub-inspector Carr, was suspected of the shooting, but managed to shift the blame onto another unionist who was jailed for six years. A subsequent report on Carr advised that he 'seems to have lost his head' and should 'be allowed to retire from the service'. He did so seven weeks later.

By August thousands of men were in strike camps throughout the eastern states, again putting immense pressure on the finances of the cash-strapped unions.

On 26 August a paddle-steamer, the *Rodney*, carrying forty-five strikebreakers up the Darling, tied up for the night and her cautious skipper set a guard around her. It made no difference. In the darkness 100 armed men boarded her, sent the non-union labourers running for their lives and set the vessel alight. It burned to the waterline then went to the bottom.

Arrests soon followed. According to William Spence:

> S.C. Robinson, James Fox, James Pender, W. Duncan, W. Goadie, J. Evans, R. Strudholme and T. McDonal were arrested and tried for burning the *Rodney*. Thirty witnesses came forward and proved an alibi and the accused were let off. A second lot were run in and found not guilty, and eventually they arrested Thomas Bonner for the offence and gave him seven years. He was not within 100 miles [160 kilometres] of the steamer when it was fired, but that did not matter to the authorities.

The situation was just as ugly in Bourke. There, it was reported, thirteen jaws were broken in one day.

On 1 September 1894, an extraordinary article appeared in *The Bulletin* magazine. It was titled 'The Anarchists of the Bush' and detailed the distribution of anarchist literature in Queensland, and the spread of anarchist symbols (including a woman pointing to a building in flames with the slogan 'Anarchy is Liberty') on the roads between Sydney and Melbourne. 'These things are probably the work of a few madmen,' the anonymously written article, which may have been penned by none other than Banjo Paterson, explained, 'but that does not lessen the danger to the society which has made them mad. The swagman's usual greeting, "Old man, it ain't far off," may yet possess a more dread significance than attaches to the voice of mere idle discontent.'

The article went on:

> Thanks to their own land hunger and consequent slavery to the banks, nine-tenths of the squatters have no money to pay for labour; and farmers have even more than in the past to rely on their own unaided exertions for putting in and taking off their crops.

Unfortunately the number of wage-earners has not decreased in proportion to the shrinkage in demand. This winter men, who, a few years ago, had never to ask twice for a job, are saying in the bitterness of their hearts, "I've never begged before; and rather than live this dog's life I'll go to gaol." When the legitimate bush-worker is thus tried, it is easy to understand the damnable despair of the hordes of artisans, labourers, clerks, larrikins, and social camp-followers who are now swarming out of the cities into the poverty-cursed country districts.

The article had particular resonance in the Queensland outback. Within a day of its publication, in the early hours of Sunday, 2 September 1894, the heavily guarded woolshed at Dagworth Station, halfway between Winton and Kynuna, was attacked by a group of armed men.

That night overseer Weldon Tomlin and police constable Michael Daly were on duty, keeping watch on the shed and adjacent huts. Constable Daly later testified:

> About half past 12 I heard a volley of shots fired from the downs side about 50 yards [45 metres] from the shed. I was about 10 or 15 yards from the corner of the shed between it and the huts. I heard one shot strike the iron of a hut and several whistled past me. I fired in the direction of the flashes (2 shots). The attacking party returned the fire and one of the attacking party called out from I should say about 40 yards [36.5 metres] 'Put up your arms you bastards or die.'

Station manager Bob Macpherson also testified: 'I was aroused about midnight of the 1st by a volley of shots. I was in the hut nearest the shed, got up and procured a revolver from my brother after some time. Before that I heard a voice call out "Hold up your hands or die" and afterwards, "Hold up your hands you bastards or die."'

Outside, Daly and Tomlin were in the midst of a gunfight. Daly:

I went to a heap of earth close to the shed for cover and from there fired 3 or 4 shots in the direction of the attacking party. I then came to the nearest hut occupied by Messrs Macpherson brothers and Mr Dyer [another manager] to advise them of the position of affairs. I was joined by Mr Dyer and returned to the heap of earth. He was armed with a Winchester rifle.

Macpherson soon joined them:

Dyer went away with Constable Daly and when I got a revolver I followed. When I saw a flash of 3 or 4 shots about 40 yards away from the attacking party I returned the fire and immediately heard a bullet whistle past me. I fired five more shots – the attacking party kept up a continuous fire.

Dyer and Daly poured gunfire into the darkness:

We fired 7 or 8 shots each and then saw a match struck at the shed immediately followed by a blaze as if from kerosene. We both fired in the direction of the match. After some time the fire reached the roof of the shed, all this time the attacking party kept up continuous fire under which it was impossible to reach the shed. I heard the same voice say before the match was struck: 'Give it to the bastards. We have waited long enough for this and now we'll have it.'

Macpherson also saw the shed go up:

It was impossible to attempt to save it in consequence of the incessant firing of the attacking party. About 140 lambs and other property were burnt in the shed. The firing continued on and off for three-quarters of an hour and only ceased when the shed was fully at large.

The woolshed burned until about 2 a.m.

The following day, a union shearer, Samuel Hoffmeister, was found dead of a gunshot wound to the head at a waterhole twenty-five kilometres from Dagworth woolshed. A brief police investigation concluded the wound was self-inflicted.

Other sheds burned during the 1894 strike included Milo woolshed; Redcliffe, worth £1000; Manuka, worth £2000; Cambridge Downs, worth £5000; Ayrshire, worth £5000; and Cassilis, worth £1500. While the fires burned, the drought tightened its grip on the land. Country that could carry a sheep per hectare before the drought could only carry one to 10 hectares, if that.

In many places grass was set alight. Some reckoned it did farmers a favour as it burned off dead grass and brought up green pick. In other places, there was so little grass the fires burned out quickly. Yet other unlucky farmers lost what little feed they had left for their stock. Ebb Smith at Warriboan wrote: 'The whole of the country is on fire and has lost 300 square miles [777 square kilometres] of grass.' At Whynebah, home of Pastoralists Union president W. Allen, there were 'ten separate fires in sight of the homestead'.

In New South Wales, in Gilgandra, a female cook poisoned the food of a group of strikebreakers, fortunately without fatal consequences. At Grassmere, unionists William McLean and John Murphy were shot by a man named Baker. William Spence wrote: 'His action was highly approved by Judge Stephen and the President of the Pastoralists' Union sent him a token of approval.' McLean subsequently died while being held in prison on a charge of conspiracy.

The strikebreakers came mostly from Victoria and New Zealand. While the shearers' union espoused principles of mateship and solidarity, the woolgrowers found that appealing to naked self-interest was a recipe for success. As one letter to the *Pastoralists' Review* put it, principled workers are 'like snow in summer, not often seen'.

However, there was plenty of loyalty to be found on both sides of the dispute. Charles Emerson Robertshaw detailed events at Weilmoringle in *Wirragoona: Tales of Australian Station Life*. The station had a large Aboriginal community that provided much of its labour and was protective of its interests. On one occasion, according to Robertshaw, an Aboriginal man named 'Pintpot' proposed his own scheme to help break the strike:

> 'I ain't union. No dam fear. I tell those other fellers suppose boss give me buckboard, I drive to Boodooga, and get five, six, good black feller, muster back paddocks same as them', and he eagerly emphasised his remarks with some well-learnt and correctly accented profanity.'

Julian Stuart, despite still being on a good-behaviour bond, was also involved in the strike action of 1894. He recalled his encounter with the strikebreakers hired by the New South Wales pastoralists:

> Whiteley King was secretary of the Pastoralists' Association during the strikes of the nineties and the undesirables, free labourers and pet merinos, were called 'Whitewings'. We were told he had hired fighting men from Sydney to act as their bodyguard on the way out to the sheds.
>
> Arthur Desmond and I intercepted a coach load in the Bland River district one day and old 'Ragnar' did the talking while I held the horses. The driver whispered to me that Arthur ought to be careful as Jim Fogarty the jaw-breaker was supposed to be in charge of the 'Whitewings'. After the coach had driven on, I told Desmond of the risk perhaps he'd run.

'Why didn't you let me know?' he asked wistfully. 'It was the chance of a lifetime. I always did want to try myself with someone who could really fight.'

Still the strike ground on. Both sides could draw on the experiences of three years earlier, but the factors working against the shearers were many. The woolgrowers and government were well versed in working together to break the strike. Wages were depressed by the economy, the consequences of overstocking and severe drought.

On 10 September the strike ended in Longreach. The shearers in New South Wales battled on. Many woolgrowers were starting to feel that the savings on labour were not worth the cost of the disruption. Yet others were still determined to win.

When William Keogh, manager of Warrana Station, near Coonamble, hired forty strikebreakers, he also employed six professional fighters to ensure they weren't interfered with. He then obtained a court injunction against Australian Workers Union general secretary Macdonell, president William Smith and branch secretary Ike Smith. The three were instructed not to 'cause, induce or persuade any employees of the plaintiff by words or by any means whatsoever to violate or attempt to violate any contract entered into by him with the plaintiff'. The order was accompanied by the threat to seize the personal estates, rents, issues and profits of the men as well as those of the AWU if it wasn't obeyed.

Other leaders such as William Spence also faced actions threatening them with personal financial ruin. The strike in the southern states collapsed in November 1894.

By then in Victoria the rate for shearing was only 15 shillings and 6 pence. In New South Wales shearers had to accept a cut of 3 shillings per hundred. And yet the offices of the Pastoralists Union were inundated with men seeking work at any rate. The union eventually told members to fight for union rates of pay but to accept the best they could get. They called the years 1895 to 1897 'the dark days'.

The bitterness lived on long after. Julian Stuart recalled an incident that highlighted the lasting consequences. Presser Ben Rogers had bested the owner of Burenda on the Warrego (Cowle), who agreed to the terms but left word that Rogers wasn't to be given a job – a standard practice of victimising troublemakers. His comrades wanted to refuse to start work without him but an old hand had a better idea. Rather than lose a week waiting for the owner to see reason, he said:

> 'My "preposition" is that instead of having our moles and "flannens" laundried by dusky daughters of the soil, as we have always done, we make Ben, with the tongue of a young Demos-the-knees himself our laundryman and at the same time retain his services as our Fidus As-kates . . . our guide, philosopher and friend. He'll earn as much as he would at the woolpress and he can breathe the free air of heaven unbeholden to our herry-dettery enemy the squatter.'

The 'squatter' had a fit when he found out but could do nothing. In the end Ben's cheque equalled that of the shed's ringer.

Others incidents weren't as humorous. In 1895, shearers both union and non-union who had broken the strike at Queensland's Bowen Downs the year before were given first preference for that year's shearing. Unfortunately, someone was waiting for them.

In mid-July 1895, first eight shearers, and then forty-nine, were poisoned. An urgent telegram sent from Aramac, the nearest town to the station, reported: 'Strychnine is suspected, and it is believed the poison was put in the meat and sago puddings eaten by the men. The poisoning only affected those who ate in the shearer's mess.'

A subsequent letter, reported in the *Brisbane Courier*, described the suffering at the station:

> Scenes at the shed at Bowen Downs are beyond description, human beings contorting themselves in all shapes and forms in all directions. A man called 'Thomas' has succumbed. He is unknown; it is thought that his name was an assumed one. Richardson, one of five brothers, reported to be the son of Mr. W. Richardson, of the Hit-or-Miss Farm, near Barcaldine, and Christie Schulz, both well-known shearers, are said to be very bad.

John Henry Thomas had died screaming in agony. Within days, the Queensland government offered a reward of £2000 for information leading to the conviction of his killer. The station's management added a further £500. The station had employed seventy-two shearers, of whom only twenty-eight were able to continue the shearing, while four police mounted a guard on the station's kitchen. Arsenic was eventually identified in the kitchen's flour and a sago pudding.

At the end of August, three union shearers were arrested in connection with the poisoning: Robert Langhorn; Michael Maher, alias Baxter, alias M'Mahon, alias Alick Piper; and George William Bristowe, alias Porter. Bristowe was noted as a union activist, especially during the strikes of 1891.

Maher was subsequently released, while Langhorn and Bristowe were committed for trial. However, the cases don't appear to have proceeded, probably due to the evidence against them being circumstantial, if not speculative. In October 1896, a correspondent to *The Worker* noted that 'Bristow [sic], who stood his trial in connection with the Bowen Downs affair in Queensland, is now shearing for 17s per hundred at Yarralla Station, in N.S.W.'

***

About the only good thing to come out of the strike of 1894 was a song. In January 1895, Banjo Paterson paid a visit to Dagworth Station. In fact, he'd been at Dagworth the month before the woolshed was set ablaze. He was a frequent visitor to the station as he was courting a young woman, Sarah Riley, who lived in the nearby town of Winton. Sarah was a friend of Christina Macpherson, who was living with her brother, the owner of Dagworth, after the death of their mother.

Accounts vary widely as to what exactly transpired during Banjo's trip to see Sarah (as detailed in my book *Outback Heroes*). Some suggest he didn't go to Dagworth at all, while others suggest he not only went there, he went to a picnic at Combo Waterhole, 30 kilometres from where the original Dagworth homestead was located, and where a farmhand was supposed to have drowned. Other accounts suggest he was shown the waterhole where union shearer Sam Hoffmeister's body was found the night after the gunfight at the Dagworth woolshed.

In later years Banjo detailed his knowledge of the events that had occurred at the station prior to his January 1895 visit. According to his essay 'The Dog', from the collection *Three Elephant Power*:

> Dogs, like horses, have very keen intuition. They know when the men around them are frightened, though they may not know the cause. In a great Queensland strike, when the shearers attacked and burnt Dagworth shed, some rifle-volleys were exchanged. The air was full of human electricity, each man giving out waves of fear and excitement. Mark now the effect it had on the dogs. They were not in the fighting; nobody fired at them, and nobody spoke to them; but every dog left his master, left the sheep, and went away to the homestead, about six miles [10 kilometres] off. There wasn't a dog about the shed next day after the fight. The noise of the rifles had not frightened them, because they were well-accustomed to that.

He went into further detail (although his recollection wasn't perfect) during a radio talk he gave on the ABC in 1938. The talk was titled

'Golden Water', a reference to the discovery of seemingly limitless amounts of artesian water beneath the arid country out west:

> I do not know that I have properly conveyed the feeling of excitability which possessed everybody in the early days of the bore water: people seemed to be looking out on to limitless horizons and except (very occasionally) in a mining camp I can remember nothing like it. The shearers staged a strike by way of expressing themselves, and MacPherson's woolshed at Dagworth was burnt down and a man was picked up dead. This engendered no malice and I have seen the MacPhersons handing out champagne through a pub window to these very shearers. And here a personal reminiscence may be worth recording. While resting for lunch, or while changing horses on our four-in-hand journeys, Miss MacPherson, afterwards wife of the financial magnate, J. M'Call MacCowan, used to play a little Scottish tune on a zither and I put words to the tune and called it Waltzing Matilda. Not a very great literary achievement, perhaps, but it has been sung in many parts of the world. It was the effect of the bore water.

To say that burning down Dagworth woolshed engendered no malice was a bit of a stretch, and he was also in error about Christina. She, like Sarah Riley, never married. In 1896 Christina's sister Jean married Sam McCall McCowan, the manager from adjoining Kynuna Station. Indeed, Jean and Sam's relationship may have been the reason for picnic trips in the direction of the Diamantina waterholes, which lay between the two properties. Yet despite the inconsistencies, this talk certainly shows that Banjo was well aware of the event and even late in life was still linking it, if tangentially, to 'Waltzing Matilda'.

Regardless of exactly what occurred, the events surrounding the song do provide a context in which to understand it. 'Waltzing Matilda' was written in the midst of one of the worst economic depressions in Australia's history and one of the ugliest industrial disputes it had ever seen. It was written about a swagman, possibly a union shearer, at a time when the countryside was haunted by thousands of them, many in rags and starving, with many more Australians threatened by the same fate. It describes how three policemen were involved in the swagman's arrest, which again refers directly to its times, when the Queensland bush was gripped by the heaviest hand of authority it had ever known. As detailed previously, arresting striking shearers for stealing sheep (then summarily sentencing them for stealing cattle) was one of the government's tactics for strikebreaking.

There are many mentions of people hearing 'Waltzing Matilda' or getting copies of it from early 1895 onwards. Paterson biographer Sydney May detailed how it was sung at the North Gregory Hotel in Winton and at the Winton races, and proved instantly popular.

'Waltzing Matilda' is undeniably a depression-era song, and a very good one. However, it also owes its genesis to shearers and their great struggle with woolgrowers during the bitter strikes of the 1890s. It's about hard times, endurance and freedom, and both squatter and worker could immediately identify with all those things. Ever since, it has been the song that has united us, in good times and bad, from the sporting field to the battlefield.

7

RISE OF THE MIDDLEMEN

(1894–1908)

If the relationship between shearers and woolgrowers had been a marriage, they'd have separated in 1894. In what amounted to an unregulated industrial-relations jungle, two entrenched, antagonistic positions had evolved and any hope of a reconciliation was remote at best.

At the same time, the inherently disorganised employment of shearers continued. Up to 50 000 workers wandered between thousands of shearing sheds spread over a third of the continent. There were ongoing arrangements between some shearers and stations but in many cases there was an element of pure luck in whether enough shearers would be available when sheep had to be shorn, or whether there would be too many, and some would miss out.

In 1895, a young New Zealander decided there had to be a better way. John (Jack) Henry Young had come to Australia in 1891, aged twenty-one, and started work in the Pastoralists Union of New South

Wales, organising strikebreakers. He soon had plenty of experience in getting shearers from one shed to the next on time.

Coordinating shearers was a key element in breaking the strikes of 1891 and 1894, but it occurred to Jack Young that there didn't have to be a strike for such organisation to continue.

As it happened, a centralised contracting system was already being operated by the Pastoralists Union of Victoria and serviced that state and the southern Riverina from the early 1890s onwards. It had 7000 registered shearers but in a typical year fewer than 1000 were utilised by about fifty sheds. A similar scheme in New South Wales was even less successful. Meanwhile, unionists such as the Australian Workers Union's William Spence also thought a centralised employment service had advantages, but only if it was organised by the AWU. In an environment of mutual distrust the situation was tailor-made for a middleman.

In 1895 Jack Young asked a select group of stations if he could supply the shearers, rousies, cooks, classers and pressers, plus machines and rations, required to shear their sheep for a fixed price per sheep. All the stations had to do was muster their stock, have them ready on an agreed starting date, then take the bales away when the job was done.

Initially, three sheds in the Walgett area agreed to the arrangement, and in the first year J.H. Young and Co. shore 50 000 sheep. Among the three stations was one owned by prominent pastoralist W.F. Jacques. The influential sheep man liked the arrangement and word soon spread.

Young's idea also suited the shearers. He provided ten of them with three sheds in a row, which meant they got a cheque for shearing about 5000 sheep each. That was as much as many shearers could hope for in an entire season. As previous chapters have shown, some might get more sheds, while others might only get one. For top-quality shearers, it was an ideal arrangement.

Young never looked back, although he soon had plenty of competition. By 1899, ads for shearing contractors were appearing in prominent newspapers. It's estimated that within twenty years ninety per cent of all sheep in Australia were shorn under some kind of contract-shearing arrangement.

The shearing contractors may have taken the headaches out of getting a station's shearing done, but the years after 1894 were extremely difficult in other ways. The worst drought in Australia's history, particularly in the northern parts of the country, devastated the wool industry. Queensland was particularly hard hit. In 1892, there had been 21 million sheep in the state. By 1902, there were only 7.2 million. It would take another decade for the numbers to recover.

While sheep numbers were falling, membership of the shearers' union and of pastoralists' unions was on the rise. In a curious twist, the troubles of the drought eventually led to rises in the rates for shearing. Initially, the dire situation prompted many shearers to head for the newly discovered goldfields of Western Australia. Many didn't return and shortages of shearers ensued.

So, in New South Wales, where pastoralists had set the shearing rate at 18 shillings and 6 pence per hundred, in 1901 most sheds were paying 20 shillings to attract enough shearers to get the job done. Shearers and the unions weren't slow to take advantage of their renewed leverage and minor disputes became more common.

One of the key tensions was between the younger brigade of machine shearers and the old guard of bladesmen. It was soon to give shearing contractors a taste of what it was like to be the meat in the sandwich, not just between shearers and woolgrowers, but between the two shearing factions.

In 1900, shearer Jim Davidson (a Shearers' Hall of Fame inductee – see page 265) got a taste of the animosity between the two groups when he did a tour of Queensland and New South Wales to promote Wolseley's new bicycle-powered shearing plant (developed in 1899). The idea was that it would greatly reduce the cost of installing a machine-shearing plant. For starters it didn't require an expensive steam engine, although it did present a new challenge in working out a rate for paying the bicycle rider. Was it per hundred sheep or per hundred kilometres?

Davidson soon discovered that small shearing sheds were the last bastion of the blade shearers. As the Wolseley company had done when first demonstrating machine shearing in 1887, Jim would take more wool off sheep already shorn by the local bladesmen. However, on more than one occasion the shearers didn't take kindly to being shown up. At Malvern Hills in Queensland Davidson would have been sent on his way in a hail of stones but for the intervention of the station manager. At Piedmont, in northern New South Wales, the station manager also had to step in to protect the enterprising salesman.

Of course, the tension between machine shearers and bladesmen wasn't the only one in the shearing sheds. There could also be a shifting pendulum of respect among the shearing team. At the start of shearing, when the shearers were all well rested and stronger than any of the other workers in the shed, the other hands treated them in a manner appropriate to a tough lot who knew how to use their fists.

However, as the shearing progressed and the relentless work wore the shearers down, the rouseabouts and other workers started to find themselves on a more even playing field. They could afford to give the shearers a bit of cheek. In any test of strength, playful or not so playful, they started to get the upper hand.

By the end of the shearing, some shearers would be pushing themselves to keep going, and they'd ignore all but the most blatant provocation. However, if it happened to rain, and the shearers got a day or two of rest, the pendulum of respect shifted back. The smart shed hands treated the shearers with due deference. Anyone else got put back in their place.

While Jim Davidson's three-month trip didn't result in many immediate sales of the bicycle-powered Wolseley plant, the station managers were sufficiently won over that every station he visited installed machines before the next season.

Of course, some shearers were quite at home with both blades and machines. On his trip, Davidson had the satisfaction of meeting the best of them, none other than Jack Howe. And even one of the popular songs that emerged in this era, 'Flash Jack from Gundagai', revolved around a shearer who claimed to use both Wolseley's and B-bows (meaning both machine and blade shears):

> I've shorn at Burrabogie and I've shorn at Toganmain
> I've shorn at Big Willandra and on the Coleraine,
> But before the shearing was over I wished I was back again,
> A-shearing for old Tom Patterson on the One Tree Plain.
>
> (Chorus): All among the wool, boys, all among the wool
> Keep your blades full, boys, keep your blades full
> I can do a respectable tally myself whenever I like to try,
> But they know me round the back blocks as Flash Jack from Gundagai.
>
> I've pinked 'em with the Wolseleys and I've rushed with B-bows, too,
> And shaved 'em in the grease, my boys, with the grass seed showing through.
> But I never slummed my pen, my lads, whate'er it might contain,
> While shearin' for old Tom Patterson, on the One Tree Plain.
> (Chorus)
>
> I've shore at big Willandra and I've shore at Tilberoo,
> And once I drew my blades, my boys, upon the famed Barcoo,

At Cowan Downs and Trida, as far as Moulamein,
But I always was glad to get back again to the One Tree
    Plain. (Chorus)

I've been whalin' up the Lachlan, and I've dossed on Cooper's
    Creek,
And once I rung Dadjungee shed, and blew it in a week.
But when Gabriel blows his trumpet, lads, I'll catch the
    morning train,
And push for old Tom Patterson, on the One Tree Plain.

The Tom Patterson referred to owned Merool Station, now Ulong, in the southern Riverina, from the 1870s until his death in 1902.

The year Tom died, New South Wales became the first Australian state to establish an arbitration court, based on a model pioneered in New Zealand. After the grim industrial-relations battles of the 1890s, it was hoped arbitration could assist in negotiating wages and conditions between employers and employees without the necessity of bitter, costly, unproductive strikes. It seemed to be preferable to fights to the death in the industrial-relations jungle. However, both sides were wary of the new system, with good reason.

No sooner was the New South Wales court established than the Australian Workers Union lodged an extravagant claim for a shearing rate of 25 shillings per 100 that was clearly aimed at giving the union room to negotiate. (In later years the tactic became known as an 'ambit claim'.) This while the drought was still hammering woolgrowers, many of whom were going to the wall. Then it was found that a new union claiming to represent shearers had registered with the arbitration court. It was called the Machine Shearers and Shed Employees Union. The MSU wanted everything the AWU didn't: 20 shillings per 100, support for contract shearing and support for shearers owning their equipment.

The AWU smelled a rat, especially when the pastoralists' unions refused to meet with the AWU but were only too happy to talk to the MSU. Bogus or not, the very name of the new union highlighted the 'turf war' between contract machine shearers and old-union blade shearers. There was a perception that machine shearers focussed on efficiency and speed while the old blade shearers nitpicked over union rules and called meetings over trivialities.

The problem for the AWU was that the machine shearers were the future of shearing while the blade shearers were becoming relics of its past. How could it embrace the new while maintaining support among a membership that was in danger of going the way of the dinosaurs?

The AWU had also badly miscalculated with its claim for 25 shillings per hundred. It was never going to happen, but to come out with a figure more in line with both reality and the MSU rate would involve an embarrassing back-down. The AWU was eventually forced to revise its shearing rate to 22 shillings and 6 pence. It then called for strike action in support of the new claim. Strike camps were formed and while there were some colourful confrontations, the action that really made the difference was when a woolgrower sued the AWU for £1800 for loss of income due to the strike. Shortly after, in September 1902, the strike was abandoned.

However, Donald Macdonell wasn't finished yet. He waited until 3 a.m. on 3 September 1903 to make his move. By then the general secretary of the AWU was also the member of the New South Wales Legislative Assembly for the electorate of Cobar, and in the wee small hours, while the Legislative Assembly was sitting but the house was almost empty, he moved a motion for the establishment of a royal commission into the MSU. Macdonnell himself was the commission's chairman.

Not surprisingly, MSU secretary John Leahy and shearing contractor Jack Young refused to appear when invited to give evidence at the royal commission. Other pastoralists were fined for not gracing the royal commission with their presence. Despite the lack of cooperation, the commission found evidence of a conspiracy between the MSU and the pastoralists.

While the union and woolgrowers threw their weight around, it made little difference out in the bush. In 1903 it was apparent that when shearers succeeded in making good money, they could lose it in spectacular fashion. In Broken Hill at that time, miners and shearers were reputed to be gambling on a grand scale. Some two-up games saw hundreds of pounds won and lost on the toss of a coin. That year sixty-three gamblers were arrested and fined one pound for being at the town's Tattersalls Club without lawful excuse. The fine, compared to the stakes being played for, was a pittance.

On a more productive level, the Australian Workers Union put renewed effort into bringing machine shearers into its ranks. In this it was helped by the easing of the drought in 1904, which led to increasing sheep numbers and demand for shearers. Many woolgrowers were also employing locals in preference to those in the MSU, who were often outsiders.

Employing people they knew gave woolgrowers some certainty about the quality of the workers they were getting. However, employing a shearer based on his name and reputation was no guarantee that you'd get what you paid for. Name-swapping was commonplace. In 1904, a shearer named E. L. Barnes did a trip to New Zealand, where he took the stand of a shearer who couldn't make it, shearing under the other man's name. When he asked for a reference at the end of the work, the overseer asked, 'And what name will I put it in?'

With its membership gradually recovering as more machine shearers came into the fold, the AWU couldn't help making more rules. In 1904 it added a new one that at first appeared perfectly reasonable: 'Members are not permitted to provide machines, and must not use any other than those provided by employer.'

However, the best shearers preferred to use their own tools for the obvious reasons: they were of better quality, better maintained, and better suited to their individual preference. It was a classic case of the individualism typical of many shearers versus the solidarity embodied in unionism.

Even as the rule was being made, it was suspected that it would be more honoured in the breach than the observance. In Queensland, which was already doing most of its shearing with contractors, it was estimated that half the shearers had their own handpieces. The old union men didn't like it and union organiser T.J. Lonsdale reckoned the lagoon on Toulby Station was home to twenty handpieces thrown there by anti-'scab' shearers.

A year after the rule was introduced, in 1905, the AWU's Donald Macdonell admitted: 'The best men are now penalised for their loyalty in sticking to the rule; while the disloyal not only [earn] more by having superior machines, but – what [is] more galling to many men – they are unable to compete on even terms with other shearers carrying machines whom they [know] they could beat on their merits.'

Not long after, the ban on carrying one's own machine was quietly dropped.

Meanwhile, contract shearing was going from strength to strength. In 1905 Sydney-based Young and Co. was employing 2000 shearers and shearing six million sheep a year (an average of 3000 sheep per man).

However, problems were starting to emerge. At times, the contractors faced the headache of finding enough shearers for all the sheds that wanted to shear. There was no problem in cooler months but come spring there were shortages. In Queensland's Darling Downs, shearing coincided with harvesting, which meant many shearers were called back to their family holdings to help bring in the crops, adding to the difficulties.

It didn't help that some woolgrowers were inflexible. The Australian Pastoral Company's William Young (no relation to Jack Young), who had stations all over Australia, was typical of many when he stated:

'I must have my shearing done about the same time. It must be got over in six weeks.' At times, he had up to four sheds shearing at once.

There were also problems over wages when contractors failed. When the National Shearing Company went bankrupt, the AWU attempted to collect their shearers' pay from the stations involved. The action failed because, legally, the stations weren't the employer.

Of course, when it came to handling shearers, shearing contractors needed a great range of skills. In particular, when shed conditions were bad and shearers wanted to walk away, the contractor had to convince them to endure the worst with the promise of good sheds to come. It was similar in areas where sheep were hard to shear and tallies were low.

Then there were problems dealing with shearers who had shadowy backgrounds, or were 'wife-starvers', whose reliability was subject to their proximity to officers of law enforcement. The term originated from the prison slang for inmates who were convicted after missing maintenance payments. Accordingly, if the police suddenly appeared at a shearing shed, the existence of 'wife-starvers' could be indicated by their equally sudden disappearance. On the other side of the equation, the contractor might have to help out a shearer who had diligently sent his income home for months only to find his wife had disappeared with the lot.

Meanwhile, the industrial landscape was undergoing more change. In 1905, the Commonwealth Arbitration Court was established, despite the existence of arbitration courts in the states. National awards made more sense in achieving consistency of rates and conditions for a shearing workforce that often travelled between states to work. It also brought about the unification of Queensland's Amalgamated Workers Union with southern Australia's Australian Workers Union, the AWU, retaining the latter's name.

In many ways, arbitration spelled the end of 'freedom of contract', much to the chagrin of the financial institutions that had fought so hard to crush organised labour and set the wages bar as low as possible.

It also theoretically meant the end of strikes. All unions had to do was successfully negotiate in the Arbitration Court to justify their membership fees. In theory, once the court had made its decision, no one could argue. What could possibly go wrong?

As it turned out, even as shearers' and bush workers' unions amalgamated in this brave new world, with 30 000 members, the seeds of discontent were being sown. There was still a radical streak in many of the AWU's members, especially in the big-station country of Queensland and north-west New South Wales. From 1905, branches in those regions were infiltrated by members of an American-based organisation called the Industrial Workers of the World. The 'Wobblies', as they were known, were left-wing socialists whose agenda harked back to the idealistic socialism of the early days of the 1890s shearers' strikes. Their aim was to overthrow the capitalist system – if necessary, one sheep at a time.

Never mind that many shearers, especially gun machineshearers working for shearing contractors, aspired to be capitalists themselves. In the regions where the big stations had survived the ravages of drought and economic calamity, there was still a culture of us and them, a tension that could erupt at any time.

**

While the wounds of the 1890s were still healing in Australia, over in New Zealand, the country that had pioneered arbitration, extraordinary shearing feats were being performed. In November 1906, nine Maori shearers on Raukawa Station in Hawke's Bay, using narrow-comb machine shears, averaged 266 sheep over the course of a nine-hour day (5 a.m. to 5 p.m. with three hours off for meals and smokos).

Among the men was one of New Zealand's finest Maori shearers, Raihania, who shore 332. Later that month, at the same station, ten Maori and European shearers averaged 219, with Raihania again the ringer with 301.

Maori shearers made a lasting impression on woolgrower, station owner and shearer Bob Mills. He'd learned the language from a Maori he once went mustering with. Later, as a manager, he sometimes didn't let on when the shearers turned up, and enjoyed the honest opinions expressed about him. Regardless of what he may have heard, he thought Maori had a natural flair for shearing and a work ethic that meant both shearers and shed hands put in a solid effort from the start of the day to the end.

They were just the sort of people that Australian contractors were looking for, but while a few New Zealand shearers made the almost week-long ocean voyage to Australia each season, they didn't do so in such numbers that they had a noticeable impact.

***

In 1907 the Commonwealth Arbitration Court took evidence to determine the first federal shearers' and farmhands' awards. Among the witnesses who gave evidence was shearing contractor Jack Young.

The AWU had long harboured suspicions that contractors weren't interested in giving men a 'fair go', and Jack had no qualms about confirming them. If a man couldn't machine-shear one hundred sheep a day he was 'of no use'. South Australian shearers were 'a wretched bad lot. If we had these shearers again, we would give up contracting'.

Young's preference was for Queenslanders, although he may have meant gun shearers from New South Wales and Victoria who made their way to Queensland to shear. Said Jack:

> They are the finest shearers in the world. They are the only shearers in Australia... In Queensland they shear from January to December, and are professional shearers. There [are] certain months when there [is] a slight difficulty in getting shearers in Queensland. The difficulty [begins] about August and September. There [are] over 40,000 shearers required in Australia during

these months, but there [are] really only 20,000 men who follow it up regularly, while there [are] 10,000 who [do] casual shearing … on the bosses' station.

Young went on to explain that the key to making money, from the contractor's point of view, was keeping wool up to the wool pressers, who needed to do twenty-plus bales a day to be kept fully occupied. With that and twenty shearers, a contractor's profit was threepence per sheep. If there were more shearers than that, he might make fourpence a sheep. It was potentially better money than the shearers were making.

However, that was the outcome when things were working well. He concluded: 'A great deal [depends] upon the quality of the shearers employed. Twenty good shearers would turn out between forty and fifty bales. Twenty bad shearers might turn out only 20 bales.'

Little wonder that contractors were always on the lookout for the best. If a shearer wasn't quick and clean enough, or was a troublemaker, or was in the twilight of his shearing career, contractors simply couldn't afford him.

The evidence at the 1907 hearing also sounded the death knell for blade shearers, particularly if they couldn't manage one hundred a day. However, they still formed the nucleus of a culture within the AWU that resisted the notion of speeding up. There was more than a grain of nostalgia mixed in as well.

'Blade shearing is quiet compared to machines,' some said.

'You can sit on a kero tin when your back goes,' they added, referring to the limited positions possible while shearing with machines.

The old men also saw the passing of a set of skills that were once highly valued. Setting up a pair of blades, grinding them to razor sharpness, even knowing what to look for in a good grindstone were all disappearing.

***

While the bladesmen were struggling to survive, so were many of the stations in the outback. It wasn't until 1907 that the drought that had held northern Australia in its grip for so long finally ended. The toll it took on many stations tells the story. Before the drought, Momba Station was carrying 420 000 sheep. After the drought, it had 74 000. Weinteriga started with 150 000 and finished with 49 500. Between them Nuntherungie, Grassmere and Netallie stations had 150 000 before the drought but only 40 000 after. Gnalta had 100 000 and finished with 9000. Billila had 70 000 and finished with 16 500.

Much of the country that had once carried millions of sheep looked more like desert. There was a feeling that perhaps the deserts were expanding. However, the Western Lands Commission studied the situation and concluded that the deserts were being created because up until the 1890s people had been stocking land with the most sheep it could carry in a good season, not with the most it could sustain over many seasons, be they good or bad.

By 1907, many pastoralists had learned that the hard way. They had gone broke, then the banks had come in and taken their stations. In many cases, the owners who lost their stations were left in place to manage them because no one wanted to take them over. Some of those people eventually got to see the properties become viable once the rains returned and the place wasn't burdened by crippling debt.

Of course, an old pioneer on the Darling River had another theory: 'I sometimes think the drought came upon the squatters as a retribution for the wickedness that has been done.'

With many big stations going broke, the stage was set for one of the biggest land redistributions the world has ever seen. Some stations that survived the drought and depression were also broken up, but with the majority in the hands of the banks, there was little resistance to the land-redistribution programs, particularly in the vast outback of Queensland and New South Wales.

The banks, meanwhile, were actually in favour of any scheme that grew the potential pool of people who were prepared to take over the land and challenges faced by those who had failed before them. Inevitably, an increasing army of battlers meant more homes, woolsheds, yards, machinery and facilities. Building them would require more mortgages. And so the cycle of debt and desperation could begin again.

As seen in the case of Jack Howe and his family, the viability of the smaller holdings was questionable. However, land-redistribution schemes did give aspirational rural workers the hope of one day owning their own property. Well-paid shearers had the best chance of all, and many went from worker to owner in the course of their lives. And once they had their block, they could supplement its income with occasional stints of shearing.

It wasn't long before there was a new expression to describe such farmers. When they cleared their block of a few hundred hectares, put a fence around it and sowed their crops, more often than not, enormous flocks of cockatoos swept down and devoured the seeds. Sometimes paddocks would be so thick with cockatoos that the birds looked like they were the crop. So the smallholders became known as cockatoo farmers, cocky farmers or cockies for short.

***

While the Arbitration Court was considering the wage claims of the shearers and woolgrowers, at the same time, in 1907, the court's head judge, Justice Higgins, set the course of wage cases for the next century with what became known as the Harvester Agreement. It involved Sunshine Harvesters and their employees and established the concept of a basic living wage for all Australian workers.

The basic or minimum wage is now taken for granted by most Australians but when it was introduced it left economists and business operators scratching their heads over the disconnection between what had to be paid to workers to produce things and what they could be sold for. For example, if wool prices went through the floor, shearing rates would only go down to the minimum set by the court.

Stuart Svensen, author of *The Shearers' War*, described the culture of the times that had led to such a decision: 'The strikes of 1890–94 had profound and long-lasting effects on political attitudes and policy, especially with the Labor Party. Three main areas of policy to be influenced were industrial relations, the financial system and land policy.' [Shearers' War *quotes reproduced by kind permission of Hesperian Press and Stuart Svensen*]

The shearers may have felt they failed to achieve their goals in 1891 and 1894, but the arbitration award of 1907 can be seen as the 'triumph in the end' that William Lane had described at the conspiracy trial of 1891. It's worth noting that the shearers' struggle of those times also made a significant difference to the living standards of all Australians for decades to follow. As Svensen wrote: 'Australia was a far better place for a worker to live in the twentieth century than it was in the nineteenth, and the men who stood and fought in 1891 should be given due credit.'

However, the position still had to be defended. In 1907, the Western Australian Pastoralists Association was formed. It may not have been a response to the federal pastoral award, but the coincidence is worth noting.

In the eastern states, many of the pastoralists' associations were evolving into graziers' associations. The cocky farmers, who had none of the history of the squatters or pastoralists, formed farmers' associations to represent their overlapping but at times divergent interests. Many of the farmers' associations, such as those in the small acreage areas of Western Australia's south-west, also operated outside the federal award, either because they did their shearing themselves, or because they used local shearers under local arrangements.

In 1908 the AWU decided to take a stand against shearing contractors. The contractors had long been seen as doing the woolgrowers' dirty work but a new trend was emerging where shearers saw the possibilities of organising themselves into teams and negotiating contracts themselves (and so keeping the contractor's profit). This 'group shearing' meant small groups of shearers could collectively bargain for their wages and conditions. That, to the AWU's way of thinking, was its job.

Fearing potential irrelevance, the AWU decided to ban group shearing. As yet another example of the union attempting to stand in the way of shearers making money, it had as much chance of success as the ban on shearers carrying their own handpieces. This while there was growing evidence of the value of contractors.

One area where they were showing their worth was in ensuring that the machinery used by shearers worked effectively. At the time, much of the equipment installed in the early 1890s was wearing out. By way of example, in 1908, at Talavera Station, near Roma in Queensland, the constant breakdowns provoked the shearers to walk out. Where contractors were ensuring the machinery was well maintained and operating properly, such delays were reduced.

As early as 1906, shearers such as Thomas Kerr were turning up with an entire shearing plant and not only shearing, but filling all the functions of a contractor. At the time, Kerr was exploiting the niche between the ban on carrying machines that was lifted in 1905 and the one on group shearing that was brought in in 1908.

He wasn't the only one. In 1908 the AWU noted that: 'On the Murrumbidgee last year there was a party of four shearers with a little plant of their own, who were a cooperative company, doing the whole of their own work, and taking contracts with farmers in the district.'

These small-scale, entrepreneurial shearers also started transforming the cocky sheds that were the last bastion of the blade shearers. Such sheds may have lacked the prestige of the big sheds, as highlighted in songs such as 'Flash Jack from Gundagai', but small operators with their own shearing plants could make a good living by travelling from place to place in their local district.

While the big sheds had led the way in mechanising their operations, gradually sheds with from two to six stands were being equipped for machine shearing. As time went on, such sheds became the norm. Blade shearing persisted in pockets for decades more, but it was increasingly rare. However, the displacement was as much due to entrepreneurial shearers as it was to woolgrowers.

A year after the Western Australian Pastoralists Association formed, the AWU belatedly set up a branch in that state as well. Its focus was the big pastoral areas of the north-west. The region involved was huge and encompassed some of the most lucrative runs in Australia. Working from station to station, shearers could find themselves in work for ten months or more, shearing from 4000 to 6000 sheep per year. In eastern Australia, that number might be only 2000. With so many sheep to shear, and so much money to be made, it was considered by many to be a shearer's paradise.

Also in 1908, union figurehead William Spence (by then also a federal MP) reflected on the tumultuous events of the previous twenty years in which he had been involved. What his years of experience appear to have taught him was the value of mutual self-interest. He wrote:

> Shearing sheds employ a varying number of hands, ranging from half-a-dozen to upwards of 200. Each shed, therefore, can be likened to a factory. Generally, it is far from any centre of population and is only used at shearing time, being locked up during the rest of the year. Counting each shed as corresponding to a factory, it is safe to say that more strikes have taken place in connection with shearing sheep than in all other industries combined. Probably 10,000 cases since 1886 would be the number. These lasted from one hour to eight weeks. But one hour meant that the Unionists were prepared for a much longer term if necessary.

> Sometimes the employer would be merely trying the men, and if they gave in, he profited; but if they held out he was not prepared for the risks of delay, so would come to Union terms. Up till 1890 there was no collective unity amongst pastoralists except the 'natural class feeling'. Each had been so accustomed to having his own way that he took any interference unkindly, even though he admitted that the union demands were reasonable. Some came to terms at once, and did well for themselves, as they got the pick of the men, who on their part showed their appreciation by more carefully looking after the employer's interests.

Other views suggest shearers had evolved a group psychology that led them to consider themselves superior to their fellow workers and even the people who employed them. That, too, would explain 10 000 strikes in twenty-two years, or more than one a day.

The spirit of the times, however, meant that an attempt was even made to settle the question of wet sheep. In 1908, R. O. Blackwood, president of the federal pastoralists' association, and AWU leader William Spence sat on a committee selected to ascertain the 'extent the shearing of wet sheep affected the health of shearers and especially as to what precise amount of moisture in the wool is harmful'. Prime Minister Alfred Deakin allocated £500 to the investigation.

After nearly a year of interviews and canvassing medical opinion, the committee could find no hard evidence of a precise effect that wet sheep might have on shearers. However, there was a suggestion the increased humidity caused by wet sheep might contribute to problems with shearers staying cool. It was decided that more than eight per cent moisture in merinos and ten per cent in other breeds should be the cut-off for shearing. That should have settled the question. However, as the next chapter reveals, in the case of shearing, if it came to a contest between self-interest and logic, self-interest was a safe bet.

'Smoko' (a rest break) during shearing in a shed in Queensland between 1860 and 1879. The technology may have changed but the exhaustion after two hours of shearing remains unchanged.
(Image: National Library of Australia, an24474523, photographer unknown)

A sketch by Frederick Grosse of blade shearing in a Victorian shed c. 1873. While wool is baled in the background, the shearing proceeds all over the 'board', the shed floor.
(Image: State Library of Victoria)

Aged shearer Eli Goodridge demonstrates how closely sheep can be blade shorn at Burra c. 1880.
(Image: State Library of South Australia, B33568, photographer unknown)

Shearers at a South Australian shearing shed c. 1880. While many stations relied on Aboriginal labour, in this instance racial segregation appears to have taken place among the shearers.
(Image: State Library of South Australia, B10724. Photo: Samuel White Sweet)

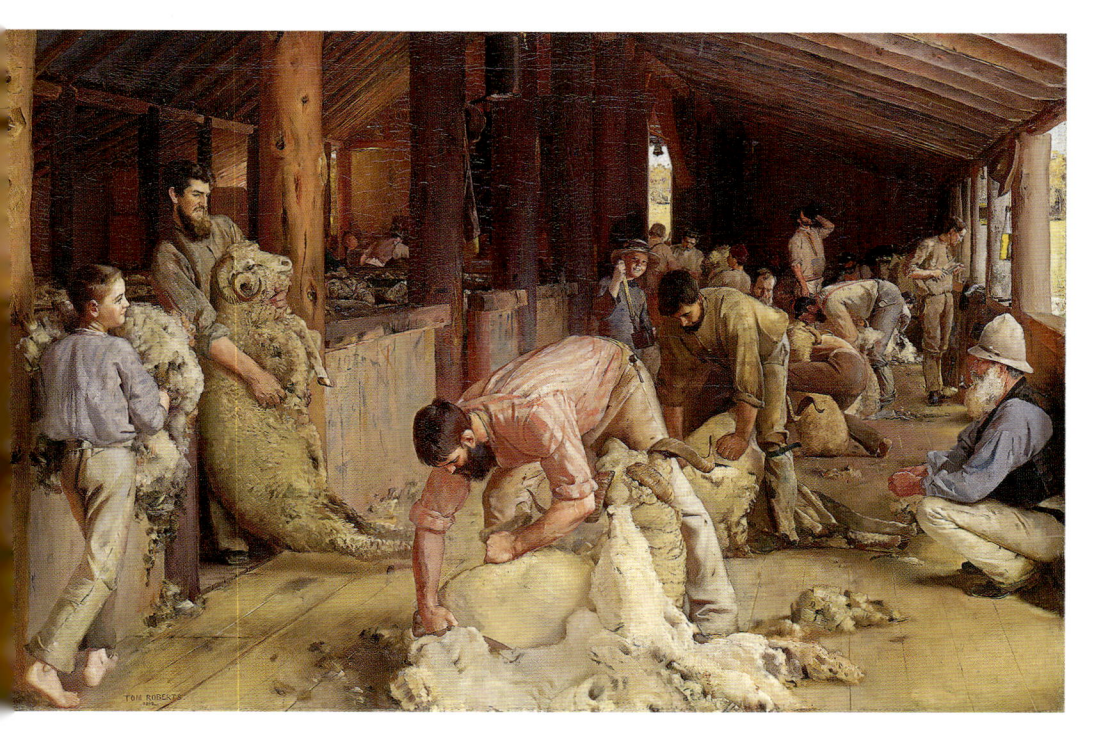

Shearing The Rams (Tom Roberts, born Great Britain 1856, arrived in Australia 1869, died 1931 *Shearing The Rams* 1890 oil on canvas on composition board 122.4 x 183.3 cm National Gallery of Victoria, Melbourne Felton Bequest, 1932)

Jack Howe in his prime in the 1890s when he set the record for blade shearing 321 merino sheep, a record that still stands. (Image: State Library of Queensland, photographer unknown)

The 1938 shilling, the first to bear the image of Uardry station's prize ram Hallmark. The iconic image reflected the reliance of the Australian economy on income from the wool industry.
(Photo: Michelle Havenstein)

One of the earliest images of machine shearing, showing shearers and tar boys at Nive Downs Station, Queensland, 1892, just six years after machine shearing was successfully demonstrated.
(Image: State Library of Queensland, photographer unknown)

Troopers guarding the woolshed that was subsequently burned at Dagworth Station during the Shearers' Strike in 1894. Events around the station during the strike may have inspired Banjo Paterson's 1895 song 'Waltzing Matilda'.
(Image: State Library of Queensland, photographer unknown)

A BICYCLE SHEARER ON THE TRACK.
WEIGHT INCLUDING MACHINE 110lbs., AND INCLUDES THREE DAYS' TUCKER.

A shearer with his bicycle in Queensland in 1910. The caption on the photo explains that the weight of bicycle and luggage was more than 50 kilograms and included food for three days. Bicycles were the preferred transport for many shearers for several decades around the turn of the century.
(Image: State Library of Queensland, photographer unknown)

A camel train loaded with wool approaching the town of Farina, north-east South Australia. The size of bales was determined by the amount of wool camels could carry with one loaded on each side of their hump.
(Image: State Library of South Australia, B23999, photographer unknown)

Brenda Station, 2012. During shearing, sheep have to be mustered from the far corners of every station. Their movement has to be managed so they don't all spend days around the shed, eating all the available feed until unshorn sheep are left starving.
(Photo: Scott Bridle, scottbridle.com)

A team of sheep dogs 'pushing up' penned sheep on Willamurra Station, 2014. Sheep handling is still almost impossible without good working dogs.
(Photo: Chantel McAlister, chantelrenaephotography.com)

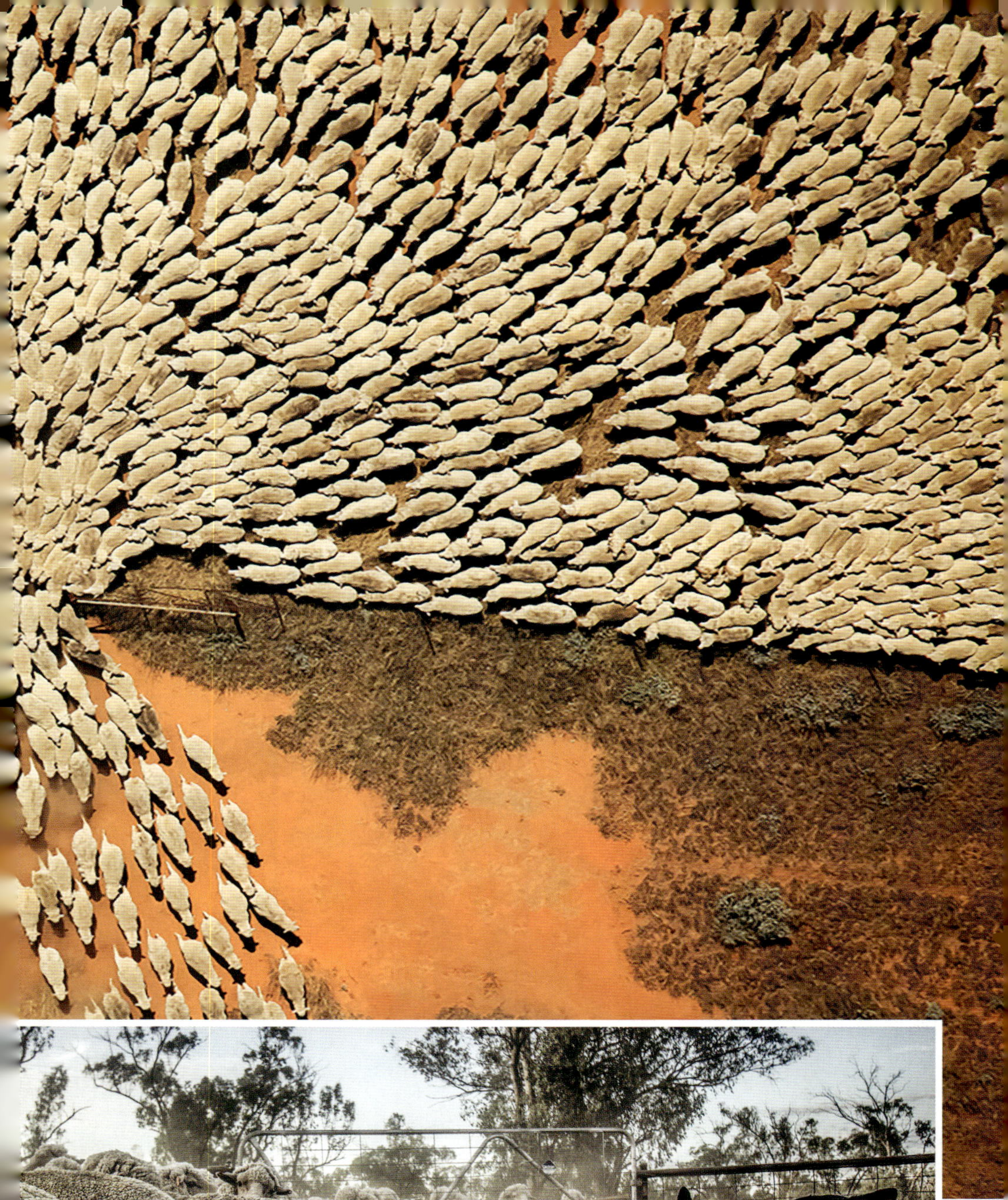

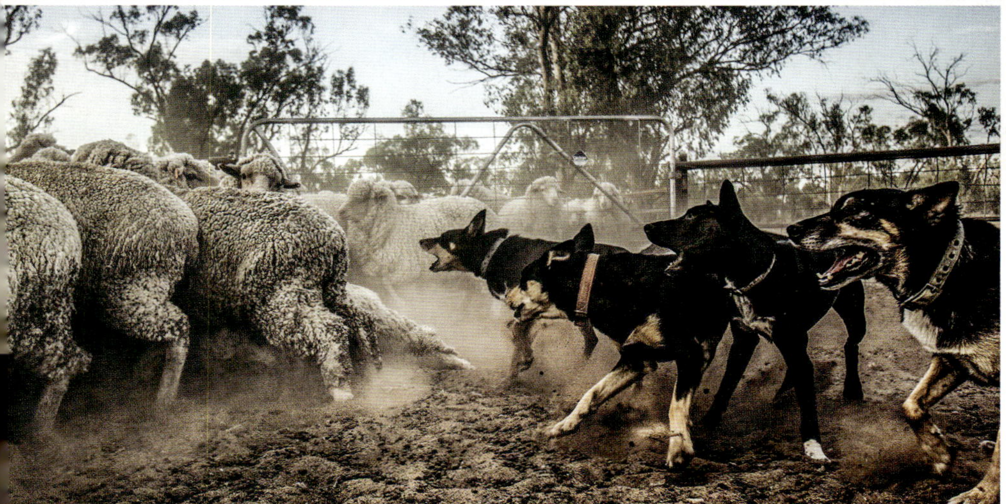

The hands of Barry Wells, injured in a pump accident on his farm. Despite being told he would never shear again, he went on to become a gun shearer. (Photo: Andrew Chapman, andrewchapmanphotography.com)

Mechanical handpieces require frequent lubrication and adjustment to keep them operating efficiently. Maintenance also affords shearers a brief respite from their back-bending work.
(Photo: Chantel McAlister, chantelrenaephotography.com)

A shearer tackles a heavily woolled merino in 2001. As sheep have grown larger and more heavily woolled, backslings have relieved some of the additional strain for shearers. Pevensey Station, near Hay. (Photo: Andrew Chapman, andrewchapmanphotography.com)

A shearing team in full flight on a station near Burren Junction, NSW, in 2013. (Photo: Chantel McAlister, chantelrenaephotography.com)

Away from the board rouseabouts deliver fleece to the wool classing tables, where it's tidied and assessed. It is then sent to the appropriate bin prior to being pressed. Brenda Station, 2012.
(Photo: Scott Bridle, scottbridle.com)

The historic shearing shed on Woolmers Estate, Tasmania, in 2014. Woolmers is now a heritage listed museum in central Tasmania, for nearly 200 years one of the world's finest wool producing areas.
(Photo: Michelle Havenstein)

A pen full of freshly disrobed sheep on Bendee Station in 2014. The sheep are counted and the number in each pen is added to the relevant shearer's tally before the sheep are returned to pasture.
(Photo: Chantel McAlister, chantelrenaephotography.com)

A typical shearing sequence demonstrated by shearer Glen Jamieson at the Shear Outback Museum, Hay, in 2014. First the belly wool is shorn and separated from the fleece, then the first side is taken off from the hindquarters to the shoulder. Next come the long blows along the sheep's back, and finally the remaining side is removed from the shoulder to the hindquarters. The result should be a fleece that is removed in one piece. (Photos: Michelle Havenstein)

The result of repeating the process on the opposite page hundreds of times a day is clear in this image of exhausted shearers at the end of a run on Uardry Station in 2001.
(Photo: Andrew Chapman, andrewchapmanphotography.com)

Research into machines that would shear sheep, never get tired and never go on strike was carried out in Western Australia and South Australia in the 1970s and 1980s. At the University of WA, engineers devised the shearing robot above, which was able to shear a sheep in four minutes. While the system was never commercialised, a number of technological spinoffs have benefited everything from shearing to car manufacture.
(Photos: James Trevelyan)

The Shear Outback Museum at Hay, NSW, was opened in 2002 to celebrate the contribution shearers and the wool industry have made to Australian life. The displays include a collection of shearing equipment ranging from early blade shears to modern wide comb machine shears. (Photos: Shear Outback)

The Flood family of central Tasmania in 2014 (from left, Winston, Lindsay and Thomas) have been shearers for generations, encompassing blade shearing and machines. Winston now judges shearing competitions at international level.

Boonoke operations manager and blade shearer Justin Campbell in 2014. Many studs still blade shear their rams because the wool looks better and it allows shearing to the exact length required if an animal is to be put on show.
(Photos: Michelle Havenstein)

Cameron Griffith taking off the belly wool – while avoiding taking off teats or pizzles – at Avondale, Queensland, in 2013.

(Photo: Chantel McAlister, chantelrenaephotography.com)

8

THE GOLDEN FLEECE

(1909–1929)

Charles Bean is best remembered as the official historian for the Australian armed forces in World War I and the writer who contributed to the establishment of the legend of the Anzacs (he landed with the troops on Gallipoli on 25 April 1915). Less well known, however, is that in 1909, as a thirty-year-old journalist with the *Sydney Morning Herald*, he was given an enviable assignment to explore every facet of the Australian wool industry, from the paddocks of the outback to the woollen mills and the clothing makers (and tennis-ball and billiard-table makers) of the world.

What resulted is an erudite time capsule of the entire industry in the era when the Australian economy truly rode on the sheep's back. Bean spoke to wool men of every social strata: squatters and selectors, shearers and rouseabouts. He travelled by train and boat, following the men on the way to the sheds and the wool on the way to the London markets.

The story so fascinated Bean that he returned to it over subsequent years, updating his book *On the Wool Track* in several editions as time wrought change on the industry and its people. When he first came to the subject, Australia was still a young nation that retained a touch of innocence. At the time, Bean saw shearers as the embodiment of the Australian spirit: indomitable, with a larrikin swagger and carefree outlook.

In the ensuing years, as Australia endured the horrors of total war and the slaughter of almost a generation of its youth, shearers were joined by another iconic figure, the Aussie digger, who mirrored their determination and swagger but added a willingness to endure and a readiness to sacrifice their lives that raised them to heroic status. Yet it wasn't lost on Charles Bean that many shearers had gone to war and become diggers.

In 1909, however, all of that was in the future. Back then, Bean's shearers bore closer kinship with the shearers of Tom Roberts' painting *Shearing the Rams* and songs like 'Flash Jack from Gundagai'. Their life was readily romanticised, although Bean also sensed 'undercurrents' of tension that persisted just below the idyllic surface.

Most of his journeys were out to the big stations along the Darling River, where paddle-steamers still followed the winding watercourse, carrying supplies upriver and wool back down. The landing stages of huge stations might be marked by something as inconsequential as a tin can hanging from the branch of a tree.

As William Spence described in the previous chapter, Bean found that many of those stations operated on an industrial scale. The woolsheds were factory buildings, in both size and the noise as the machinery woke in the early hours of the morning and ran until the final bell at the end of the day.

He was at one of them, Dunlop Station, when the shearing began. The date for the start was well known to everyone in the bush who had hopes of finding work there, and as it neared, shearers, cooks, rouseabouts, pressers and others started to converge on the place.

It was a similar story as sheep were brought in from the outlying areas of the station. It would be a disaster if 100 000 head arrived at the shed all at once, without enough food and water to hold them there, but it would be worse if the shearers cut out all the sheep in the vicinity and the next mob was still hours away. If work stopped, the shearers would stop earning money. So would the contractor, while most of the other shed hands he employed would still be costing him money for their weekly wage. Wrote Bean:

> Orders had to be sent out weeks before to the back stations to have the different detachments of sheep marched in to certain places at certain dates. Mass after mass of them had to be shifted in, like battalions or brigades in a military concentration. The stages by which they came were left more or less to the overseers and their musterers. But the main outlines of the campaign had to be sketched by the manager. He might perhaps alter the dates as the shearing progressed, ordering them to slow down or advance their times by a day or two, but there was generally little change. When the final order arrived to have the sheep from White Dog paddock in at Emu paddock on Wednesday week, at Emu paddock on Wednesday week the sheep must be, or somebody would hear of it.

At any one time, 5000 or 6000 head would be in the woolshed paddock. Some might go straight into the woolshed itself. Others would be housed under the raised floor to ensure that they remained dry, especially if rain threatened. Many thousands more would be walking in, mustered by stockmen on horseback. At one station, a manager told Bean, 'There's one lot moving in at the present time from a paddock on a back station ninety miles [145 kilometres] away.'

Bean also described the great annual wave that rolled across the outback, in New South Wales usually from July to November:

> At that time of the year there began ... a great movement, away back in the heart of Australia. Far out there the back country was mobilizing. Much later we, too, in the big cities on the sea would begin to feel the effects of it – indeed those effects went travelling on still farther, across the sea, like an extending wave, and eventually lapped into every corner of the world, though few of the people concerned realise the fact.
>
> Each year from July to November, the shearers come across New South Wales. At the time when we went through, the sign of them was their bicycles. It is true some still came on horseback, some in sulkies, some on foot. But before our visit the bicycle – the 'safety' push-bike – had spread through the country as fast as the rabbit.

The value of the bicycle for an itinerant workforce was that, unlike a horse, it didn't need feeding or a supply of water. It didn't wander off while you were working. It might get broken but it didn't get sick or die, or perish during a drought. It did have the disadvantage that it struggled on terrain that a horse could traverse with ease but it soon became the transport of choice in the era before motor vehicles became widely affordable.

Charles Bean's description of a bush bicycle is particularly memorable:

> It looked like an overloaded towel-horse. It stood in the grass-choked gutter, and leaned against the decrepit grey veranda-post of the hotel. Everyone who stirred from time to time down that straggling, wide, very sleepy street stopped just for a moment to look at it. There was a sort of horse-collar of weather-beaten

canvas looped over its forepart, another looped over the back part, and a bulging triangle of canvas packed in between. Hooked on ingeniously to various angles of the frame or handles were a billy, pannikin, water-bag, and one or two unconsidered trifles. From somewhere in front and somewhere behind protruded a segment of rubber tyre. There was scarcely anything else to guess by. But those who went down that street turned their heads and smiled. They knew it well enough. They were looking for a sign of the seasons, much as others watch for the returning swallows. And here it was – the advance guard in the invasion of New South Wales.

Bicycles laden with swags, waterbags and the bare minimum of personal effects were to be seen leaning against some of the most remote woolsheds in the country. Some had crossed sandhills, gibber deserts (vast regions covered in sunbaked red stone) and flooded rivers.

Bean also noticed that there was a subtle social distinction that set those who travelled by bicycle above those who turned up on foot. 'It was one of the most puzzling things in the West,' he wrote, 'for it cut utterly against the whole grain of the people there to recognise any social distinction at all, except, perhaps, that between a sound man and a useless one.'

In stories of the time, the bicycle (sometimes broken, sometimes in perfect working order) was often found near the body of a shearer who had lost his way, run out of water, or both, and perished in a lonely paddock between one woolshed and the next.

The greatest enemy of the bicycle was burrs. Bean made mention of bindi-eye, a small, many-spiked burr that is the Australian bush equivalent of Velcro. It hooks onto everything that touches it, especially wool and bicycle tyres, where it cuts a shearer's hand on the former and the tyre on the latter.

However, there are other bush burrs that make the bindies look tame. Cathead burrs, for example, look like they were invented by the devil. They have only four needle-like spikes but they're long, sharp and arranged so that no matter which way the burr falls, one spike is pointing straight up. They'll go straight through a boot, and even more easily into a tyre. Noogoora burrs are like catheads, except they've got even more spikes.

Puncture-proof tyres were eventually developed in an effort to counter these menacing plants but not before shearers on the move used their skills to devise other solutions. Some replaced worn-out tyres with strips of kangaroo hide bound around the wheel rim. Others stuffed tyres with rags or grass. The Shear Outback Museum in Hay has a bicycle on which a length of rope has been used as an alternative to a tyre. Then there's the bush myth of the cyclist who wrapped a snake around his wheel, pushed its tail into its mouth and hooked the tail onto the snake's fangs to hold everything tight.

However, even this couldn't compare with a bicycle repair that demonstrated the sheer ingenuity of bush mechanics. Wrote Charles Bean:

> The most hopeless accident that can happen to a bicycle is for the front fork to snap off ... When a front fork breaks, the average cyclist would conclude that his only resource was to walk. But there has wobbled up to a Western shed before now a strange thing – a complicated arrangement of tree branches and fencing wire. A front wheel waggles like a drunken man between two solid supporting saplings, which are bound with winding after winding of fencing wire to the debris of a bicycle fork. Across the drunken wheel itself are two battens of wood, nailed like a cross.

It is still possible to hear today an expression that first circulated in the days when bicycles became the chosen transport of many outback workers. When people were so tired that all they wanted to do was collapse, they would describe themselves as being punctured. Of course, the continued usage of the term may have something to do with the fact that the replacement of bicycles with motor vehicles in the bush hasn't resulted in a significant change in the frequency of getting punctured tyres.

By the end of the first day of shearing at Dunlop Station, there were plenty of punctured shearers. Bean noticed one in particular, the shed's learner, who was struggling more than the others. He was making a mess of the sheep he was shearing and the overseer was trying not to notice. The young man's back, unused to the relentless strain, was causing him immense pain, but Bean noticed that all along the board, there was a lot of checking and lubricating of handpieces going on among the other shearers after every sheep shorn.

Eventually the young fella hung up his handpiece and put on his jacket. Knocking off early wasn't strictly allowed, but on the first day of shearing, in a good shed, there was a bit of leeway. The overseer went over and gave the disconsolate lad a few words of encouragement before he left the shed.

Not long after, an older shearer hung up his handpiece, too. Then all along the board the men followed his lead. The men decided that the sheep that were coming through were too wet to shear. Again, on the first day, with more than just the learner's back feeling the strain of returning to the board, there wasn't a lot of argument from the boss.

As mentioned in the previous chapter, in the year before Charles Bean toured the outback, 1908, a special committee had investigated the health risks of shearing wet sheep. It was a question with a long and dispute-ridden history. Bean encountered the most common attitudes, he maintained, among three men with shearing experience he met during a train journey.

The three just happened to represent three different types of shearer. The first was a carefree rural worker, currently working as a drover.

The second was an older man, a well-educated farmer, travelling to the western New South Wales sheds looking for extra work during his property's quiet season. The third was a taciturn, nuggety Cornishman, also a farmer, who could quote the union rules like they were the Ten Commandments (except they numbered more than a hundred).

The drover reckoned he had experience of a shearer becoming ill after shearing wet sheep:

> 'E was a young fellow, and 'e shore 'em when they were wet and 'e was hot. 'E took ill after. His fingers and legs and arms w's all cramped up. 'E was in the hospital twelve months and 'e come out crippled for life.
>
> The worst of it, it's very 'ard to know when the sheep are wet. It's only those that knows can tell it. They feel 'em on the brisket. I couldn't tell myself if a sheep was wet or not, and the shearers can't hardly tell themselves sometimes.

The educated farmer had a more developed view:

> I've seen men shear wet sheep scores of times, especially towards the end of shearing, when they have booked stands in another shed and want to get away to it. The sheep are never wet then.
>
> It's when the shed is near a town or hotel that the sheep get wet. Someone hangs up his machine, and no one likes to stand out. There's a majority, and they knock off. I've seen them knock off three days for a point or two of rain when a shed started. At the end of the same shearing it rained heavily, but one day was enough to dry the sheep then. It all means that a fellow who doesn't want to work gets his way, and the fellow who's there to knock out a big cheque loses two or three days. You may reckon this as a safe thing, anyway – that if the wool is dry enough to press, it is dry enough to shear.

Finally, it was the Cornishman's turn. He knocked the ash off a cigarette that Bean reckoned was made from a rolled piece of paper from his own *Sydney Morning Herald*, and gave his opinion in a slow, quiet Australian accent:

> I think wet sheep are a myth. I don't think anyone suffers through shearing them. I don't think most shearers believe in them. They do when they want a spell. Two doctors followed the question through from Riverina to New Zealand last year, and said that every time they had received a report of a suspected case of illness from wet sheep, the illness could be traced to some previous trouble. There's hundreds of men besides shearers has rheumatism, aren't there? If a man is inclined to rheumatism, he naturally gets it after getting wet – or even before, if there's rain in the air – whether he's a shearer, or whether he's not. So it works out this way: There might be thirty men in a shed who could all shear wet sheep without any danger and one that the wet would affect. Well, they all have to knock off for him. That's what 'wet sheep' is.

There was general agreement, however, that when it came to shed politics, it didn't matter what your opinion was about wet sheep. If the majority thought the sheep were wet and shouldn't be shorn, the whole shed stopped shearing. Not even the station manager could change that.

Of course, there was a point where wool became so wet that there was no point in shearing it because it couldn't be pressed into bales. If it were, the wet wool would either rot or, in extreme cases, generate enough heat while it broke down that it spontaneously combusted. However, this state was well beyond what shearers considered a wet sheep.

As detailed previously, some shearing agreements attempted to give managers authority in all decisions involving shearing but when it came to wet sheep, shearers still had wiggle room. The autocratic rule of the station manager was challenged by the democracy of a majority voting to knock off due to health concerns. Regardless of the legitimacy of those concerns, wet sheep became a useful tool for shearers in their dealings with managers. As a wool-classer put it:

> There's no love or affection and harmony between us. You see, if I was to make myself more friendly, he'd begin to try on. I have to be on the lookout for them trying on from the first day of shearing to the last. It seems to go pleasant enough on the surface, but it's fight, fight, fight all the time underneath. That's what a shed is.

Sometimes, fight really meant fight. Many independently minded bush people were unlikely to accept the manager's authority without one. Wrote Bean:

> It was much better to avoid fighting; but there are times when it is an incalculable advantage to the boss to be able to use his hands. In one shed we visited there had been a row. A shearer wanted to fight the overseer. It happened that the boss came along; he was not a big man, but he could fight like a game-cock, and people knew it.
> 'I'll have no fighting in the shed,' he said quietly to the shearer, 'and you can leave Mr Jeffries alone. If you want to fight, and care to come outside, I'll accommodate you.'
> But the shearer didn't want. He took his cheque and went.

In matters of wet sheep, and many other matters, every decision the shearers made was the result of a vote. Even if the decision was won by only one vote, every shearer was obliged to accept it. And so, theoretically, was the station. In this grassroots adherence to a democratic ideal, Charles Bean saw 'great independent currents that flowed underneath the surface and largely affected not only the greatest industry in Australia but the outlook of many Australians of that time'.

The danger, of course, was that everyone had to go along with what the majority decided, even if it was wrong. If some shearers wanted to 'knock out a big cheque' while most wanted to get on the grog, work stopped.

Self-interest wasn't one of the undercurrents Bean specifically identified, but he noted that some shearers were starting to branch out into contracting, and considered it one of the better developments in the wool industry of his era. This while it was against union rules, suggesting the notion of group solidarity was not always binding.

In some instances, it wasn't clear whether the rules were being broken. In the Goulburn district, in the New South Wales Southern Highlands, for example, in 1909, trusted shearer Joe Coves was given the applications for shearing stands on several stations to sort out. He was probably the best person to decide who was worth having and who wasn't but it put him in the position of working as a labour agent. It wasn't clear whether that meant he was engaged in group shearing.

Meanwhile, as land reform continued to transform much of the rural scene, particularly in the eastern states, there was a steady increase in sheep numbers across the country. By 1900, sheep numbers had fallen to 90 million, but over the next seventy years they would double to 180 million. The growth was helped by the developing skills of Australian woolgrowers in farming dry land (and the strains of merino suited to it) and the clearing of more land for grazing.

In 1909, Charles Bean could already see some of the results:

By the time of our survey there was already coming in the 'inside' country a system of little stations of 4000 to 10 000 acres [1620 to 4050 hectares] in good country, exceedingly well-managed, so that two sheep could feed where one fed before; the fences well kept, the gates strong, the paddocks clean. The effect of such methods on the

> hands employed is incalculable – the 'share farms' that sprung up there should be models compared with those on a slackly managed run. We found some 'outside' stations managed that way too.

This development was precisely what the land reformers wanted. When it worked, everyone was happy. When it didn't, there was much more suffering as many more people were involved. Where the big pastoralists preferred to be left alone to make money, cocky farmers lobbied for government support and had the numbers at the polls to have their voices heard.

The relationship between cockies and shearers was also different. While many shearers aspired to become cocky farmers themselves, they often looked down on struggling woolgrowers. The cockies, in return, weren't fans of the Arbitration Court's fair day's pay for a fair day's work for shearers. This was especially the case when they toiled for returns that fell well short of what shearers made.

The situation was highlighted in the book *On Our Selection* (1899). Son Dan Rudd was welcomed home as a hero when he returned from shearing with tales of having rung the sheds out west, while shearing beside the best. But when it came to the endless work to be done on the family's struggling property, he wasn't interested. After he'd loafed around the place for a month, his overburdened father finally did his block and chucked him out.

***

Another source of tension that seemed inconsequential at the time was wide combs (before World War II, they were referred to as broad-gauge combs). Up until the time when Charles Bean was writing about shearers, the width of machine combs was restricted by the engineering problems involved. Those problems appear to have been solved around 1904, in New Zealand, and the use of wide combs soon spread throughout that country. It's worth noting that in the same era

Aboriginal inventor David Unaipon devised an improved mechanism that was soon incorporated in most shearing handpieces, for which he received little in the way of royalties.

In Australia, as early as 1909, wide-comb usage was noted at Conomodine woolshed, in the Molong district of New South Wales, where they were shearing 6500 sheep. A year later, at Brindingabba woolshed, in farwest New South Wales, three shearers were found using wide combs.

While these may have been cases involving genuinely wide gear, the practice of 'pulling combs' – bending the outside teeth of the comb outwards, so as to capture more wool – was widespread.

In 1910, the AWU considered the question of wide combs for the first time. Some of the union's delegates feared that using wide combs might cause injury to shearers and they would have to work harder to push the comb through the wool.

The new type of comb would also present problems for shearers going from shed to shed. They could easily find themselves shearing with narrow gear one week and wide gear the next. This would give an unfair advantage to the shearers who carried their own handpieces and shore with the comb that best suited them, week in, week out.

The other concern was that wide gear had the potential to erode shearers' earning power by making them more, or less, productive. The convoluted argument ran along the lines of if they shore less sheep, they'd earn less, but if they shore more, the rate they were paid would go down, and so they'd earn less.

In the end, the union decided on a new rule, Rule 103: 'No shearer shall use a broad gauge machine unless all other shearers employed in the shed are supplied with similar machines.' The fine for breaking the rule was only a pound, less than a day's wages for even an average shearer.

The rule didn't exactly specify how wide a comb had to be before it was considered too wide, but at the time narrow combs were 6 to 7 centimetres across while wide gear was up to 9 centimetres.

One thing that wasn't considered, and appears not to have been noticed, was that the points of a pair of blade shears were almost exactly the same distance apart as the outer teeth of a wide machine-shearing comb. Both could gather in the same amount of wool. At the time many blade shearers could match machine shearers using narrow combs in the number of sheep they shore, although possibly not in the quality of shearing. As it turned out, it took until the 1950s for Australian shearers using narrow gear to match Jack Howe's blade-shearing tally. With wide gear they passed it easily. This, of course, was well in the future.

In the early 1900s, the wide-comb question ran a distant second to what the AWU was coming to consider the great evil of the time: contracting. In 1911, the shearers' award came up for renewal, and Justice Higgins took ample evidence on contract shearing's impact. His summing-up encapsulated the situation:

> In the other states the shearing usually takes place in the latter part of the year, but in Queensland there is shearing all the year round, in all the months; and there has arisen a special class of professional shearer, men attracted by the early season and the prospect of many sheds, men who come to live in the various centres of Queensland, and who, by frequent shearing, acquire exceptional dexterity and speed. In Queensland there are also, perhaps as the result of the same causes, partly also because the stations are generally larger, far more sheds than elsewhere in which shearing contractors are employed. Of the shearing fixtures for this year in Queensland, I gather about seventy per cent, or more, are contract sheds. In New South Wales, I am told, not one-fifth of the sheep are shorn contract, and the proportion of contract sheds is still smaller. The contractors have the pick of the sheds and the pick of the shearers, and attract them by the steady run and rapid sequence of sheds. In Queensland there are

also many cooperative parties of shearers, who go from station to station, bringing engines and other plant with them; and the tendency of such parties to 'speed up' is apparent as in the case of butty-gangs [small teams that put in competitive bids for work on various job sites in other industries]. The effect of contract shearing on the tallies is very marked in certain instances where it has been introduced after the station has been doing its own shearing.

This suggests contractors had it pretty good. However, consider the challenges of Broken Hill–region contractor Charlie Flavel, who organised shearing for cattle king (and woolgrower) Sidney Kidman, renowned for running his properties on a tight budget. Maintenance of the shearing machinery was haphazard and spare parts a rarity, but Flavel got equipment going and seldom charged Kidman for his repairs.

Then there were the shearers. The 'corner country' of New South Wales breeds some very tough people and Flavel had to be just as tough to keep his teams in line. But he was a former Broken Hill shearer himself, born and raised there. The fact that he thrived, and eventually was contract shearing 450 000 sheep a year, says a great deal about his ability, both as a manager and in being able to stand up for himself.

The concerns of the AWU didn't end with the 1911 arbitration case. At the union's annual conference, the representative for Charleville, Jack McNeill, called for contracting to be abolished. Late in 1911 a plebiscite was held by the union to discern members' attitudes towards contract shearing. Of 27 397 respondents (the AWU had 47 000 members at the time), only 3487 (thirteen per cent) supported contract shearing. However, the union leadership's response was to do nothing. They may have realised contracting wasn't going away whether the membership liked it or not.

It probably didn't help the union aversion to speeding up that 1911 was the year that the earliest known shearing contest was held, on Boxing Day, at the Sydney Showground. Queenslander Dan Cooper and South Australian Bill Day competed against each other in shearing fifty sheep. Not surprisingly, the Queenslander was faster. However, the contest was scored on both speed and quality. Day shore his sheep cleaner and edged out Cooper by a single point.

Over in Western Australia, such developments were overshadowed by tragedy. Just three months later, in March 1912, Western Australia lost an entire team of its finest gun shearers. They were aboard the steamship *Koombana* en route from Port Hedland to Broome, from where they were to make their way to Liveringa Station. Koombana is a Noongar word meaning calm and peaceful; sadly, however, the voyage was anything but. The *Koombana* was caught in a severe cyclone and sank. There were no survivors among the 150 people on board.

The deaths of the shearers were remembered by bush poet Jack Sorenson (1907–1949) in 'The Lost Shearing Team':

> From far off Queensland, Lockwood came
> (a bladesman gun was he)
> To shear more sheep and earn more fame
> In Western Kimberley.
> And Grand Old Lawrence too was there,
> He realised his dream
> When he took his sons to learn to shear
> With the Liveringa Team.

In 2012, a ceremony was planned to mark the passing of 100 years since the sinking of the *Koombana*. However, it had to be postponed due to Cyclone Lua.

***

Back in western New South Wales, while Charles Bean was noticing the emergence of cocky farmers, it was less obvious that at the same time the giant sheep runs were disappearing.

As in other areas, attempts were being made to break up the big properties, although they were less successful than elsewhere. Nevertheless, the properties along the Darling that once ran 15 million head were down to only a million by 1913, due to low prices and drought. These days the figure is around 3.3 million.

Bean did encounter one cocky farmer who was making a go of it on a small 'selection' totalling just under 10 000 hectares:

> Near the house was a large drafting-yard, apparently built long ago. And in the shed leading off it, at the door of one of a few small catching-pens, with the shears in his hands and a heap of belly-wool on the floor at his side, was a man. There was a half-filled bale of fleeces in the shed and an old wool-press just outside.
>
> He was his own shearer, picker-up and tar-boy. He was rouseabout, presser, station-hand, brander, roller, piece-picker, and classer all in one. And he seemed to be satisfied.
>
> 'There's some reckon you can't make it pay,' he said – without being asked, so one could tell what was the current topic out there – 'but I know you can. The only thing is, never borrow; go without rather. The man that borrows is broke.' He had two leases, of 10,000 acres [4046 hectares] each, one on the River, the other 30 miles [48 kilometres] back. He kept about 30 cattle, some horses, and 1200 sheep.

In other areas where land distribution was more successful, many of the cockies couldn't afford the high cost of a large shearing shed and its equipment. In many towns, shearing and wool-scouring operations were established to wash and shear their flocks. Not only were such operations successful, they were tailor-made for contract shearing.

In 1913, for example, the Longreach scour shore 777 000 sheep. Flock after flock, month after month, all being shorn in one place meant shearers could set up a home, raise a family and find sufficient work that they never had to leave town.

In fact, by that time, cocky-shed shearing and cooperative shearing already accounted for three-quarters of all the sheep shorn in Australia. Big-shed shearing in the pastoral zone may have created the image of the wandering professional shearer but they were no longer the norm; suburban shearers, locals working around their district, were.

Others shearers were suburban in that they were actually based in the cities and travelled to the bush for seasonal shearing work. Charles Bean noted the message two of them left on an outstation door: 'William Smith (Balmain) and George Kelly (Rosedale), cycling to Delano, found everything clean and food good.'

Balmain is an inner-city suburb of Sydney. Rosedale is a small town 180 kilometres east of Melbourne.

The itinerant nature of shearing may have been reduced as cocky farms replaced the big properties but there was still opportunity for travel, especially among top shearers looking to extend their working season. From the 1880s onwards shearers were crossing the Tasman from both sides to secure twelve months' work: New Zealand from December to February, Queensland and western New South Wales (starting in January, and peaking from April to June), central and northern New South Wales (July to September), Victoria (October to December).

The severe drought that hammered the Australian inland for a decade from the late 1890s tipped the balance towards Australians going to New Zealand, where the increasingly wrinkly merinos discouraged New Zealanders because they were becoming harder to shear. There were, however, some merinos in the New Zealand high country suited to Australian shearers' skills and the time of year (around February).

There was already a distinct cultural difference between shearers from the two countries. Both groups were unionised, but New Zealanders tended to be from farming backgrounds and had the work ethic to match. Australians going to New Zealand tended to be the more expeditionary style of worker, nomadic larrikins with no fixed address. Australia had more than its share of cocky shearers but there was ample work within their own localities to satisfy most of them.

Union solidarity ran stronger among the Australian shearers while working fast and clean suited the New Zealanders. They could also divide along other lines, including race. In one instance a white shearer working in a team of Maori shearers refused to use the stand he'd been given, stand five, because the handpiece on that stand had a bad vibration. He insisted the team draw their stands by picking numbers from a hat. One of the Maori shearers organised the draw. The white shearer drew stand five. It was later revealed that every number in the hat had a five on it.

***

The outbreak of World War I disrupted much of the pattern of shearing in both countries. Australian wool was such a vital part of the allied war effort that the entire clip was put at the disposal of the British government for the duration of the conflict. To prevent profiteering, prices were fixed; nevertheless, the arrangement provided a bonanza of good, assured income for woolgrowers. Shearing was considered an essential industry although many shearers enlisted anyway.

However, as the war dragged on, and with it the slaughter of thousands of young Australians, the undercurrents of the shearing industry started rising to the surface.

While drought once again affected the clip in the eastern states of Australia, in 1915 a shortage of shearers still became evident. More noticeable for the AWU, membership was falling. The reasons should have been obvious, among them enlistment and a preference among youngsters to go to war instead of to the shearing sheds. However, in 1916, some Queensland union representatives thought otherwise. As one put it:

> The real cause is the contractor, who has a monopoly of sheds and who employs none but fast shearers. I have known men that could shear a hundred sheep turned down. The men he employs start shearing in January and finish in December, and that is what they call getting a big run. You can't blame the men getting all they can, but the system is to blame. I have known a large number of shed hands, shearers and cooks who have left the pastoral industry because of the contract system. The smaller the shearing plant the greater the evil becomes. A small plant of five shearers were shearing near here last year. They shore 20 000 sheep, and none of those men had a ticket [a union membership]. Abolish the contractor, and our membership would be doubled. More shearers, shed hands and cooks would be required. The shed hand would then have a chance to learn to shear; now he has none. A plebiscite of members was taken a few years ago, and the abolition of the contractor was carried by a large majority, but the executive took no action. By not doing so they blundered greatly, and the pastoral industry remains in the grip of the middleman and monopolist.

Meanwhile, the union was getting a lesson in economics. The award rate for shearing had been set at 24 shillings per hundred back in 1911. When the award was to be re-examined, in 1916, the case was postponed due to the war situation. The existing award was simply extended for the duration.

Out in the woolsheds, there was inevitable discontent. Woolgrowers were banking large cheques thanks to the guaranteed price from the British government. The shortage of shearers meant that some of them were paying above the award. Or rather, the contractors were.

The going rate for a good shearer was more like 30 shillings per hundred.

The AWU, however, was bound by the award. Matters came to a head at the annual conference early in 1916. The union's great figurehead, William Spence, was again re-elected despite being a member of Prime Minister Billy Hughes' pro-conscription Labor government at a time when the AWU opposed conscription.

However, a group of union representatives, primarily from central Queensland and north-west New South Wales, attempted to establish a new set of union rules that would radically alter, and radicalise, the AWU. In essence, they wanted to scrap arbitration in favour of direct negotiation, make membership petitions binding on the union's executive (they hadn't forgotten what had happened to the vote on contracting), and make all changes to union rules subject to-rank-and-file approval.

The group were identified as members of the Wobblies, and the union leadership went on the attack. The motions were defeated, but if the union thought that was the end of the matter, it was very much mistaken.

In April 1916 meetings of shearers were held in the Queensland towns of Winton, Hughenden and Charleville. The meetings were organised by AWU delegate and Wobblies supporter Mick Kelly. At the meetings, shearers detailed various grievances that had either been ignored by the union or that the union could do nothing about because it wasn't covered by the current award. While the AWU insisted on adhering to the award process, the Queensland shearers demanded a shearing rate of 32 shillings and 6 pence and an increase in pay for shed hands from 37 shillings and 6 pence a week to 50 shillings.

Mick Kelly and the other Wobblies may have been rebels with a socialist cause but they were also bush unionists who had a good understanding of the people they represented. In May 1916, Queensland was treated to the spectacle of shearers from Cunnamulla on the Queensland–New South Wales border to Cloncurry up near the Gulf of Carpentaria going on strike against the wishes of their union. Shearers in Western Australia also went on strike in 1916 for better pay, again against the AWU's orders. Times had certainly changed since the strikes of 1891 and 1894.

On 18 May 1916, the AWU met a delegation representing the strikers in Rockhampton to discuss the situation. When newspapers covering the dispute realised the union didn't actually represent the strikers, they reported that a breakaway union had formed. If that wasn't bad enough for the AWU, a short time later the strike succeeded, with an increase in the shearing rate to 30 shillings per hundred, in part because what the militants were demanding was what woolgrowers were paying anyway.

Two things were evident after the strike of 1916. The award rate wasn't set in stone. And the AWU couldn't always control its members. The former point may have been novel but given the independent anti-authoritarian streak many shearers possessed, the latter should have come as no surprise.

Belatedly, the Arbitration Court considered the shearers' award and in 1917 set the shearing rate at 30 shillings per hundred. Not everyone was happy. Pastoralist W. E. Abbott in particular lashed out:

> The woolgrower has taken a lot of killing because he grew up strong and sturdy without coddling or protection, but now I think the politicians, with the help of Judge Higgins and the AWU, have got him down and will give him the 'coup de grace' before long. Then Australia will have to look to the coddled and protected irrigationists of Yanco and Victoria to pay the interest on her debts with their exports of produce.

The 1917 award hearings provided further insights into the way shearing operated at the time, especially when it came to contractors.

Shearer Frank Lysaught gave evidence as a witness for the AWU about the need for slower shearers such as himself to be given a fair go.

'The slow man has to live as well as the fast man,' he told the court.

He didn't think it was right for contractors to favour the fast shearers. When challenged that it was common sense for them to do so, he disagreed.

'Supposing you were going to get anyone to do anything for you, you would get the best men you could, wouldn't you?' Frank was asked.

Frank replied, 'I do not think I would. I believe in giving a fair deal.'

While Frank was prepared to give the mediocre a fair go, there was nothing fair in another piece of evidence presented to the court. It was a letter replying to a shearer's application for a job:

> Yes, I will handle the team at 'Crower' this year, but in picking the men have to be quite satisfied they are out to work and not lie in the hut because of two or three points of rain. I remember you and your shearing, but don't remember if you are what we call a wet sheep shearer or not. If you will guarantee that you will vote right and not make one to hand up the job, I shall be pleased to receive your 1 pound deposit and put your name on the list.

***

Over in Western Australia, such machinations were of little interest to a young farm lad named Don Munday. At the age of fourteen he'd begun blade shearing around his cocky-farming district of Toodyay, 100 kilometres east of Perth. Some farmers wouldn't employ able-bodied men who weren't at the war, so willing youngsters like Don had plenty to keep them busy.

Munday had only learned to shear the year before, on his family farm. He'd started out practising on the odd sheep during the afternoon tea break. He reckoned his first fleece would have looked better in a butcher's shop than an art gallery, but he had to start somewhere. The next year, 1917, with a bit more experience, he shore at half a dozen small sheds, and by the end of the season he considered himself a real shearer.

Munday's introduction to shearing was typical of many cocky farmers. He went on to shear all over the world in the course of a colourful career detailed in his book *Tin Dog, Damper and Dust*, but his attitudes reflected his upbringing. Any militant tendencies among the cocky farmers were apt to be variations of a determination that resulted from being battlers since birth.

In 1918, Don shore 4000 sheep at a rate of sixty-five per day – this for a youngster of just fifteen. As he went from local station to local station in the southern Western Australian districts, his relationship with the owners was one of equality. He wrote of being made to feel at home. On most places the owner's wife was the cook and the shearing team comprised just a handful of people.

That year there was only one property where he felt like he was treated as a 'necessary evil'. Don left after one night and never went back. Over the next few years, as detailed in following chapters, Munday met woolgrowers with similar attitudes but there were others who left a lasting positive impression. He was also destined to become one of a new breed of cocky shearers who were savvy enough to cut out the middleman in the sheds and become a contractor themselves.

***

For woolgrowers in the eastern states, the strikes of 1916 had been something of a wake-up call. The decade of arbitration leading up to them had brought a period of relative stability. Now, with World War I over, additional measures were considered necessary to ensure that industrial peace was maintained as well.

In 1919, a group of graziers in New South Wales formed their own contract-shearing organisation called the Graziers Co-operative Shearing Company. It would soon become known simply as Grazcos.

Its first chairman, W. F. Jacques, explained its rationale: 'Contractors as a body are a source of weakness rather than strength as the rivalry between them is not in the owner's interest so that it is desirable in the future that we should secure control of the shearing through our own organisation.'

To set the company up and manage it, Grazcos got none other than Jack Young, pioneer of contract shearing, to come out of retirement. He gave the Grazcos board a typically blunt assessment: 'Judging from my experience during the past month of the state of the labour market, you have not formed this company a day too soon. I find the condition of the labour market almost in a worse position to-day than it was twenty-five years ago when wages were one half.'

Charles Bean also made his return at this time, visiting the shearing sheds he'd first toured a decade before. It may have been that the rural idyll gave him a welcome respite from writing about his terrible experiences during four long years of war.

One of the things he noticed was a change in the character of the shearers he encountered. In particular, they had become much more careful about what they did with their money, especially when it came to the practice known as lambing down. As he explained: 'When sheep were lambing, station hands used to be sent into the paddocks to see that everything went smoothly. The process is still called "lambing down". By a gentle metaphor the words were transferred to the assistance which in the old days publicans gave men who came in to get rid of a cheque.'

Up until the end of the nineteenth century, he reckoned, whenever the sheds in western New South Wales finished shearing, in the surrounding towns there would be 'Pandemonium for a fortnight, but matters had improved before the First World War. By then, if the shed cut out at 4 p.m., most of the shearers would be hull down on their bicycles, and the wool-classer on his way to Melbourne, by 6 p.m.'

Some shearers might have a couple of beers, or a single big night out, but they weren't as likely to be 'lambed down'. Out in the back country, the itinerant shearers were more worldly than other rural workers. Many were accustomed to city life and could handle themselves in places like Sydney or Melbourne, let alone one-horse outback towns.

However, from Bean's perspective, there were actually two kinds of towns in the outback. The first was the industrial town, the collections of houses and buildings that comprised a sheep station and where wages were earned doing the many jobs associated with wool production. The only industry of the other type of town was to take the wages earned in the first type of town.

It was easy to tell the two apart. In the latter: 'There is no ghost of a sign of any shop or factory that can excuse a town for existing in the red desolation – except one big, well-kept, stoutly-built, prosperous centre of industry – or perhaps two or three – around which the place has obviously grown up. That is the hotel.'

The publicans who 'lambed down' the workers weren't particularly evil. They could be seemingly kind, generous and even sober. However, their motives were always the same.

'If we don't get their cheques cashed here,' they said, 'the next place will.'

Some of the techniques for lambing down were unscrupulous. A cheque would be handed over the bar, drugged liquor was then served, and the hapless victim woke up some time later to discover that he'd bought champagne for the whole town until his cheque was gone. Sometimes it might even be true.

Then there were cases of scrupulously honest lambing down. In South Australia a publican helped an old boundary rider drink his cheque by allowing him one drink an hour until it was gone. The old man came in every year, handed over his earnings and the drinks started coming. It would take a month for the money to run out, during which the man was never quite drunk and never quite sober.

What had happened to the hard-drinking shearers? The land reforms of the previous twenty years had wrought a profound change in many of them. Charles Bean recognised some of its consequences: 'There did exist flash, raw shearers still. And of course many youngsters came back with full purses, roaring like lions, who went up-country like lambs. But a fair proportion of shearers were employers themselves – farmers or farmers' sons, shearing in their slack season.'

The same attitude curtailed the losses shearers faced from another popular vice that was harder to avoid: gambling. Often the only entertainment in the sheds was a game of cards or two-up. A friendly wager added more interest and that could be all it took. In many sheds, throughout shearing's history, the gambling followed the shearing like night followed day.

Inevitably, professional gamblers were drawn to the possibility of preying on cashed-up shearers. If they could get into a shed in some capacity or other, their gambling school was in business. They were sometimes referred to as 'forties', a reference to Ali Baba and the forty thieves, as they stole away the wages of unsuspecting shearers and their teams.

Typically for gamblers, though, in many accounts the gambling was always more excessive in days gone by, never in the present – that or it was only the younger hands who went too far.

One thing that didn't seem to have changed as the years had gone by was the undercurrent of rebellion. It may have moderated in some areas, but in others even union rules were considered an unwanted intrusion. In Queensland, that rebellious attitude was starting to take concrete form as a breakaway from the union, threatening to undermine the orderly settlement of disputes through arbitration.

In 1920, to deal with the local militants, the Queensland branch of the union applied for a state award. With support from woolgrowers, a rate of 40 shillings per hundred was agreed, 10 shillings higher than the Commonwealth award. The justification was that the sheep of Queensland's outback were bigger, dustier and harder to shear. Whether that was true or not, Queensland was treated separately for the rest of the century.

Not surprisingly, shearers elsewhere wanted what the Queenslanders got, but rather than go through the lengthy process of arbitration, the AWU and the woolgrowers' representative body at the time, the Graziers Association, met to consider the situation. The forty-shilling rate was agreed, as was a reduction in working hours to forty-four a week.

In the post-war years there was still much hand-wringing over the issue of contractors, and the evils of speeding up. The reality, though, was that it was shearers who ultimately controlled the pace of shearing. While ever they were paid by the sheep, and had a bloke beside them who was shearing just that bit faster, they'd all be trying to ring the shed. At times some union representatives suggested the AWU should campaign for a universal tally, a fixed number of sheep each shearer should be paid for each day, but not even the AWU thought it could entrench mediocrity to that extent.

The prevailing attitude was encapsulated in Henry Lawson's 'The Boss's Boots':

> The 'rouser' has no soul to save. Condemn the rouseabout!
> And sling 'em in, and rip 'em through, and get the bell-sheep out;
> And skim it by the tips at times, or take it by the roots,
> But 'pink 'em' nice and pretty when you see the boss's boots.

***

Matters took an interesting turn on the industrial front in 1922 when the Arbitration Court's new judge, Justice Powers, considered the latest award. In his opinion, the post-war wool market was still fragile and wage restraint was required. And yet, the shearing rate set in 1917 at 30 shillings was well below the market rate of 40 shillings. Justice Powers tried to achieve a compromise. He set the new rate at 35 shillings per hundred, 5 shillings less than shearers had been getting for the last two years.

If Justice Powers thought shearers would accept the new rate, he was wrong. To be fair, had he lifted the rate from 30 shillings to forty, he'd have gone down in history as the bloke who preached restraint and pulled the trigger on a 33.3 per cent increase. As it was, 5 shillings was still around seventeen per cent.

Woolgrowers, who felt they were in a better bargaining position now the war was over, seized on the ruling and insisted the AWU and its members should be bound by the award. Legally, the union had to accept it.

The situation was tailor-made for the latest incarnation of the Wobblies. Again strike action flared in the militant areas of western Queensland and north-west New South Wales. This time, however, Grazcos brought in strikebreakers from the southern regions and sacked anyone identified as a troublemaker. Making matters worse, union supporters who followed the union's directive to accept the award rate and not strike were labelled as 'scabs' when they defied the Wobblies.

In the bitter fight that ensued, without the support of their union, the shearers endured for as long as they could. Many of the union's regional representatives tried to give tacit support to their members but had to be cautious or risk legal action for inciting the strikers.

Grazcos publicised any prosecutions and fines that resulted, emphasising the point that the strike was illegal, and making it clear to strikers that shearing was continuing without them. The company also tackled any graziers who didn't toe the line. Quantambone Station wanted its sheep shorn, no matter what, and was happy to pay the shearers' rate, whereupon Grazcos sued the station. The judge refused to impose an injunction on the shearing.

On 2 September 1922 the workers' poet, Henry Lawson, died. *The Worker* republished his poem 'I'm Too Old to Rat', which at the time was more relevant than ever.

> I don't care if the cause be wrong
> Or if the cause be right –
> I've had my day and sung my song
> And fought in the bitter fight.
> In truth at times I can't tell what
> The men are driving at –
> But I've been union thirty years
> And I'm too old to rat.

Ultimately, the 1922 strike was doomed. If it achieved anything, it was a legacy of bitterness and confusion. With the AWU held prisoner by arbitration, shearers were justified in wondering what good the union was doing them. Woolgrowers may have wondered the same thing when they were hit with strikes that showed how arbitration could fail.

In 1926 the question of wide combs arose once more, this time for consideration by the Arbitration Court. Once again, the matter came up because of a new invention, the Cooper double bent-tooth comb. Curiously, the AWU supported its use but woolgrowers were concerned that the comb would leave ridges in the wool and could potentially harm sheep, especially lambs.

It may have been a case of whatever the woolgrowers wanted, the union instinctively opposed. Nevertheless, shearers gave evidence that in reality bending teeth was common practice in the sheds. The court found that the double bent comb gathered more wool than a standard comb, therefore cutting more wool with each blow. Single bent combs, on the other hand, were only considered 'useful as a guide' for the handpiece.

The court eventually added a new clause to the 1926 award: 'The shearer shall not, without the consent of the employer, use any comb wider than the standard size of 2½ inches [6.35 centimetres, or exactly what was in the union rules], nor shall he use any double bent teeth comb.'

There may well have been evidence that supported the clause. However, it was the first time in its history that the court had brought down a ruling that directly restricted productivity. Wide combs would continue to be illegal for the next half-century.

By this time, there were more rules in the shed than ever before. In 1926, an English jackaroo discovered how some of them worked. He was managing a shed for a wealthy old woolgrower who knew better than to hang around all day and instead had his overseers do his bidding for him. He told his 'pommy jackaroo', who wasn't particularly experienced, to stamp out rough shearing.

It wasn't long before the Englishman noticed one shearer making a lot of second cuts. So he sacked him. The shearer took absolutely no notice. The jackaroo started shouting at him but the shearer just kept on shearing. Then the shearer who was the union representative stopped shearing his sheep and came over.

'Serves ya bloody right,' the rep said. 'You can't just walk up and sack a man, mate. That's union business and has to be done through me as the men's rep.'

The representative then went back to his stand and his sheep. Eventually he finished the sheep he was shearing, released it and hung up his handpiece. He then walked down to the shearer whom the jackaroo had tried to sack.

'Hang it up, mate,' he said. 'Too much second cut.'

The shearer didn't argue, nor did he ignore the union representative. He stopped shearing, gathered his belongings and walked out of the shed.

The jackaroo later concluded: 'A simple job – once one had learned the thousand and one rules the shearers have . . . and had become able to condense them into the Shearer versus The-Rest-of-the-World-Theme.'

The following year, Grazcos explained its operations during hearings for the 1927 award case. They admitted that cards were kept detailing every shearer's ability. The year before the hearings, 1926, they'd employed 1706 shearers. Every one of them had a card, even if they only shore one sheep.

The company also had a zoning system for the areas in which it operated, in order to manage the workflow and teams it employed. In New South Wales and Victoria, sheds were colour-coded according to the months of the shearing season, so contractor teams could be rotated from place to place: July sheds were yellow (the north-west of New South Wales), August was blue (the central-west and Riverina) and so on, ending up in November, coded brown, in Victoria. Each shed also had a spot indicating the number of shearers it required.

***

Despite the turmoil, shearing was still an attractive career for young Australians. Down in Victoria, in September 1924, one of them was a seventeen-year-old named Henry Salter (another member of the Shearers' Hall of Fame – see page 278). Like a lot of people in the southern states, Salter started as a rousie in the local sheds. He got some experience finishing off bits of sheep for an older shearer, Frank Clinton, then got his first stand as a shearer.

For his new job he rode his bike into Cohuna and bought trousers, boots, a flannel shirt, and some combs and cutters. He told the shopkeepers with pride that he was starting shearing the following week. On his first morning he no longer walked to the shed in the company of the other shed hands. He walked up with shearers Frank Clinton and Alan Peel. Not even the fact that he only managed forty-one sheep on his first day, while the other two topped 100, could dampen his pride.

He shore even less on his second day as muscles made sore by the previous day grew steadily worse. It was only towards the end of his first week that the pain started to recede and his tallies started to rise. It didn't help that he slept in a hut with a brick floor and no beds.

'We put three wool packs on the floor and three blankets and lay on that,' he told *Australian Shearing* in 1991. 'After two or three weeks on the floor, you get used to it.'

Soon he was earning £6 or £7 a week, with tallies still below 100. Nevertheless, for a youngster, it was 'good money'.

Salter may have noticed that some of the best shearers from his district were joining the annual migration to Queensland. That was where they could get the long runs that would earn them far more than just good money. However, it also earned them the resentment of Queenslanders.

In 1924, the AWU organiser for Charleville, Sam Brassington, detailed the reasons locals were bitter:

> As usual the men recruited by the contractors in the Southern States have returned to their homes, after having enjoyed the pick of the shearing. Year after year the number of southerners increases, much to the detriment of local workers.
>
> Western towns have declined under its blighting effects, and there has been a steady drift of bushmen to the cities during recent years. The contract system has ably assisted centralization in the cities.

Brassington didn't make any allowance for the fact that sheep numbers in outback Queensland had stagnated, while the Queensland award was higher than elsewhere, naturally luring shearers north. He also took little notice of the increasing trend for contract shearing to be carried out by shearers themselves. In the post-war period, that trend led to the contract system becoming less centralised, not the other way around.

Young Henry Salter was one of the shearers who branched into contracting. Coming from a struggling cocky farm, he needed to help support his family. So in the mid-1920s, when he was only nineteen, he bought a Cooper Little Wonder two-stand shearing plant and got into the small-scale contract-shearing game. The shearing season in his home region of northern Victoria wasn't very long but just over the border, in New South Wales, the bigger sheep runs of the Riverina beckoned. He mostly employed family and friends to help him, and he also shore himself. With a focus on making money rather than trouble he was soon finding plenty of work. He also always shore union.

Over in Western Australia, Don Munday was also discovering contract shearing. He started working for a contractor, still cocky shearing, in the Murchison district at 40 shillings a hundred. He also got work blade-shearing stud rams, for which he was paid 100 shillings per hundred. Munday was essentially self-taught with the blades but he could shear up to 100 a day. The contractor he was working for reckoned he could double that if he switched to machine shearing.

Don said 'righto' and was soon on his way by slow train to his first machine-shearing shed. He showed up on the Monday morning, having never handled a machine before. He didn't know how to load the handpiece so he tried to learn by watching his pen mate.

The shearer he was paired with, nicknamed Bob the Terror, quickly realised Munday was out of his element, so he showed him how to put on a comb and cutter and adjust the rocker. Bob spent most of the first day teaching Don how to shear with machines, especially keeping the sheep in position – the key to clean, fast shearing. By the following Thursday, Munday was getting the hang of it and managed a tally of 101. Bob, who was turning out to be anything but a terror, called it the lavatory tally (two sticks with a hole in the middle).

A few sheds later, Munday was shearing at Narndee Station and found out what it was like to get 'wool bogged'. The big Western

Australian merinos were cutting 5.5 kilograms each, and he was back to struggling to get a decent tally, and a decent income, each day. However, it turned out to be a worthwhile experience; in a few years' time all the sheep he encountered were well woolled.

Further north, shearer Lardie Fleay was discovering the significant contribution Aboriginal people were making to shearing in the pastoral zone. As he told author Patsy Adam-Smith:

> There were blacks in the sheds up until recent times. I started shearing up north in 1925. At Nookanbah black women would come in and sort locks. Fifteen or twenty of them sitting there pulling, draggin' sheep shit out of the little tufts of wool. Wool classers used to have little blackfellows to throw the wool into the various bins. Some of WA's best shearers were black. There was one 80-year-old who shore 200 in a day. He died in the shed that old man. I was shearing with his son. [*Reproduced by kind permission of the estate of Patsy Adam-Smith*]

Down at Cleveland, in central Tasmania, shearing was an occupation that spanned generations. I got to have a cuppa and a yarn with two generations of the Flood family – Lindsay and his towering sons, Winston and Thomas. (It would have been three generations but for the fact that Lindsay's grandson Shane, a good 200-a-day shearer, was working in the mines.)

Lindsay was born in 1925, in a shearing shed at Valley Field Station, on the Macquarie River.

'I was about to be born and the house got a fire,' he told me in a gruff, down-to-earth working man's accent, 'so they rushed Mum across to the woolshed, and that's where I was born.'

He learned to shear at Valley Field before getting his first pen in a shed down the road at Boswell.

Dad showed me a bit when I was younger. There was a lot of blades and then the machines came in and sort of took it over. They still shear a few here with the blades, studs like for the shows, Hobart show and Launceston show, Campbell Town show.

I was shearing with the old handpieces down out of Hobart there, the old blade shearers shearing down there and this bloke managed it for these people that owned it and he said, 'Lindsay Flood, take a bit more off the top knot. You're not takin' enough off.' And he put his finger in where it was and I made a blow with the blades and nearly cut the end off his finger. He never come back at me no more.

Blade shearing survived longer in Tasmania than in other regions of Australia as it took longer for electricity supplies to reach some of the more remote areas. That may sound like an opportunity to disparage Tasmania for being backward, but it says more about how wild and rugged parts of the state can be.

***

That kind of country produced people to match. One of the longest runs, in terms of distance, in the 1920s and for many years afterwards was the one for Tasmanian shearers. The island state's short season allowed shearers from the Longford, Cressy, Campbell Town and Ross districts of central Tasmania to range far and wide in search of more work opportunities. It still does.

The most epic shearing trip involved travelling by ship to Melbourne, then by train to Adelaide, then north on the Ghan to Farina. There the shearers unloaded their Cressy bicycles, made by a local bicycle maker named Tapley, and headed cross-country to Innamincka, a distance of 450 kilometres. Their route traversed enormous red sandhills and an area they called The Cobblers. Explorer Charles Sturt called it Sturt's Stony Desert, which is a more accurate description. For shearers, though, a cobbler is a sheep that is particularly hard to shear.

The intrepid cyclists followed the tracks of the camel teams and slept each night in the 'Star Hotel', meaning outdoors. Eventually they would arrive in Innamincka, a flyspeck town on Cooper Creek, in the far north-east of South Australia. From there it was a simple matter to travel the 175 kilometres north to Cordillo Downs Station, one of the most remote sheep properties in Central Australia. Or as simple as it can be out in the arid regions of the continent. The route from Innamincka to Cordillo passes through the country that killed explorers Burke and Wills. As recently as the 1960s a family of five died in the region after losing their way on the Birdsville Track. In modern times, the roads from Innamincka to Cordillo and across to the Birdsville Track are still challenging, even with four-wheel drives. They're particularly hard on tyres.

The family of one Tasmanian shearer told author Patsy Adam-Smith about his experiences:

> Uncle Bob Greig was riding his bike up to Cordilla [sic] and he came on a lonely boundary rider.
> 'How far to Cordilla?' Uncle Bob asked.
> 'Aw,' drawled the man, who rarely saw another man to converse with. 'As far as the crow flies about two hundred miles.'
> 'Bugger the crow flying,' says Uncle Bob, 'if the crow was on this bike, how far is Cordilla Downs?'

Once they got to Cordillo, where you wanted to be sure of a stand to have travelled such a long, hard road, some of the Tasmanians would start the very long run of shearing back down through Queensland and South Australia, into New South Wales and Victoria, then home. Others crossed over to the Queensland coast to pick up work cutting sugar cane, then worked their way back south.

These extraordinary adventures saw shearers away from their homes and families for eight months of the year. The run to Cordillo only came to an end in the 1940s when the station went over to cattle. The property lay outside the dingo fence and the sheep-fed dingoes bred to such large numbers that sheep were no longer viable.

In the mid-1920s, however, Australia was riding high on the sheep's back. It took until 1926 for sheep numbers in Australia to return to 100 million, the number before the droughts of the 1890s, but by then sheep were clipping much higher wool weights. In that year the clip totalled 440 000 tonnes while in 1892, 106 million sheep were clipping 290 000 tonnes. Wool was generating three-quarters of the nation's income from agriculture and a third of the total export income.

While the federal government was establishing a new national capital in the prime wool country of the New South Wales Southern Highlands, in 1927 consideration was given to renaming Canberra Woolgold. The name reflected an appreciation of Australia's dependence on its modern version of the golden fleece.

Much of the wealth was flowing to the shearers who harvested the wool. In 1928, Western Australia's Don Munday followed the lead of entrepreneurial shearers like Henry Salter and started his own contract-shearing business. He organised with Wolseley's Western Australian agents, Dalgety's, to set up a vehicle with a portable electric shearing machine.

It was a three-stand affair with a 5-horsepower engine, a 50-volt generator, three motors, downtubes and other equipment. It cost £250 (including accessories and spares) and the company let Munday have it on a sixty-day trial. The plant worked perfectly, and with a team of three it handled 400 sheep a day for the sixty days. At £2 per hundred (and very few expenses), Don and his mates finished well in front (about £230, in fact, even allowing for the total cost of the plant). The little electric plant was still working when it was sold forty-five years later.

Not so good for Munday was a bad case of yolk boils – sores that became infected after prolonged exposure to the grease in sheep's wool, and not helped by poor diet. He recalled:

I'd been plagued for about ten days with a crook bout of boils on my left arm (what we shearers call the rousie arm, because it's used mostly to control the sheep). We were shearing wethers at the time, and big rough ones at that, when I picked one of the most fidgety swines it's ever been my bad luck to grab. He kicked all the time and shook his head with such vigour that his left horn caught the top of one of my boils, ripping it right open. Puss [sic] and muck ran everywhere, and I was in such great agony that for once I lost my temper and hit that sheep with a hell of a whack under the jaw with my handpiece. [*Reproduced by kind permission of UWA Press*]

The owner saw what he did and warned him not to do it again.

'No need to,' Don said. 'One hit from me is enough for any bloody sheep you can breed.' Nothing more was said. At the time Munday was shearing a very respectable 175 sheep a day.

Further north, some shearing was being done in an entirely different manner, as described by H. M. Barker in his memoir, *Droving Days*:

Although instances of stock thriving better through the absence of fear can be quoted by most people in the outback pastoral country, a full and satisfactory explanation of the reason is not to be had. Sheep, especially, are unpredictable, and a certain amount of a certain kind of upset even makes them quieter instead of wilder. A typical instance of that I saw when blacks used to shear the sheep in the north-west of Western Australia. It was on a station called Yarrie on the De Grey River. The shearers were mostly women, big and fat. One would lay her sheep out on the floor and squat beside it, her legs tucked underneath her somehow, and she'd lean over on it shearing away, making small snips with only the tips of the shears. Each one would do about four sheep an hour but they'd make a perfect job of it. The most surprising thing of all was that the sheep did not kick. They lay quiet as if they were enjoying it. If a white man tried to do the same they'd struggle and lash with their hind legs from start to finish. The blacks got their sheep from a pen and sheared them anywhere on a big wide floor. When a sheep was finished it was allowed to get up and find its own way outside. It would do that in a hesitating way, picking its way quietly between the other shearers. The shorn ones would assemble about the door for a while. Occasionally one would remain standing after it was shorn and I'm sure that meant it had enjoyed the operation and would like it repeated.

Black children played about amongst the shearers picking up wool but adding to the homely atmosphere. The owner, a man over eighty, sat on a bale of wool supervising. I asked him why the sheep remained so passive throughout such an unorthodox procedure. He said one reason was that 'these blacks shear for pastime or pleasure but a white man shears only for money'. The blacks, he said, had a friendly approach that fitted the temperament of sheep. He pointed to a gin shearing in front of him, sprawling over the prostrate sheep with her big soft breast holding it down.

'Gawd, look at that,' said the old man, 'that would stop any man from kicking, it's the same with a sheep. If that was a white shearer he'd hold that sheep down with his knee and it would be a wooden-headed sheep that couldn't tell the difference and show it.'

We watched her finish that sheep, the points of the blades working only a few inches from her nose.

'You likeum cokenjarri?' said the old man.

'Yes, I likeum cokenjarri all right,' she said, holding the sheep's face up and pressing it with her cheek. (Cokenjarri was their native word for a sheep.)

'Gawd, they're a happy lot,' said the old man. 'Keep them occupied and they're right.'

The happiness of the women may have been confined to the eye of the beholder but the depiction of an idyllic rural scene was typical of the wool industry of the late 1920s. Prosperity was everywhere.

In the same era, shearer Ray Stibbard, who had also started shearing in cocky sheds, went into contracting. He ended up with thirty-nine sheds shearing 450 000 sheep. He later said that the key to his success was that he treated the men who worked for him as equals. That may not have been too difficult in a time when, as another shearer put it: 'By the time a rouseabout reaches town with a few bob in his pocket he's a gun shearer!'

It seemed that the prosperity of the 1920s would never end. However, there were ominous signs if you knew where to look. Prime Minister Stanley Bruce was trying to get the Australian economy working more efficiently, in part by dismantling the two-tiered arbitration system that allowed unions to shop around for the best award. The experiment with cocky farming had some notable successes but for many battlers, especially war-scarred soldier-settlers, their cocky farms went by another name: starvation blocks. Various schemes evolved to support them, many supported by government debt that was in turn supported by overseas borrowing. To a degree, the income that wool earned paid the interest on those overseas borrowings. Wool was subsidising industries that were protected by tariffs from the realities of the wider global financial system. Many other countries had gone down the same economic road. The party couldn't go on forever.

9

A MATTER OF SURVIVAL

(1930–1945)

In mid-1929, Prime Minister Stanley Bruce attempted to dump the federal Arbitration Court. Instead, his government fell and the nation went to the polls. Arbitration and industrial relations became the main election issue and led to Labor winning in a landslide on the back of fears of a return to the pre-arbitration capitalist jungle. The election was effectively a referendum on the arbitration system. 'It Will Never Again Be Threatened', declared a headline in *The Worker*.

Stanley Bruce became the first prime minister to lose his seat while in office. Incidentally, the second prime minister to lose his seat, John Howard in 2007, also did so in an election fought over industrial relations.

Yet it may have been that Bruce could see what was coming and had to act quickly. As it happened, in September 1929, global stock and commodity markets started to fall. In October, the US stock market crashed. As confidence fell, spending slowed and shrank production with it. Rather than recover, things grew steadily worse. By May 1930, the worst-case scenario for the Australian economy was realised. The world wool price collapsed.

Rory O'Malley explained the consequences in *Mateship and Moneymaking*:

> The sheltered sector – and this included development-mad state governments – borrowed for all it was worth when wool was high, but there was nothing [anyone] could do to shield them from savage credit squeezes when wool slumped. The savagery of the economic collapse in the 1930s is the outstanding illustration of this flaw in the post-Federation financial architecture. Another flaw was that it assumed world prices for wool would always carry the burden of costs imposed on it. [Mateship and Moneymaking *quotes reproduced by kind permission of Rory O'Malley*]

As the old battler on the Darling told Charles Bean, 'the man who borrows is broke'. Only now it applied to the nation. One grim set of figures tells the story. In 1925, wool was earning 55 pence per kilogram. In May 1930, it was earning 11 pence per kilogram. That alone goes a long way to explaining the depth of suffering experienced across Australia during the Great Depression.

The crash in the wool price didn't cause ripples throughout the rest of the economy – it was a tsunami. For example, in the late 1920s the government had been encouraging struggling cocky farmers to 'Grow More Wheat' with a subsidy of 4 pence a bushel. As its money supply disappeared, the government discontinued the scheme. Wheat prices immediately fell below the cost of production. Many cockies were hammered twice, as they were growing both wheat and wool.

It didn't take woolgrowers long to share the pain with their old adversaries, the shearers. The pastoral award was set to run from 1927 to 1931 but in May 1930 the collapse of wool prices led woolgrowers to urgently request a variation.

In the Arbitration Court Justice George Dethridge reflected on the increasingly desperate times: 'Whatever the court may do, the market prices of a product of an industry must, in the long run, be the main factor governing the share of wage earners.'

This was a very different view from that of Justice Higgins back in the early days of the court. Higgins had thought it better to set wages based on what people needed to survive, rather than what the industry needed to survive.

Justice Dethridge added that while some industries could have their prices subsidised, when it came to wool 'there is no power in Australia that can control prices'. He noted, however, that 'if the wool industry is crippled, all other industries will be more or less lamed'. It was the mainstay of the Australian economy, 'not a parasite that Australia can afford to allow to wither'.

It didn't take Justice Dethridge long to reach a decision. In July 1930, the shearing rate was cut by twenty-five per cent. Compared to the eighty per cent drop in wool prices, it wasn't too bad, but in places like Queensland it meant shearing at 30 shillings per hundred, instead of forty.

Once again, the old battlelines were drawn. The AWU prevaricated, fearing the legal consequences of striking against the award. The secretary of the Graziers Association of New South Wales, J. W. Allen, who had been instrumental in using legal action to defeat the 1922 strike, came out swinging. When the *Labor Daily* ran the headline 'Sixty Thousand Shearers May Go on Strike', Allen's graziers' association got an injunction to stop the paper publishing 'anything by way of encouragement or incitement to strike'.

The AWU eventually took the position that shearers should accept the award rate, but try to bargain for higher rates if they could get them.

The shearers went on strike anyway. In north-west New South Wales, there were soon 1000 shearers in strike camps. Grazcos, meanwhile, started bringing in shearers from areas further south.

Given the dire unemployment situation, there were plenty of willing and capable hands. By the end of August, the futility of the shearers' situation was abundantly clear, and the strike collapsed.

However, out of the ruins the Wobblies emerged in their latest incarnation, the Pastoral Workers Industrial Union. With the support of the fledgling Communist Party, it turned its focus to Queensland for 1931.

On 2 January 1931 the shearers at Longreach voted to strike. Violence in the district was not long in coming. As one account described it:

> Shortly after 5 o'clock yesterday morning, the twelve men who constitute the shearing gang at Norrindoo shed, 10 miles from Surat, were roused out of their sleep by an invasion of about 40 strikers who had travelled from Surat in seven motor cars. The men swarmed into the hut and in threatening tones ordered the men to pack their swags and 'clear out'. Several of the men were defiant, and a fierce fight was soon raging, the strikers endeavouring to forcibly eject the men from the shed. Although hopelessly outnumbered, the loyalists stood off their assailants with their fists as well as they could but they were roughly handled by the enraged strikers. The floor was soon a mass of struggling figures and boots were freely used to supplement fists. Amid the confusion several shots were fired. A number of the strikers were armed apparently with revolvers. Fortunately, the shots went wild, no one being injured by the shooting. In the middle of the turmoil, two members of the police force from Surat, who had followed the strikers, arrived by car. They were powerless to prevent the ejection which followed, although their presence undoubtedly had a restraining effect. Vainly they exhorted the strikers to depart, but all attempts at conciliation were useless. The strikers compromised by sending a delegate to warn the men in the hut

that unless they left immediately, firearms would be resorted to, and that, in effect, they would be literally shot off the premises. Deeming resistance hopeless, and overawed by the threatening attitude of the strikers, the men immediately packed their swags and left the shed.

While the Queensland shearers battled each other, the Queensland AWU insisted shearers work at award rates. Once again, though, those who did were labelled scabs. Grazcos again proved decisive as it organised special trains to bring shearers and shed hands up from the south. There were plenty of willing takers and once again the strike soon collapsed.

As the Depression ground on, unions advised their members to take any rate they could get. And many shearers were realising that shearing at any price was better than no job at all.

Entrepreneurial shearers like Henry Salter fared slightly better. He had successfully expanded his small contract-shearing operation over the Victorian border into New South Wales and while things were very tight, there were enough sheds to keep him going. He was also canny enough to cultivate an agent in Swan Hill who let him know who was in a position to pay for his work and who he should avoid.

Meanwhile, trainloads of workers were pouring out of the cities, heading for the country, hoping for any kind of work. The days of swaggies tramping the roads returned with a vengeance. At Weilmoringle Station, some recalled, the only work they had was cutting wood to fuel the steam engines during shearing.

During the Depression it was said that Tasmania's primary export was shearers. As contractor Fred Cotterill told Patsy Adam-Smith: 'All the Tasmanians were good. You could always pick a Tasmanian. They dropped their haitches at Hamilton and picked them up at Ararat. Whenever you pointed out a pretty bird to them they'd say, "Can you eat it?"'

Tasmanian shearer Ray Watley recalled his experiences in Queensland: 'When I first saw the Cordillo flock I said, "Sheep! They're more like bloody mountain goats." Kynuna shed was a bough roof over a bullock hide floor. We shore 210 000 there one year. It looked like a bodgie set up but it was cooler than the big iron sheds.'

Over in Western Australia, Don Munday was enjoying mixed fortunes. He still had his small contract-shearing operation but in 1930 his family had harvested a bumper wheat crop. With the loss of the wheat subsidy it was worse than worthless; it had cost them more money to put the crop in than they got when they took it off. Munday decided to leave the family farm near Wickepin and find more work shearing to cover expenses until the Depression eased and prices recovered.

That year he did the Wiluna run with contractor Tom Ellis, using two portable two-stand Cooper Little Wonder shearing plants. The Little Wonders weren't really suitable for shed work but under the circumstances Munday and the other shearers didn't have much choice.

While shearing at Lake Way Station, Don found grazier Bert Lukin a 'proper squatter snob'. When Bert discovered Don was a cocky farmer he started sniping at him about wheat prices, subsidies and the preferential treatment he thought the battlers were given. It became so petty that Bert misspelled Don's name as Mundy in his tally book. Don pointed it out and said, 'My name, like your sheep, would look a lot better with a little "a" in them.'

Their next station was Granite Downs, but before they started shearing, contractor Tom Ellis told his shearers their rate had fallen to 31 shillings and 6 pence a hundred. Munday sent a telegram seeking advice on what to do to the Perth branch of the AWU. Eventually he received a reply that read 'Carry On'.

At Paroo Station, Munday encountered one of the eccentric characters of the north-west, a young manager named Clarrie Clews.

Every morning Clarrie greeted the men and then said, 'The nor'west squatter's a hardy bird, he has a face like a sun-baked turd.'

While at Paroo, word came through that all shearers in the state were going on strike. Munday pulled out, intending to return to Yealaring where he could get work cocky shearing for 40 shillings a hundred. He didn't consider this strikebreaking as the rate was far better than the rate the strike was about.

As in eastern Australia, the Western Australian strike was short-lived. After two months it was over, but plenty of bitterness remained. The shearing rate had ended up at 26 shillings and 6 pence a hundred. It wasn't bad money, considering the times, and while Don was prepared to accept it, others wouldn't.

Munday got more shearing work in the Gascoyne district and was flown to Carnarvon by contractor Harry Doyle. The reason for the expense soon became apparent. At Yardie Station Don found himself shearing alongside the worst shearers he'd ever seen. Some may have talked up their ability hoping they'd at least be given a chance. At the end of the shed, Harry sacked the whole team, except Don.

Back in Carnarvon, the strike may have been over but there were still clashes between union shearers who wanted to stay on strike and the men they considered strikebreakers. Munday sympathised with the latter: 'The poor cows coming in were dead broke and flat out to get a job away from the depression-hit city.' As for Carnarvon, after the strike it was 'a spiteful brawling joint'.

One good thing that came out of the Depression was that it put a dent in the drinking and gambling that was associated with some big-money shearers. In the years before the Depression, it has been suggested, £2000 could be wagered on the roll of a dice, £1000 on the turn of a card. After the Depression, such excesses became a thing of the past.

They weren't particularly missed. According to some contractors, gambling could make sheds harder to run. If shearers lost badly, and ended up owing other shearers money, they'd often take off during the night. Next morning, the team was a shearer short, more if those owed money gave chase.

Don Munday was the kind of shearer who had no interest in squandering his hard-earned wages. Early in 1931 he went to see Bill Synnot, manager of Western Australia's top shearing contractors, Synnot and Dunbar, for a job.

'How many can you do?' Bill asked.

'Two hundred and twenty-seven,' Don replied.

'How did you do them?'

'I haven't got the sack yet,' Don said.

Synnot gave him a job on the Myroodah run: eight months, 25 000 sheep per man.

On the way out of Synnot's office, Don ran into one of the company's top shearers, Duncan Muir, who was good enough to give him some tips on what to expect. Duncan showed Don what to take, rolled in his swag, which could double as a seat. It comprised a groundsheet, a blanket, a sheet, moccasins, two pairs of shearer's pants, two shearer's shirts, socks, shaving gear, a mosquito net and ammoniated tincture of quinine for dengue fever.

A few days later Munday boarded the MV *Koolinda* and set sail for Derby. When they arrived, four teams were assembled: forty-two shearers, forty-two rousies, five pressers, five cooks, four experts, four classers, and one piece-picker. The teams set out for Noonkanbah, Myroodah, Mount Anderson and Quanbun Downs in five trucks. The teams sat in the open air on benches that ran the length of each truck. The wet season was only just ending so Don's team had to drag their truck through mud for the last few kilometres to the Fitzroy River, which was still in flood.

Once the shearing started at Myroodah, it didn't take Munday long to realise why Synnot and Dunbar were the best contractors in the state. All their shearers were totally professional. There was no joking or wasting time on the board. Everyone was there to shear as many sheep as possible as fast as possible. Don was more than satisfied with how he went. He rang the state for the year with his best tally of 286, and shore 7849 of Myroodah's 54 000 sheep.

In early May the team set off on the next leg of a 2500-kilometre journey that would take in Wallareenya, Indee and Pippingarra at Port Hedland, Byro and Yuin on the Murchison, and Karara near Perenjori.

At Pippingarra Munday encountered Ted Richardson, the first pastoralist he met who acted like a normal person. He'd talk to anyone with never a sign of snobbery. His two sons behaved the same way. Pippingarra was the only shed where Don was sorry when it cut out. The whole team felt the same way. They gave Ted a thank-you gift of a box of cigars for all his support.

While shearing around Port Hedland, tourists used to visit during the shearing. One day the cry went up, 'Ducks on the pond', meaning a woman was on the board and that appropriate decorum should be maintained. That was until the woman in question bent over to see what one of the shearers was doing. The opportunity was too good to miss. One of the other shearers placed his still-running handpiece on her buttocks and she almost jumped out of her skin.

When the team moved on to Byro Station, in the Murchison, what Munday noticed most was the sheer isolation. The shearing shed and quarters were good but totally isolated from the homestead, or anywhere else.

The next station was Yuin, 200 kilometres from Byro. While the station area was an oasis, the country around it was parched. The Yuin sheep were in such desperately poor condition that the shearing wasn't about speed, it was about minimising the stress on the blighted creatures. When the shed cut out, owner Charlie Foulkes-Taylor thanked the shearers for handling his poor sheep so carefully.

In his memoir, Don makes a point of refuting Patsy Adam-Smith's description of shearers' relationships with the north-west's Aboriginal people. She'd quoted sources saying, 'More than half the men who went up there were having a bit. The natives up there were more animal than human. One night one was going to have a baby. She lay down on the ground and had it and caught up with the mob later.'

Munday reckoned nothing could be further from the truth. After a hard day's shearing, all he ever wanted was a shower, a meal, a Scotch and a bed. Others were the same. Most young women were very shy and 'wouldn't come within coo-ee of a white man'. He went further: 'To suggest that those innocent kids cohabited freely with old shearers is utterly false. And it saddens me to think what could've been had they been shown a good example and even a little respect, instead of being treated like dirt.'

Munday's shearing career lasted for sixteen years. In 1934 he gave it away to go back to working his farm. In his view, shearing was 'No job for old men'. As it was, he was still demonstrating shearing decades later, in the 1980s, aged in his eighties.

While Don was shearing his way through Western Australia, Jim Scullin's federal government was having far less success negotiating the political minefields hampering its response to the economic crisis facing Australia and the world. During 1931 the government had taken the bold decision to devalue the Australian pound, which effectively increased the export returns for agricultural products in local currency.

Faced with a hostile senate and a divided caucus, the government adopted a watered-down version of its economic strategy that at least had some support. The Premiers' Plan, as it was known, had three main points: reduction of government deficits, a 10 per cent wage cut and, most revolutionary of all, an interest-rate cut. However, the root of many of the country's worries, protectionism, remained. Warren Denning later wrote in *Caucus Crisis: The Rise and Fall of the Scullin Government*:

> Canberra became a happy hunting ground for tariff 'touts': an unpleasant name bestowed on a group of importunate people whose purpose was to impress on the government and the party the dire importance of Australian-made silk stockings, or razor blades, or toilet paper, receiving the whole of the Australian market ... The doormat at the entrance to the Customs department was worn thin by their feet.

Denning wrote that in 1937. In modern times, it still has a ring of familiarity. Wool, of course, was still exposed to the vagaries of world prices, which, by the end of 1931, were showing signs of having bottomed and were beginning the long road to recovery.

Even in those dark days, there were still plenty of shearers who were prepared to back themselves, whether by desire or necessity. In 1932, in Lockington, Victoria, not far from where Henry Salter's contract-shearing business was based, shearers Frank Sarre and Ron Arnold got themselves a two-stand shearing plant and started working in small sheds around their district. Their operation kept them going during the Depression and put food on the table for their families, including Frank's son Kevin (a Hall of Fame inductee – see page 279), born in 1933 and destined to become one of the most influential shearers of his generation.

* * *

It may not have been noticed in Australia at the time, but across the Tasman, the skills of New Zealand's shearers were continuing to develop. In 1933, Percy de Malmanche shore 412 sheep in ten working hours. The record wasn't recognised due to the longer working day involved; New Zealanders usually shore for nine hours in a day. So the next year he had another go and shore 409 ewes in nine hours (which meant he'd have beaten Jack Howe's 321 in seven hours and twenty minutes by a dozen sheep), while clipping an average 4.3 kilograms of wool from each.

Both tallies are impressive, but the 412 may be more so for one simple reason: during the ten-hour course of removing the wool from the sheep, Percy also removed the contents from a bottle of rum. Percy wasn't sure if the rum helped him or slowed him down but it was far from the ideal strategy for a record attempt. Nevertheless, it says a great deal for his ability to shear and/or handle his grog.

Back in Australia, one of the first shearing competitions in Victoria was held in November 1934. It was conducted by the Pyramid Hill Agricultural Society and was judged on a combination of speed and quality. The winner was local shearer and contractor Henry Salter, who took home five pounds. The local paper said it was the first championship in Australia, although as noted previously, competitions had been held elsewhere in the early 1900s. However, from this date on competition shearing became a regular occurrence, particularly in Victoria and the Riverina region of New South Wales.

Through the 1930s shearers gradually regained some of the ground they'd lost on wage rates. In Queensland, in 1936, this was helped by a plague of flies. The flies were so bad that a lot of shearers, who didn't have a free hand to swat the pests, gave up and went home (as someone who has endured Birdsville's flies for a year, as detailed in my book *Birdsville*, I can sympathise). The resulting shortage put upward pressure on the shearing rate.

Wool prices were also on the rise, giving Australia much-needed foreign income. In 1938, the Australian Mint acknowledged Australia's debt to the merino when it issued a new Australian shilling. It featured the Uardry stud ram Hallmark, the 1932 Royal Sydney Show grand-champion ram. With his triple-chin wool folds he was one of Uardry's proudest products, and one whose genes have been passed on to dozens of other sheep studs and commercial wool flocks across Australia. The importance of wool to the Australian economy was underlined in a Queensland government inquiry held not long after. It found:

> The Australian Wool industry is ... entirely unsheltered and dependent on overseas trade. It is exposed to any economic blizzard that blows in any wool-consuming country of the world ... It has to accept world parity for its product, and this fluctuates according to the ability of the customer countries to pay, as well as their desire, or disinclination, to buy. While its income is determined by the purchasing power parity of low wage countries overseas, all its costs of production are inflated by the high living standards of Australia.
>
> Anything that is done in Queensland and Australia to help the industry function efficiently, and to reduce its costs, should ungrudgingly be done in order to advance not only its interests but the interests of the whole community.

That year, too, Don Munday was demonstrating his shearing skills to the world. He had gone on a visit to Britain and ended up staying, doing shearing demonstrations and working for the Wolseley company making shears. He was demonstrating at the Empire Exhibition when he managed to shear a fully woolled sheep in just eighty seconds. He believed it was a world record for shearing such a sheep under world-championship conditions, and that it wasn't bettered during his lifetime.

Also in 1938, while the Depression may have dented the gambling instincts of shearers they certainly hadn't disappeared, as shearer Percy Gresser discovered at Weilmoringle, in northern New South Wales. In writing of the shearing at that time, he also echoed Don Munday's views regarding the relationships between shearers and Aboriginal women:

> For several weeks each year there would be 60 or more men employed during the shearing at Weilmoringle, and practically every night the gamblers among the shearers and shed hands

would play poker or hazards in the dining room of the shearers' quarters. Also a two-up school would be in progress during much of the daylight hours and at weekends and during time lost owing to wet weather. The aborigines [whose community lived and worked on the station] were inveterate gamblers. Whenever there was a game on, day or night, some of them would be present. Instead of finishing up winning the shearers' money, they invariably parted with what money they had. Every now and then one or another of them would not be seen for a couple of days or so. When he appeared upon the scene again it would be with a pair of carved emu eggs or a walking stick made from ringed (fiddle backed) gidgee, or several carved boomerangs, a couple of clubs or a shield to sell to the shearers or raffle, in order to get a few shillings with which to again join in the gambling school. It was said that the aborigines would save up what money they earned for weeks beforehand in order to gamble it during the shearing.

They did not make it a practice to frequent the shearers' quarters except to take part in the two-up, hazard or poker games. The women never did so during the occasions I happened to be shearing there. In fact, the general attitude of the aborigines was one of aloofness (but) they are bitterly opposed to anyone going to their camps and taking photographs of them and their women and children without asking leave of permission.

At the same time the question of wide combs continued to have a life of its own. In 1938, the Arbitration Court revisited the question, and made the clause restricting their use more specific. It now said: 'The shearer shall not use any comb wider than 2½ inches [6.35 centimetres] between the points on the outside teeth.'

The suspicion at the time was that some contractors were getting their shearers to use wide combs.

The new wide-comb rule provoked little comment, which may have been due to the proliferation of rules by that time. The extent to which shearers were governed by rules is reflected in the experiences of Broken Hill contract shearer Charlie Flavel. During the Depression years, one of his teams was told that the ceiling of the shed they were working in was 15 centimetres lower than was allowed in the award. The men took a vote on whether to keep shearing. Eight voted to shear, twelve voted to strike. Rather than follow their companions into their strike camp, the eight went on with the shearing, cutting out all the sheep. On their way off the property, a month later, they passed the twelve, still in their 'strike camp'.

'Got enough head room now,' Flavel chided them.

Despite being a contractor himself, Flavel had no illusions about their place in life. He considered contractors crawlers. If their shearers were rubbish, they crawled to the owner. If the owner was a pig, they crawled to the shearers.

Despite such views, there were still plenty of people willing to take on the job. Some thrived. In 1939, Victorian Henry Salter was doing so well that he expanded his shearing plant to four stands. He still shore himself and used family to help him where he could. In 1942, his colleagues in small-contract shearing Frank Sarre and Ron Arnold also upgraded to a six-stand plant.

***

The outbreak of World War II again saw shearing made a protected occupation and the entire wool clip purchased by the British government. The war situation favoured well-organised contractors, and while the likes of Henry Salter, Frank Sarre and Ron Arnold struggled to find shearers, Grazcos built its business until it was shearing eight million sheep from Victoria to Queensland.

The company was also ready to deal with any threats of strike action. It had perfected a tactic of isolating militants then prosecuting them into silence. Grazcos stuck to the award but as prices rose during the war, so did wages. Private contractors reflected the market by paying above award.

Elsewhere in Australia, other tensions were swirling. Early in 1942, in the north-west of Western Australia, a group of 200 Aboriginal elders from twenty-three tribal groups representing workers on the sheep stations in the region held a meeting to discuss ways to secure better conditions. Many were being paid rations only, were forbidden to leave the stations where they worked and were housed in the most rudimentary of structures. In effect, they were slaves. The meeting was organised by people from the Pilbara community (including Clancy McKenna, Dooley Bin Bin and Peter 'Kangushot' Coppin) and white labourer and prospector Don McLeod. Discussions ran for six weeks before the decision was made to take strike action at twenty-seven stations covering an area of 10 000 square kilometres. The strike was to begin on 1 May, International Workers' Day and the beginning of the 1942 shearing season. However, it was decided to delay action until after the war was over.

Western Australia's Aboriginal workers weren't the only ones dissatisfied with their rates of pay. Towards the end of World War II, while new alterations in the federal and Queensland awards were being negotiated, there was a militant strike in Queensland. In April 1945 it spread to northern New South Wales. At the time, much of the strike area was facing a drought and most woolgrowers were anxious to shear.

The Arbitration Court stood its ground and refused to hear the award case until the strike was over. This may have carried weight with the AWU but many militants regarded arbitration as the problem, not the solution. The strike didn't last long, but once again, the undercurrent of tension remained. The war may have made such undercurrents run deeper below the surface than usual but when world peace returned, the renewal of battle between shearer and woolgrower wouldn't be long in coming.

10

SUNDAY TOO FAR AWAY

(1946–1975)

> So you're off to Riverina, where the sun is shining clear,
> And the ewes and lambs are bleating, calling shearers far and near;
> Where the musterers are busy and the grass is waving high,
> And the July fogs are climbing up the sunbeams to the sky.
> – 'John Drayman'

Up in the Pilbara, the Aboriginal workers were mobilising. With the war over, the time had come to try to get a better deal. Maybe they'd even get paid. To ensure that every station's workers went on strike on the same day, a novel system was devised to get around the fact that many couldn't read English. Well before 1 May, the day the strike was to begin, organiser Dooley Bin Bin went 'visiting relatives' on each station. While there, he distributed calendars printed on the labels of jam tins. All his 'relatives' had to do was cross off a box on the calendar at the end of each day until there was only one box left. That was the day to strike.

On 1 May 1946, 800 Aboriginal workers walked off twenty-seven north-west stations. They formed strike camps and outlined their demands for wages and better conditions. Many of the stations were paralysed by the actions. No mustering, no shearing, none of the labour needed to get sheep to the sheds and bales pressed and carted away. Strikebreaking wasn't easy either, as non-Aboriginal labour would expect to be paid, which would have meant conceding the core demand of the Aboriginal strikers.

The dispute should have been an easy win for the workers but the stations dug in and held out for the next three years. So did the workers. They resorted to traditional hunting and food gathering to keep themselves going. Meanwhile their employers came to the realisation that they were living in the twentieth century and the days of happy natives kissing sheep and saying 'likeum cokenjarri' were over, if they'd ever really existed. The strike became the longest in Australian history, and one of its least known.

At the time, Western Australian sheep numbers were just short of 10 million. Half those sheep were in the wide-open country of the north-west, while the other half were in the cocky-farming country sprawling to the south and east of Perth. As previous chapters have shown, teams of shearers from the cocky country travelled north to shear on the long runs of sheds but Aboriginal people were also employed as shearers, musterers and rousies. In fact, they were the backbone of many stations' operations.

When the stations eventually conceded the key demands, for many Aboriginal people there was no going back. Decades-old relationships couldn't be renewed. For many of the stations, it was the beginning of the end. Without slave labour the economics of isolated sheep stations simply didn't stack up. When they had to pay their workers award wages (which would eventually be the case for all Aboriginal workers when they were included in the federal pastoral award in 1968) they became more vulnerable than any other woolgrowers to falls in wool prices.

* * *

Over in the eastern states, the Royal Melbourne Show held its first shearing competition and the growing popularity of these contests saw the Sydney Royal Easter Show stage competitions at around the same time. However, most of the competitions put a low value on speed, awarding it only a quarter of the points while the rest were for other aspects, mostly relating to quality. Basically, if you could shear a sheep in three minutes and thirty seconds, you got maximum points for speed.

Many gun shearers, able to shear a sheep in around two minutes, in shed conditions, didn't bother entering such competitions as people they could shear rings around were beating them for reasons that didn't apply in the real world.

The emphasis on quality over quantity was also evident in the Arbitration Court, which in 1948 extended the clause regarding wide-tooth combs so contractors couldn't push shearers to use them. It now said: 'The shearer shall not use, *nor shall the employer permit a shearer to use*, any comb wider than 2½ inches [6.35 centimetres] between the points on the outside teeth.'

In Australia, at least, it seemed the battle over speeding up had been won. Unfortunately, no one thought to tell the New Zealanders. For the next twenty years there was barely a murmur about the use of wide combs in Australia. Meanwhile, over in New Zealand, wide combs were standard issue, and the idea of only going as fast as the slowest shearer definitely wasn't part of the culture.

Of course, money could still provide the best shearers with enough motivation to shear prodigious numbers of sheep, no matter what they were using to do the job. And after 1949, there was plenty of money.

In that year, the AWU finally won a point that many of its members had been seeking for years: the shearing rate was linked to the price of wool.

According to the Wool Value Allowance, for every penny that the price of wool went above 39.5 pence per pound [86.9 pence per kilogram], 9 pence per hundred sheep was added to the shearing rate for the next season. This should have settled the long-running argument that when wool prices went up woolgrowers never raised the shearing rate, but they always wanted to drop rates when prices fell. Of course, there seemed to be an assumption that wool prices would only ever go up, and history had shown that if there was one thing shearers hated most, it was a cut to the shearing rate.

For a time, all was well. In 1945 the shearing rate was 45 shillings per hundred. By 1950 it had risen to 100 shillings. Shearers had to be happy with that.

Shearer Ted Reick certainly was. In 1950 he finally matched Jack Howe's 1892 feat by machine-shearing 326 merino sheep in eight hours. The average wool weight for the sheep was 1.36 kilograms heavier than Jack's had been. Dan Cooper had also overtaken Howe's record in 1949, machine-shearing 325 in Victoria, the distinction being that the sheep were easier-shearing Corriedales.

Even New Zealander Bob Mills was impressed with Reick's achievement:

> A comparison may be made here between Godfrey Bowen's nine-hour tally of 559 of possibly the fastest and best shearing sheep in the world [Welsh mountain sheep, shorn in 1960], and Reick's eight-hour tally of 326 of the slowest and toughest shearing breed in the world, using the narrow gear. Which is the better machine-shearing performance? An impartial study of all records and high tallies brings me to the inevitable conclusion that Reick's is the best of them all.

As detailed previously, Mills also considered Jack Howe's feat with the blades to be the greatest blade-shearing achievement of all. Score two for the Aussies. However, Godfrey Bowen's achievements will be considered shortly, along with the consequences when many New Zealand shearers discovered they could shear rings around their Australian colleagues.

Meanwhile, with such good money to be earned as a shearer, it was little wonder that there was keen interest in getting into the business – not a simple matter at the time. The usual entry method was barrowing: getting into a shed as a rousie, then getting to shear a bit of a sheep here and there, finishing them off for a shearer after the bell and slowly learning the tricks. Eventually, you might get a stand as 'the learner' and go from there.

By the late 1940s, however, Henry Salter had built up sufficient notoriety from shearing competitions and his business that he finally responded to frequent requests for lessons. He started out doing some instruction on his own then hit upon the idea of running proper lessons through a local school. Over at Lockington, fellow contract shearer Ron Arnold was doing much the same thing, at the very same time.

In 1950, at Kerang High School, Henry organised a formal nine-week shearing course that included practical experience in local shearing sheds. The fee was 7 pounds 10 shillings, and the course was unsubsidised, meaning students or their families had to come up with the money themselves. Detailed shearing notes were included:

> You first enter catching pen, and catch a sheep by putting your left arm under sheep's neck near brisket, and with your right hand grab a handful of wool on right side flank, you then lift sheep off floor and back out of pen to where your handpiece sits on the floor. You sit sheep on rump and between your legs, hold knees firmly against sheep, pick up right hand foreleg, push backwards,

catch it on your side and holding it there, this leaves your left hand free. Your sheep is then ready to shear.

Pick up your handpiece, put machine into gear, proceed now by placing handpiece on front flank, push downwards on side of belly keeping the comb on skin, do one blow or stroke down to the back left flank, break out the wool with a forward thrust with your arm, turning handpiece downwards, shear belly wool off with diagonal blows. When belly is shorn break wool off with left hand and throw belly wool away from you.

The notes went on to describe the whole shearing process. There were plenty of applicants for Henry's and Ron's courses. Over the next twenty-two years, Henry taught nearly 5000 shearers.

In 1950, the idea of a national shearing competition also gained support after America started organising a world shearing championship. As Australia was the world's largest producer of wool, especially fine merino wool, even the AWU believed that an Australian should win it. While it was being organised (format, type of sheep, rules), the Americans suggested using wide combs. The idea went no further in Australia.

As for the price of wool, and the amounts shearers were paid to shear it, the rises of the late 1940s were nothing compared to what happened at the beginning of the 1950s. On the Korean peninsula, the growing tension between north and south erupted in the early hours of 25 June 1950, as thousands of North Korean troops launched a massive offensive over the border. Within a week, the South Korean capital, Seoul, had fallen.

As an international coalition of forces set about driving the North Koreans back, the US government secretly approached the Australian government led by Robert Menzies to inquire about purchasing the entire Australian wool clip. The Americans hoped their allies would do them the same favour they'd done for the British in both world wars, whereby the clip was compulsorily acquired to ensure supply and prevent profiteering. Despite the fact that America had saved Australia's bacon in the Pacific just a few years earlier, the Australian government refused. If America didn't want its soldiers to freeze to death defending world peace, they'd have to pay the market price.

Which they did. Or as the chief American wool buyer put it, 'We will have to use the long purse.'

In 1950–51, the average wool price, which usually sat below a shilling a pound (2 shillings and 2 pence a kilogram), went to 14 shillings and 7 pence (32 shillings and 1 penny per kilogram). It peaked in May 1951 at 31 shillings and 3 pence per pound (68 shillings and 9 pence per kilogram). Those who recall the times refer to wool getting a pound (in currency) a pound (in weight). In May it was way beyond that, at more than one-and-a-half pounds in currency to one pound in weight.

That year some woolgrowers received cheques that were the equivalent of half what they could expect to earn in their entire lives (assuming they worked on the land for sixty years). The smart money recognised that such prices could never last and invested the lot (or at least most of it). The stupid money assumed the good times had finally arrived and blew the lot. The ensuing orgy of spending left little doubt about the wisdom, or lack of it, that prevailed. Money flooded Australia and while the beneficiaries rejoiced, economists looked on aghast.

In August 1951, the newly launched *Financial Review* newspaper, in only its second issue, noted: 'The froth has been blown off wool prices ... the economy has been jerked up to a new price and cost basis only sustainable at the higher level of wool prices.'

With the shearing rate linked to the wool price, shearers also shared in the bonanza. In 1951, the shearing rate was set at a massive 174 shillings per hundred.

It wasn't until the budget of September 1951 that the government reacted. By then, imports and inflation were skyrocketing. According to the anecdotal evidence, up until 1951 well-off woolgrowers might splash out on motor cars. In 1951, they all bought planes. In fact, aerial mustering dates from this time. On 26 September, treasurer and Country Party leader Arthur Fadden brought down what was described at the time as a horror budget. By then, though, the damage was done.

The Americans put away the long purse in 1952, invested much more in the development of synthetic fibres made by companies such as petrochemicals giant DuPont, and the long decline of the wool industry began. In hindsight, the cost of Menzies snubbing the Americans probably outweighed the benefits. However, it's interesting to speculate, with the Korean War wool boom as a guide, how much money woolgrowers would have made from the two world wars if the British had been treated the same way as the Americans.

The party may have been over, but someone still had to tell the shearers. In 1952, the Arbitration Court made the brave (if not foolhardy) decision to hear some of the latest pastoral award cases in the northern New South Wales towns of Moree and Coonamble.

According to the Wool Value Allowance formula, with the price of wool falling, the new shearing rate should have been 127 shillings and 6 pence (a nearly 50-shilling cut). Some woolgrowers may have been quietly muttering, 'Welcome to our world, fellas.' Had his honour explained that to the militant shearers in either town, he'd have found himself living in interesting times. However, the blow was softened somewhat by a rise in the base award rate to 140 shillings per hundred.

Undercurrents of resentment may have remained, but even at that rate there were plenty of shearers who were motivated to shear big numbers of sheep. Not surprisingly, interest in shearing was intense. In 1953, the first Australian Shearing Championship transformed annual competition at the Royal Melbourne Show. Henry Salter was the first winner. Second place was taken by Kevin Sarre (son of Frank Sarre and nephew to Ron Arnold). The Victorians were practically neighbours. Henry's winner's medallion was donated by the AWU.

Cocky shearers like the Sarres, Henry Salter and Ron Arnold had plenty in common with the other star shearer of 1953, New Zealander Godfrey Bowen. On 6 January 1953, he set a new all-time record by shearing 456 sheep (eclipsing the hard-drinking, fast-shearing Percy de Malmanche's 1934 record of 409) at Akers Estate, Opiki, Manawatu. Godfrey's brother, Ivan, had a go at the record in December of that year, and the plan was that he'd aim to equal, not pass, his brother's tally. In the end, due to a miscount, he beat him by one sheep. The women's world record was also held by a New Zealander, Grace Johnson, who had blade-shorn 120 sheep.

Woolgrower Bob Mills witnessed Godfrey's achievement and thought other shearers would benefit from being taught his technique. He also thought Godfrey would make a great instructor. During 1953 he convinced the New Zealand Wool Board to approve a training scheme involving Godfrey. Mills had argued that, while other schemes had failed in the past, it would be different if it involved a champion that other shearers looked up to.

There was some resistance from the New Zealand Shearers Union, but after influential union rep Bob Tutaki attended one of Godfrey's demonstration days, he spoke in glowing terms of the scheme's value to the industry, and congratulated Godfrey on his ability as a shearer and as an instructor.

Then there were the shearers. At one shed, full of Maori shearers, the antagonism threatened to spill over into violence. The owner had a word to the men. 'See first, judge afterwards,' he said. Godfrey won them over.

That just left the sheep. At one demonstration where Ivan was standing in for his brother, it was discovered that the only sheep available were merinos, tough-looking wethers. The situation smelled of an ambush. Before giving his demonstration, Ivan found a shed where he could watch merinos being shorn, then had a go at shearing one and found out what combs and cutters to use.

Back at the demo, the sheep seemed as mean and defiant as many of the spectators, most of whom looked like they wanted to see the great Ivan Bowen taken down a peg or two.

The crowd was silent as he started on his first sheep, which took him three minutes and thirty seconds to shear. There was scattered applause and a glimmer of interest as Ivan started his second sheep. It took three minutes. When he shore the third sheep in two minutes and thirty seconds, the crowd broke into spontaneous applause. Ivan was both fast and clean, even with some of the hardest-shearing sheep in New Zealand.

Eventually, Bob Mills and Godfrey Bowen hit on the idea of doing demonstrations at night, which allowed shearers to come in from other sheds after they'd knocked off for the day. In one crowded shed, someone fell from his vantage point and managed to rip out all the lights. Godfrey was already shearing his sheep when the shed was plunged into darkness. He just kept shearing. When the lights came back on, the sheep was standing there, perfectly shorn. Western Australian cocky shearer Don Munday demonstrated a similar ability in England by shearing sheep blindfolded.

Significantly, all of the shearing achievements of Godfrey Bowen and his brother were done with wide combs, and mostly on fast-shearing sheep. Narrow gear was so rare that Bob Mills, writing in the 1950s, felt the need to explain to New Zealand readers what it was:

> Narrow gear is a handpiece with a comb and cutter not more than 2⅜ inches [6.3 centimetres] in width. Such gear is hard to find anywhere today, though some may be tucked away on the back shelves of machinery stores or perhaps kept as treasured possessions by some old-time shearers as reminders of their former prowess. The narrow gear later gave way to a comb of wider dimensions, known as medium gear, which in turn was replaced by the much broader comb which is almost exclusively used in

this country today. Maori shearer Raihania's tally established with the original narrow gear deserves the admiration of all present-day shearers. Any shearer who would evaluate his effort should ask himself whether he would like to hook his machine, loaded with narrow gear, to a downtube and attempt to shear 332 sheep.

The other place you could find narrow gear, of course, was everywhere in Australia. And it could still achieve some impressive tallies. As Western Australian shearing contractor Marcus Synnot told Patsy Adam-Smith:

> At Noonkanbah 101 000 sheep were shorn in five weeks in 1954; 44 men in the shed, 20 shearers on the board. They shore 20 000 one week, 1000 per man per week. That was a world record. We shore over 4400 one day. The learner had tears in his eyes; he had shorn over 200 that day and was still dragging the chain!

The teams up in the Kimberley played as hard as they worked. One contracting team had a Chinese cook who became the butt of all their practical jokes. They put burrs in his bed and jam in his slippers. The cook took it without saying a word or openly retaliating. Eventually, he won their respect, and they decided to tell him they wouldn't play any more tricks on him.

'Are you sure?' the cook asked.

'Yes.'

'No more burrs in my bed?'

'No.'

'No more jam in my slippers?'

'No.'

'Okay, then,' said the cook. 'No more piddle in your soup.'

**

In 1955, as the interest in shearing competitions continued to grow, the AWU seized control of Australian competitions. It established the Shearing Competition Federation of Australia, which set about reconciling the running of competitions with the union's rules and the provisions of the pastoral award. For example, weekend shearing was against union rules, plus the union insisted competitors should be paid for the sheep they shore. The competition rules the union promoted emphasised quality over speed, which was a bone of contention with some organisers.

Curiously, the New Zealand Wool Board held the same view. A spokesman maintained that it wasn't interested in speed shearing. Out in the real world, shearer and woolgrower Bob Mills couldn't believe it. He wrote:

> This somewhat platitudinous assertion thus denies the importance of speed to the shearing industry, and is strangely at variance with the true situation. Clean shearing, with as few second-cuts as possible, is most important; but after that comes speed. Let any unknown shearer ask any farmer or contractor for a stand, and he will be met with the question: how many can you do? Not: how clean can you do them? All our millions of sheep have to be shorn mostly within three months, and by, in comparison, a mere handful of shearers.

It's worth recalling Don Munday's interview with shearing contractor Bill Synnot, who asked both questions: how many can you do? And how did you do them? However, the first question was about speed.

Shearer Ern Barnes had some practical advice on the subject, in his book, *Easier Shearing*:

> Some days passed, and I was still investigating the problem of why it was that one shearer could shear more sheep with less

effort than another. I would stand for a minute or so after I had let a finished sheep down the chute and try, by watching the methods of fast small shearers and slow big ones, to see what I could learn by it ...

I learned to fill the comb, to take long blows with the hand-piece and not to depend on the speed of the stroke alone; in fact to eliminate useless motions of all kinds. For no matter how fast the hand-piece is pushed through the wool, much time and energy is wasted by going over the same ground more than once.

If the AWU had concerns about where all this speeding-up might lead, in 1955 a tragedy occurred that gave them weight. Charlie Olliver was another highly regarded New Zealand shearer who was determined to beat the Bowen brothers' records. Eventually he got his chance, shearing the same breed of sheep in the same shed where Godfrey Bowen had set his record two years previously.

Unfortunately, things started to go wrong even before Olliver was halfway through his attempt. At the 11.15 break, he stumbled on a spectator rope as he was leaving the shed. He staggered and was barely able to stay on his feet. Onlookers noticed that his neck was white and his pulse was racing.

There was no doctor present, but Bob Mills, who wasn't part of Olliver's support team but had come over to help, set out to try to get one from Palmerston North, 16 kilometres away. Too late. As Bob and the doctor arrived at the shed, someone came running out, shouting: 'Have you got a doctor?'

There was little that could be done for Olliver, who had collapsed. He died later that night. The cause of death isn't clear, but it was probably due to organ failure caused by dehydration and dangerously elevated body temperature. It's why marathon runners pour electrolytes into their bodies to keep themselves going, and why they collapse when they don't get enough.

In reality, the effort involved in a normal day's shearing wasn't much different, especially in the oven-like corrugated-iron shearing sheds of an Australian summer, where temperatures can be in the high forties and even hit fifty. This, coupled with the physical exertion of wrestling an animal weighing 45 kilograms or more. One hand would be gripping a hot, vibrating, 2-kilogram handpiece while the other hand and arm might be covered in fly-blown, dung-riddled, maggot-filled wool.

Lousy sheep could be one problem; sandy sheep were another. Some shearers claim to have worn out dozens of combs while shearing them. Burrs and thistles were just as bad, if not worse. They could cause cutters to jump out of shearers' hands, to thrash wildly on the floor, or take pieces out of grease-softened skin.

At one station the shearers turned up and asked, 'Are there any burrs on the place?'

The owner said, 'No.'

When the shearing started, bang! Burrs everywhere.

'I thought you said there weren't any burrs on your station,' the shearers complained.

'There aren't,' the owner replied. 'They're all on the sheep.'

Still another problem was pregnant sheep. Good management meant they weren't normally shorn but in some circumstances it was unavoidable. At other times, pregnant sheep slipped through unnoticed. Lambs could be born in the yards and pens, or on the board, the shearers pushing afterbirth out of the way as they were trying to shear. The lambs might be crushed in the yards or have to be pushed down the chute repeatedly while they kept climbing up, trying to find their mothers, bleating pitifully as they did.

And then there were the shearers' quarters. Even as recently as the 1950s, conditions could be squalid. One station's shearing shed became so run down that it could no longer be used for its purpose. A new shed was built, but the dilapidated old shed was still considered sufficient to be turned into shearers' quarters. At another place, the quarters were used to house the station's flea-riddled dogs when the shearers weren't around. At yet another, the only shower was a bucket hanging from a tree. The owner wouldn't build a proper shower so the men waited until his wife and the station's governess were about and thirty of them stripped to have a shower in the open. A new shower block was erected forthwith.

* * *

By 1955, the wool price was continuing to drop and the resistance of woolgrowers to the Wool Value Allowance was increasing. This was especially the case following the unprecedented spike in the wool price in 1950 that resulted in the shearing rate going through the roof. The rate didn't start to drop until 1952.

In November 1955, Queensland's woolgrowers' representative body, the United Graziers Association, successfully applied to have the Wool Value Allowance removed from the Queensland award. In February 1956 the same bonus was removed from the federal award, resulting in a 10-shilling cut to the shearing rate.

There had been no great disturbance when rates fell in 1952, in line with the wool price, but the attack on the bonus and the rate cut in 1955–56 sparked what is generally regarded as the longest shearing strike in history (although the 1946 strike in WA, which involved Aboriginal shearers, rousies and station hands, eclipses it). In Queensland, the strike lasted ten months.

The reaction to the strike was mixed on all sides. Some woolgrowers were satisfied to pay the old award. On the shearers' side, there were some who just wanted to make a living without any trouble and during the course of the strike found jobs elsewhere.

There was plenty of trouble. There were black bans on wool transport, wool trucks were hijacked, there was woolshed intimidation and there were pub brawls. One brawl that broke out at Muttaburra eventually involved 500 shearers and strikebreakers. At its height, thirty-two other unions were drawn into the dispute.

Understanding of the basis of the strike was sketchy among some shearers. A good twenty-five years after the events of 1956, shearer and union organiser Laurie Walsh told Patsy Adam-Smith: 'Men who went on strike in 1956 could remember 1951 when wool-growers were getting boom prices for wool and not paying shearers a penny more to harvest it for them. In 1956, when the price dropped, they cried poor to the Arbitration Court and were awarded a reduction in the shearing rate.'

Laurie seemed to have forgotten that the Wool Value Allowance had resulted in a lift to the shearing rate in the order of 100 shillings.

In October 1956 the Queensland Labor government declared a state of emergency. So much for worker solidarity. The strike ended the following month with a settlement that was close to the old award. The AWU claimed victory, saying that the 'tables of 1890 had finally turned'. Others called it 'One of the most momentous victories during the seven decades of [the unions'] existence'. The 1975 film *Sunday Too Far Away*, a docudrama about shearers' lives that was part of the renaissance of Australian filmmaking, regarded the strike as a victory and concluded, 'It wasn't the money, it was the insult.'

With the benefit of hindsight the strike of 1956 was a hollow victory at best. A year later, the Queensland Labor Party split and then lost power to Joh Bjelke-Petersen, who headed the first of a succession of conservative Queensland governments that held power for decades after.

Union representative Alf Kain claimed the union's action in stopping trains at Longreach from carting wool was also a victory. The railways never recovered, he boasted. In fact, woolgrowers had turned away from the unionised government-controlled railways and utilised independent road transport instead. They never went back.

Taking a long view, Rory O'Malley wrote in *Mateship and Moneymaking* that the 1956 strike wasn't nation changing and, if anything, entrenched an obsolete system. The world was changing and the old animosities reflected in the strike of 1956 were being left behind. The key point was: 'The 1956 strike reflected a failure to cope with unprecedented prosperity.'

After all the pushing and shoving, the shearing rate was still quite high, and the incentive to put up big tallies was never greater. In 1957, a young Kevin Sarre, who had been taught by his uncle Ron Arnold since he was eleven years old, shore 327 merinos at Hopefield Station in Victoria. He'd surpassed Ted Reick's 1950 record by one sheep.

Sarre was considered a brilliant shearer, and had been working as one since he was fifteen, despite the fact that his father had wanted him to go to university. Sarre's feat added to the notoriety he was gaining as he and Henry Salter vied for the top honours in regional, state and national shearing competitions. What set Sarre apart was that, like the author of *Easier Shearing*, Ern Barnes, he didn't just learn to shear and then get on with it. He continued to study shearing technique to find ways that would make him even more efficient.

Not to mention profitable. In 1958, the shearing rate rose to 200 shillings per hundred. Wool prices were still down but the inflationary effect of the wool price spike was still pushing the basic wage upwards. Not surprisingly, high pay rates, and the general shortage of shearers, were tempting for the fast, hardworking shearers from across the Tasman. From the 1960s onwards, increasing numbers made the trip to Australia, finding work in particular in Western Australia, New South Wales and Queensland. They were most attracted to cocky-farming areas where the work ethic closely matched their own. And if they brought their wide combs with them, no one seemed to notice. At least for now.

In 1961 Kevin Sarre went to New Zealand to compete in its inaugural national competition, the Golden Shears. To the chagrin of Australian supporters, he didn't win. Ivan Bowen took the honours in a competition that demonstrated that the New Zealanders were on another plane compared to Australia. The enthusiasm for the Golden Shears was also unprecedented, and the annual competition, held at Masterton, has since gone on to become the Wimbledon of shearing competitions.

While Sarre was in New Zealand, he became familiar with the Bowen technique, devised by Godfrey Bowen. It was the key to the superiority of the New Zealand shearers, but Kevin didn't think it was entirely suitable for shearing merinos. Not long after, the Australian Wool Board asked Sarre to devise a technique for the merino body type. The meticulous young shearer took three years to come up with an answer.

In 1964 Sarre launched the Tally-Hi technique for shearing merinos. It was adapted from the Bowen technique and, as Godfrey Bowen had found a decade earlier, not all shearers embraced it with open arms. This despite the fact that there was ample evidence that it significantly lifted the tallies of the shearers who adopted it.

At the time, Sarre was a world-record holder for shearing merinos, but it made no difference when he demonstrated Tally-Hi to a group of shearers at a shed in always-rebellious western Queensland. Sarre suggested they put him up against their fastest shearer, and soundly beat him. Another contender stepped forward and Sarre shore rings around him as well. The shearers didn't take it well. That night, a gang of them were waiting in the dark outside his accommodation. He was forced to run to avoid being bashed.

Sarre had come up against the reality that not all shearers shared his background and motivations. He came from a region of Australia where there were shearing schools (his uncle had established one of the first), competitions, and shearers such as Henry Salter and his father who were contractors as well. He was ambushed (in every sense) by resentment towards anyone who excelled. The competitive instincts of shearers may not have extended to total equality but they didn't embrace tall poppies either.

As for the AWU, it still divided the world into us and them. In 1966, it turned its attention to the shearing schools run by Ron Arnold and Henry Salter and decided the time had come to act. What particularly irked the AWU was that the students had to pay for their lessons. It concluded, 'It is against every principle of this union to pay to be taught.' The union's view was that the woolgrowers or government should be footing the bill.

At the time, most Australians still believed that the country rode on the sheep's back. In 1966, with the introduction of decimal currency, the shilling with the Uardry ram disappeared but the new $2 note featured early wool pioneer John Macarthur, one of the first to bring merino sheep to Australia.

In April 1967 the AWU intensified its attacks on shearing schools. Henry Salter was one of the prime targets. A union representative interrupted one of his classes, saying the boys were breaking union rules: they weren't members of the union, they weren't being paid union rates.

Salter was told to report to Victorian AWU secretary Brahma Davis. Growers supplying sheep to his school were threatened that their properties would be black-banned. Not long after, the Kerang shearing school was cancelled. Salter continued to attempt to teach classes for another three years. In 1970, aged sixty-three, he retired. A colleague, Ross Hann, took over his plant and attempted to continue teaching but after he was threatened, he closed down his operations in 1975. People soon forgot the shearing schools had ever existed.

In New Zealand, shearing schools continued to turn out shearers trained in the Bowen technique. In Australia, the AWU was making it as hard as possible to break into the industry. The union denied that there were shortages (which would push up shearing rates) while shutting down schools that opened the door to young shearers and taught them how to shear faster. Of course, this made Australia even more attractive to New Zealanders, who were only too willing to plug the well-paid gaps.

There were subtle signs of the impact of the New Zealand invasion as early as 1967, when woolgrowers started asking the Arbitration Court to approve wide combs, which it refused to do. The rule banning them had gone unchallenged for the previous twenty years. It had existed in various forms without causing an issue for forty years before that. But the winds of change were blowing once more and this was just one of them.

In the big pastoral country of Western Australia's north-west, the biggest change came in 1968, when all Aboriginal people were included in the pastoral award for the first time. The gains achieved by the strike on WA sheep stations in the 1940s were now universal. Everyone had to be paid for the work they did. In effect, 1968 was the year Australia abolished slavery (it was actually outlawed by the Criminal Code Amendment (Slavery and Sexual Servitude) Act in 1999).

The impact was significant. By the 1980s many stations had shut down. As Tommy Fleay told Patsy Adam-Smith (using language this writer does not condone): 'There's no sheep from Roebourne upwards today – all given back to the niggers that land. I've seen 75 000 sheep at Mt Anderson, 80 000 at De Grey. They can't employ natives nowadays unless they pay them. And they can't get white labour up there. When the old boys were on about a quid a week it was all right, oh yes.'

Patsy Adam-Smith maintained that in the 1980s in the whole area there was only one pet lamb. In fact, some stations managed to hold on and overall sheep numbers fell from five million to roughly a million. However, the glory days of the north-west sheep industry, and the shearers' paradise of eight- and ten-month runs of sheds and sheep, were over, never to return.

North-west historian and woolgrower Jenny Hardie wrote eloquently of those days:

> Morning comes early at shearing time. First, the hollow clonk of the night horse's bell stops, next the thunder of hooves as the

plant is rounded up into the stockyards. The cleaver on the meat-house block rings out as the chops for breakfast are cut down. The bell goes, the dogs wail, the galahs screech, the engines roar into life. Another day begins. With the shearers' arrival come the familiar smells, noises and scenes of shearing. Down in the yards there's drafting and dipping, tailing and tallying. And there's dust. There's that shearing-time smell: of lanolin, sheep dip and ammonia all rolled into something strong, but pleasantly burning to the back of the nose. It wafts through the yards, the sheds and quarters, the homestead and even the bedroom, where dusty, oily shirts and trousers are carefully ostracised from routine wash. In the shed when the gong goes, all around is noise, action and sweat. The whole shearing operation is hypnotic in its synchronised teamwork. Lined up on the board the six curved shearers in black dungarees, singlets and moccasins drag, stretch and bend the lifeless lumps of woolly sheep. With long rhythmical sweeps of their hand-pieces they peel back the dusty fleeces to reveal white over translucent pink bodies that, when finished, scramble up into sheep again and leap through the race into the sun. [*Reproduced by kind permission of Hesperian Press*]

*　*　*　**

Around that time, down in Tasmania, Lindsay Flood's son Winston was getting started as a shearer. He recalled:

Left here when I was about sixteen, went rouseabouting in Victoria for about three months, south of Horsham, come home, got a job down the road here, rouseaboutin', and finished up goin' shearin'. Went to Queensland for a few years. I've been to the west, I've shorn in every state except the Northern Territory. The west is hard, that's where it's hard. Meekatharra, back of Meekatharra. Conditions, rough. Very rough. Blackall? That's paradise, Blackall.

> Back of New South Wales, too. That's pretty hard. Up around White Cliffs, Wilcannia. Hard on your vehicles, tyres, doin' tyres in and stuff like that. I came across a bloke, he chased somethin'. He had a brand new vehicle and he had four flat tyres.

His father, Lindsay, remembered the old shearer who taught Winston the ropes: 'He really struck lucky. We went down to Hobart there, eight-stand shearin' shed and he went as the learner and he drew a pen and there was an old shearer in it, Eric Harvey wasn't it, and he was a good old shearer and he learnt him how to shear. This old fella put a lot of time in with him, you know.'

That was until Harvey's lessons started to produce results, as Winston recalled: 'Once I started going around him, once I started shearin' more than him, he wouldn't talk to me. No, he was an old gentleman. His wife, his lovely wife, she had a big caravan, and a big American jeep, four-wheel-drive jeep.'

In the late 1960s when Lindsay was drawn to Queensland, Winston and his other son, Thomas, went with him. As Lindsay recalled when I visited him and his family in Cleveland:

> I used to shear around Blackall. Terrick Terrick and Barcaldine Downs, Campbells (where the Queen stayed). I wanted to have a good look around, you know. Shearers from up there would come down here. We couldn't understand what the country would look like and we thought, 'Oh, well, we'll go up.'

After shearing in Queensland, he would work his way down through New South Wales and Victoria.

For four or so years Lindsay took his family to Queensland. They did six months there and six months in Tasmania. When his boys were young, they'd go to school in Blackall, or get into all kinds of mischief with the local kids. His wife, Gwen, worked as well, as cook or cleaner. She recalled: 'The shearers were very rough up there. I know the bedrooms I used to clean out ... sometimes they were deep with clothes and all the rest of it, up round Winton and there.'

Another year, 1975 or 1976, Grazcos flew Lindsay, Winston and two other Tasmanians up to the Riverina, where they were short of shearers. Winston recalled:

> They flew Dad and I, Wally Rushton and Ernie Pitt up there to do a month's work. Four days later we was comin' home. We'd ran out of work. They wanted us to go on to this other shed at Euragabar, that was at Gunbar.
>
> I said, 'No, I'm not goin' there. Too rough, too solid, too hard of work.'Cause all our hands was all soft. There's no burr here, see. Only thistles. But when we got up there we had Noogoora and all the burr under the sun and all our arms up here was all bleedin' and cut and 'nup'. We were soft as soft, we were.

The wool was harder too. So hard that it could wear down or tear skin. Said Winston: 'And not only that, it was 45 degrees, so who wants to be up there then. Fifteen stander and old cook was rough as rough. Beer fridge? Beer was hot, so what do you want to be there for. No TV, no corner stores, no power.'

Winston, who was born in 1951, eventually spent twenty-five years based in South Australia, where he shore with machines and blades. He learned to blade-shear in Hay, in the Riverina, in the late 1980s.

While the union shearers they encountered may have been sticklers for the rules, the Tasmanians just wanted to shear. When it came to voting sheep wet and dry, Lindsay had a few tricks up his sleeve:

> They was buggers. But they'd always put me rep. And I'd have a pack of Log Cabin bacca tins, with the hole slit in the top. Put the votes in, see: wet and dry. So when they finished I'd take it

down to old Ted Carter the overseer and he'd say, 'You bugger. I bet they're all Dry in there.' I'd say, 'Yes, Ted. That's their vote.' I'd give it to Ted and there'd be one Wet in it. The rest would be Dry. And the other tin, the one I was supposed to give him, was all Wet. I'd swap 'em over. But if there was a black cloud in the sky they'd want to vote. Oh gee. No shearin'. Sittin' down. Bugger this. They put the wrong one in as the rep. But I got away with it.

The first time the Floods went up to Queensland was in 1969, when the country was in the grip of drought. It was so bad that people were walking off the land and leaving the towns. When the Floods went back in 1970, the people they'd met the year before were gone. In Charleville, Tambo and Longreach it was the same story. As the people went, so did the stock. The infrastructure – sheds and sheep-proof fencing – then became so run down that it was too expensive to repair it. The most important fence of all was the dingo fence. Winston experienced the consequences: 'I've shore up around Walcha and Armidale and them places [in New South Wales]. I've done four seasons up there. And yeah the dogs up there killin' sheep were bad. One fella claimed, that we shore for, lost 2300 fine wool merinos probably worth 120 to 150 bucks each. So that's a lot of income gone.'

Inevitably, the conversation turned to the cooking they'd experienced as shearers. Who was the worst they'd ever encountered? Over by the kitchen sink, Gwen chipped in, 'Me.'

Her sons looked down and Thomas muttered, 'Don't say nothin'.'

Lindsay wasn't daunted:

We used to go to a shed there, Terrick Terrick, and there's a great big stove and it was out from the wall about this far [he indicates about half a metre]. And this old cook would get up out of bed and he'd go and put his apron on and his cap and go to the stove and he'd say: 'What'll we give the so–and-sos this morning, greasy chops or speedballs?' [Speedballs are rissoles that have been squeezed flat in the cook's armpit.]

And he'd say, 'I'll give 'em greasy chops.'

And so there's a rouseabout there, only a little fella and we said to him, 'Now, we want you to get down behind that oven in the mornin' and when he comes out askin' do they want speedballs or greasy chops, you say, "No, it's greasy chops."'

And of course this little fella got there and when old cook said this 'greasy chops and speedballs' the little fella says, 'No, give 'em greasy chops.' And this old cook went for the lick of his life. There's a overseer there name of old Ted Carter, from Rockhampton, and this old hand rushed out and said, 'I'm goin'.'

He said, 'That stove spoke to me, answered me back this mornin'.' He was upset for a day or two until he found out what it was.

Winston warmed to the subject:

We had a good cook out with us once, out the back of Blackall, and when it rains you've got that black mud, you can't go nowhere. So this cook, he knew we couldn't sack him. We couldn't get away and no one could get there. So he started drinkin' all our grog and doing this and doing that. We weren't workin' 'cause we couldn't shear 'cause they couldn't get the sheep to the shed. Well it got to, in the finish, there was a loaf of bread and a tin of jam with a knife stuck in the top of it.

'That's it,' he says. 'Youse want it, youse can have it.'

It seemed most stories were about a cook 'out the back of Blackall', rather than the one over by the sink. Said Lindsay:

What about that old cook out back of Blackall, dirt track out to it. Anyway it rained and he made a big batch of scones to take to the next shed and he put 'em in a sugar bag. And we got bogged. So we put the scones under the back wheels so we could get out.

Of course, there are many other stories about cooks. Sometimes the cook was known as the baitlayer, the poisoner or the babbling brook. One was called the Holy Ghost, for his ability to resurrect leftovers. Another was called 1080, after a poison used to kill vermin. Most memories are about bad cooks. It seems you may appreciate a good meal, but you'll never forget a bad one.

In World War II, a shearer ended up in a Japanese POW camp. While some men were dying due to the poor diet, the ex-shearer took it in his stride. When asked how he managed it, he explained that in shearing sheds, he'd had worse.

Then there was a cook of some ability who used to hang plum puddings in bags to dry them out. The shearers couldn't resist the urge to use them as punching bags, so he put a rock in one of the bags. They only punched it once.

One New Zealand shearer could only get a job in Australia as a cook so he quickly got cooking lessons. He could already make a stew, so he added plum pudding to his repertoire. At his new job he tried to make a pudding but it was a disaster. There was still plenty of time before dinner so he put it aside and had another go. He took it to show the contractor, who said, 'I'll bet you a fiver you couldn't make a worse one.' To which the New Zealander replied, 'Hold this a minute.'

During his travels in the early 1900s, Charles Bean learned that the first thing a cook had to be good at was baking bread; the next thing was fighting. He was told of one physically imposing cook who took no nonsense from the shearers:

At the first dinner he marched into the hut with his sleeves rolled up and the knots on his arms well displayed, and planted the dinner decisively on the table.

'There's your tucker, gentlemen,' he said. 'You can have a piece of that or you can have a piece of the cook.'

There are also many stories of alcoholic cooks and the various intense distilments they concocted from methylated spirits, boot polish and lemon essence. These were embodied in the dirty, shambling cook in the film *Sunday Too Far Away*, whose belligerent manner made him difficult to sack.

Other cooks had little or no regard for hygiene. In one instance, from many decades ago, the shearers complained when they found maggots on their meat.

'There ain't!' the cook protested. 'I swear I wiped them all off.'

In the days when big sheds employed anywhere up to 200 shearers and shed hands, cooks paid by the number of men they fed could make extremely good money. Not surprisingly, there was strong competition for the cook's job at some stations. Chefs from city restaurants were attracted by the possibility of a profitable break from town.

In modern times, food-handling and nutrition regulations mean that most of the problems of the past are a distant memory. In my experience, station kitchens are spotlessly clean, and the food is plentiful and wholesome. Most cooks are justifiably proud of their abilities and meticulous in running their kitchens. They may not be cooking for the masses as they once did but most other requirements haven't changed: meals on time, plenty of variety and style, and good organisation so that nothing ever runs out, no matter how far they might be from the nearest grocery supplier. It can still be a seven-day-a-week operation, starting at 5 a.m. or earlier and often continuing through until 10 p.m.

The alcoholic cook, who may have been more myth than reality even in days gone by, is almost impossible to find these days. The only one I've encountered over more than a decade doing research in the outback was working in a mobile food van at a rodeo event in western Queensland (a bit further than 'out the back of Blackall'). He was not the kind of person you'd want to see preparing your meal; in fact, if you did you'd never eat it.

* * *

More and more New Zealand shearers were making their way to Australia in the late 1960s, but they weren't getting it all their own way. Many who thought they'd try their hand in Australia came unstuck when they got among the merinos and the wrinkles that proliferated on them, even into that era. They were totally unlike the fast-shearing New Zealand sheep. There were instances where shearers who could do 300 a day in New Zealand could only manage a dozen in Australia. They became so wool-bogged it was as if they couldn't shear at all. Only when breeding away from wrinkles started to have a widespread impact did some New Zealanders get over their dread of the hard-shearing Australian merinos.

By 1970, there were more than enough sheep to go around. By then, the total Australian flock numbered 180 million, more than fourteen sheep for every man, woman and child in the country. Such large numbers also allowed an increase in 'suburban shearing' (shearing locally) as opposed to expedition shearing. Some shearers, however, took to flying to sheds in their own aircraft, returning home to towns such as Broken Hill nightly or on weekends.

Not only was 1970 a high point as far as sheep numbers were concerned; it was also the year that a meeting of woolgrowers in Moree set the course for Australia to introduce a reserve price scheme for wool. Instead of piecemeal wool marketing, a single authority would promote and sell wool, hopefully creating a 'woolly DuPont'. The benefit for growers who yielded independence over their clip was that they would get an assured floor price.

It seemed no one remembered the words of Justice George Dethridge during the 1930 shearers' award hearing when he said: 'there is no power in Australia that can control prices'. Woolgrowers now thought they could do just that.

However, great change was afoot. In 1973, twenty-three years of conservative national governments came to an end when Gough Whitlam led Labor to victory in the federal election. Decades of insular, protectionist economic policies also came to an end as the new government set about initiating much-needed structural reform. The need for change, typified by the government's slogan, 'It's Time', was ubiquitous.

Not even unions were immune. In 1974, then Australian Council of Trade Unions president Bob Hawke said: 'Some unions are unconcerned with attempts to improve the psychological working environment of their members, and simply concentrate on registering the regular wage increases emanating from indexation. Their days are numbered.'

The next ten years would show just how right he was. For the AWU the clock was already ticking, due to two significant events.

First, 1974 saw massive floods in eastern Australia that set back shearing in many areas. When things dried out, there was a massive backlog of the country's 180 million-odd sheep, and the call went out for shearers. Grazcos took the dramatic step of chartering aircraft and recruiting New Zealand shearers en masse to avert a crisis. Even the AWU cooperated in the combined effort to get the sheep shorn.

For many woolgrowers the New Zealanders were a revelation: fast, clean, uncomplaining. They were everything Australia's unionised, nitpicking shearers weren't. Grazcos' 1974 annual report gave due recognition to the efforts of the New Zealanders: 'Their performance was particularly good, and it was only through the attitude of these men that it was possible to get all the sheep shorn.'

From 1974 onwards, Grazcos started going over to New Zealand and recruiting the best talent on offer at the annual premier shearing competition, the Golden Shears.

The other significant event in 1974 was less obvious, but just as important. In that year, Qantas took delivery of its first 747 jumbo jet. The aircraft rapidly revolutionised international air travel, in particular making it dramatically cheaper. Almost overnight it was far easier for large numbers of people to travel anywhere in the world, whenever they wanted. The flow of New Zealand shearers making the trip to Australia became a flood.

Their growing presence in places like Western Australia led many to believe that it was New Zealanders who introduced wide combs there in the 1970s. However, local shearers suggest they were bending the rules, and the teeth of their combs, long before that. One of them, Terry Harper, shore with contractor Eric Kennedy in the 1950s: 'Everyone shore with pulled combs. If they said they didn't, they're liars. When Eric Kennedy told us the union organiser was coming at about eleven o'clock and to put our straight combs on, I wouldn't.'

When Harper was caught, he was fined. The union organiser said, 'You know you're doing the wrong thing.'

Harper replied, 'You know I've been shearing with them for years and I'm not changing.' [*Reproduced by kind permission of Valerie Hobson*]

The rapidly changing situation in the shearing sheds of Australia makes *Sunday Too Far Away*, released in 1975, so much more curious. The film, set around the events of the 1956 shearers' strike, reflected the atmosphere of tension and distrust that existed between shearers and graziers, echoing Charles Bean's undercurrents of hostility. It wasn't remotely like the idyllic scene of Tom Roberts' *Shearing the Rams* but it was also nothing like the times in which it was made. In 1975, the real tension existed within the ranks of shearers themselves.

11

WHATEVER MAKES IT EASIER

(1976–1990)

As the number of New Zealanders shearing in Australia grew, so did the realisation that the outsiders were a different breed. They didn't care for union rules. They wouldn't vote sheep wet; they were used to them that way. If Aussie shearers said the sheep were wet and left for the pub, the New Zealanders would stay and cut out the remaining sheep.

The New Zealanders even regarded Australia's shearing competitions as a joke. In 1980 New Zealand competition organiser Laurie Keats said of the AWU-organised events: 'They had rules designed for old men to win.'

As for the narrow combs the Australians were using, as far back as the 1950s New Zealand woolgrower and shearer Bob Mills had considered them antiques. Wherever they could get away with it, New Zealanders shore with wide combs.

One of the hot spots was the cocky country of Western Australia. The AWU was not strongly represented there, as distances were large, union organisers were thin on the ground, and the culture of the region was antagonistic towards them and their rules.

While the 600 members of Western Australia's Pastoralists and Graziers Association were bound by the federal pastoral award, the 7000 members of the Farmers Union of WA were not. And between them they had 30 million sheep. In practical terms, if the farmers employed union shearers, they had to pay award rates and provide award conditions. However, if they employed others (such as New Zealanders), or paid above award, there was plenty of scope for the rules to be skirted.

In the late 1970s, the AWU sensed that something had to be done. It decided the time had come to clean up the West and applied to what was now the Arbitration Commission to have the Farmers Union included in the award. The farmers were happy to go along with the AWU until the question of wide combs came up. Arbitration Commissioner Pauline Barnes noted that wide combs were ubiquitous in Western Australia. Accordingly, she exempted the whole state from the wide-comb ban.

The decision was a long way from what the AWU had in mind. Worse still, shearers from the eastern states of Australia, who were also travelling to Western Australia to pick up extra work, were discovering wide combs as well.

One of them was Bob White. Bob was born and raised in the Bathurst region of central New South Wales, where he grew up to become a top-class shearer. While shearing in Western Australia he liked wide combs so much he brought some back to New South Wales. There he became a contractor and put together a strong team. It was generally known that his team used wide combs. Most of White's customers had no objections to their use (other woolgrowers still thought there was a greater danger of injury to sheep) but to the AWU, the use of wide combs in its sheep-shearing heartland was unthinkable.

White's contracting team included plenty of locals, but he had good men from New Zealand and Western Australia, too. This also antagonised the AWU, which, at one point, registered its objections to the use of foreigners with the Arbitration Commission, including Western Australian shearers among those considered 'foreign'.

In January 1980, Dave Hollis, a Western Australian AWU organiser, warned that wide combs were the thin end of the wedge when it came to protecting the pay and conditions the union had fought for over decades. He wrote a paper about his concerns, *How the West Was Lost*, in which he described New Zealand practices as a leprosy that would spread Australia-wide. Wide combs weren't the problem. New Zealanders were.

By then, New Zealand's shearers weren't just migrating to Western Australia. Muttaburra in Queensland and Mortlake in Victoria were becoming virtual New Zealand settlements. Their arrival was a mixed blessing. The decline of rural communities meant any new arrivals, especially those with children whose presence in the local school delayed its closure, were generally welcomed. Yet there was also a feeling that many shearers were enjoying the benefits others had fought for and whose livelihoods were being threatened. So some communities embraced the New Zealanders while others saw fights between Kiwis and locals that were soon depicted as having the potential to degenerate into a violent race war.

As for the wide combs, there were concerns among shearers that they could be dangerous. They called them Merry Widows, due to the risks of injury while using them, however nebulous those risks might be. When union reps appeared in areas where wide combs were banned, those shearers using them quickly dropped them down the chute. The idea was that you had to be caught red-handed to be fined.

Matters came to a head in the early 1980s. In an attempt to find out whether any of the concerns regarding wide combs were valid, woolgrowers sought permission to conduct trials. However, they would only do so with AWU cooperation. At the time, it was even against the AWU's rules to so much as experiment with wide combs. The AWU categorically refused to sanction a trial.

When the argument reached the Arbitration Commission, Commissioner Barnes continued the exemption of Western Australia but decided not to make a ruling either way regarding trials of wide combs. She put the matter back in the hands of the AWU and the woolgrowers to see if they couldn't sort the matter out between themselves.

The assumption was that reasonable people should be able to arrive at a solution through a process of considered negotiation. Instead, for the next year, the AWU used every tactic it could think of to thwart any trials and discourage any use of wide combs. Black bans were imposed on properties that used them. When Bob White's shearing team was accused of using the combs on Rockdale Station and White publicly denied it, he was black-banned for simply talking about wide combs.

By November 1981 the Livestock and Grain Producers Association of New South Wales had despaired of making any progress, and applied to the Arbitration Commission to have the wide-comb ban lifted across Australia. In response, the AWU lodged a counter-claim for wide combs to be banned in Western Australia.

On 2 December, the new arbitration commissioner, Ian McKenzie, attended a demonstration of shearing with wide combs given by none other than Bob White. The demonstration was conducted at the Sydney Showground. Someone tipped off the media, which showed up to witness the event as well. An image of White shearing with a wide comb ended up on the cover of *The Land*.

White also gave evidence to the commission. He said that he had found commercially available wide combs weren't satisfactory for shearing merino sheep. So at night, after work, he reground them so they worked better.

Not surprisingly, other shearers became interested in the results of his efforts. Soon they were finding that not only were their tallies higher when using a wide comb, but the physical strain was actually less. The commission was told that once a shearer started using White's adapted wide gear, they never went back to narrow gear (unless they were forced to). White added that Sunbeam had released a new wide comb in August 1982, the Hustler, which he thought was the first commercially available wide comb suitable for merino sheep.

White's evidence indicated that the main impediment to using wide combs to shear merino sheep (their suitability) had been overcome. Not only that, as one ex-shearer and woolgrower, Greg Charles, told me, 'Shearing hurts when you're doing it and it still hurts after you stop. Who cares what kind of comb you use? Whatever makes it easier. That's all that matters.'

If wide combs made shearing quicker, and easier, it should have been game, set and match for the wide-comb ban. And yet the AWU fought on. The last remaining defence seemed to be tradition. In the increasingly economically rational 1980s, it was just about the worst defence going.

As the commission continued to gather evidence, at one point it ranged as far as the remote outback of South Australia. At Commonwealth Hill, one of the remotest sheep stations in Australia (whose history is detailed in my book *Outback Stations*), young shearers were not 'impenetrably fixed' either way. They thought wide combs were better than pulled (bent-tooth) combs, which, because they weren't pulled in any precise manner, risked compromising quality.

Finally, on 10 December 1982, Commissioner McKenzie reached his decision. He found the evidence in favour of using wide combs 'strong and compelling', and lifted the ban.

Almost. The AWU immediately appealed Commissioner McKenzie's decision. The ban remained in force while the full bench of the Arbitration Commission sat to consider the situation. In giving evidence, one of the AWU's main complaints was that Commissioner McKenzie had made his decision without conducting properly organised trials. This from the organisation that had fought tooth and nail to prevent them. It was too much for the commissioners. Their judgement on 23 March 1983 not only upheld Commissioner McKenzie's decision to lift the ban, it savaged the AWU.

The full bench found the AWU's actions were 'calculated to smother the development and manufacture of more efficient combs'. Regarding trials: 'In light of the implacable opposition of the AWU to any such trial and its refusal to attend, should they have been conducted, the sincerity of this submission is open to question.' That may have been a polite legal way of saying, 'You can't be serious', but you didn't have to read between the lines of the commissioners' observations on the AWU's attitude in general: 'hedged in by conservatism and tinged with hysteria'.

Ouch.

The union's reaction was to call a strike. The battlelines were complex: union versus non-union, locals versus foreigners, narrow versus wide. The AWU's position was impossibly weak but there was also a glimmer of hope for the union in the fact that a federal election had just been held and a new Labor government led by former unionist Bob Hawke had swept to power. All they needed was a bit of the worker solidarity of the good old days and the wide comb would be history.

It was not to be. Australia was facing serious financial challenges that would soon see new treasurer Paul Keating suggest that without economic restructuring the country ran the risk of becoming a banana republic. The old days were over.

Behind the scenes attempts were made to get the AWU to back down. To no avail. Bloody confrontations made nightly news bulletins. Demonstrations of shearing with wide and narrow combs revealed to the general public the clear superiority of wide combs. The union's position wasn't helped by New South Wales AWU stalwart Ernie Ecob, whose public statements were so politically incorrect that, to this day, the Ernie Awards are presented each year for the worst examples of sexism on public record. One of Ecob's pronouncements was 'Women aren't welcome in the shearing sheds. They're only after the sex.'

Out on Weilmoringle Station, woolgrowers Rens and Merri Gill could see some humour in the situation. In the 1980s the station still had an Aboriginal community settled within its precincts and many of its shearers were Aboriginal. 'We were always afraid Ernie would declare us black!' Merri confided to me recently, savouring the irony.

Eventually, the new federal minister for industrial relations, Ralph Willis, called a conference chaired by Arbitration Commissioner McKenzie. A six-point plan to end the strike recognised that the question of possible injury to shearers from wide combs should be addressed. In other words, trials were needed. The AWU agreed to cooperate but insisted the wide-comb ban remain in place while the trials went on. No one fell for yet another AWU delaying tactic. Instead, it was agreed that employers weren't to discriminate against shearers who wanted to use narrow combs while the union was not to harass shearers using wide combs.

The subsequent trials provided unequivocal evidence that wide combs were the future. There were no health and safety issues. Even an occupational-safety report commissioned by the AWU undermined the union's arguments against wide combs (the AWU tried to bury the report but copies circulated anyway). The union found itself in the farcical situation of trying to get loyal union shearers to present evidence against wide combs when none could speak from experience because they hadn't used them. Meanwhile, non-union shearer after non-union shearer testified that they were easier to use.

The union continued to orchestrate resistance. On 10 May 1984, busloads of shearers protested in Canberra. In Broken Hill an angry union official was quoted as saying, 'If I was a New Zealand shearer, I would not come within a hundred miles of this town. Someone, sometime, somewhere, will have two beers too many. And someone will get killed.'

For Commissioner McKenzie there was a sense of déjà vu when he reported his findings on 5 June 1984: 'I am satisfied that the conclusions reached in my decision of 10 December 1982 were correct and to return to the exclusive use of 64 mm combs would be against the weight of evidence. I again stress that this industry cannot remain impervious to technological changes.'

The only course left to the AWU was to use threats and intimidation to force shearers to comply with the union's rules. However, rather than comply, many shearers left the union. Others left shearing altogether. One of them did so after being savagely beaten and having a wide comb forced into his mouth. He barely survived the attack.

On 6 October 1984 a Maori shearer was assaulted at Hamilton, Victoria. Not long after, two New Zealand shearers confronted local shearers in nearby Coleraine and a brawl ensued. Police eventually broke up the fight. The following day, there was another brawl between local shearers and Maori at a Coleraine house. Later in the day, vehicles again appeared at the house and shots were exchanged between the house and the vehicle. Charges were laid but the New Zealand witnesses failed to appear and the case was dropped.

On 27 November 1984, the general secretary of the AWU wrote to Bob Hawke, regarding New Zealanders. He described 'An ever-increasing animosity between our members and New Zealand shearers who, our members quite correctly believe, are being brought into the country by employers to pursue their aims of having the provisions of the award broken'.

There was a general feeling that New Zealand shearers would work for thirty per cent less than the award rate and would work overtime and on weekends.

The general secretary added that employers were 'deliberately avoiding their responsibilities of training Australian workers'. This from the union that in the 1960s had shut down the schools run by employers such as Henry Salter, who'd been made an MBE for his services to shearing.

By then, though, even union shearers were facing the fact that wide combs were here to stay – at which point the union hierarchy decided that if the rank and file wouldn't fight, the leadership would have to fight for them. In late 1984, Ernie Ecob called a crisis meeting in Dubbo, New South Wales. New national secretary Gil Barr also attended.

Barr may have realised the battle was lost when he proposed giving up on opposing wide combs and suggested that if woolgrowers tried to reduce the shearing rate due to the ease of shearing with wide combs the union should put in a claim for shorter hours to compensate for the productivity gain. It didn't occur to him that this would simply give New Zealand shearers, and other non-union shearers for that matter, even more opportunities to take sheds and sheep from shearers hamstrung by the award.

Not even that suggestion satisfied the meeting. A battle plan was devised: no wide combs, a monster meeting in January 1985 to endorse the decision, and Grazcos was to face a total ban for its role in promoting wide combs, importing strikebreakers and suspected involvement in the gunfight at Coleraine. Plus, anyone who was known to have done any shearing during the 1983 strike would be black-banned permanently. Anyone who used a wide comb before Commissioner McKenzie approved them would have to explain himself to his local committee. Anyone who started using wide combs after the ban was ended would be required to return to using narrow gear.

Those at the meeting seriously believed this plan would achieve a 'united and harmonious return' to '100 per cent union membership'. It was akin to insisting the *Titanic* was unsinkable after it had sunk.

The AWU's position guaranteed mass defections of shearers. Not only that, the fallout from the wide-comb dispute had ramifications for the entire union movement. After the wide-comb fracas, compulsory union membership came under attack in many other industries, especially where union interference was perceived as more of a hindrance than a help.

All of the Flood family were shearing when the wide-comb furore erupted. Recalled Winston:

> I was lucky at the time. I got crook and spent time in hospital and it was all over when I got out. I had cancer and I didn't shear for a long time. Then I made a bit of a comeback. I was never to shear again then I had a comeback. All these guys, they took pity on me and give me all this narra gear and I reckon I shore narra gear for the next four years. I never bought anything. Then after that I got onto wide gear.
>
> What they were frightened of was the Kiwis coming here and using wide gear and undercuttin', which they were at the time. Shearing lambs for a dollar instead of it should have been $2. Things like that. When they first come into Australia it took 'em a month or two to get an old motor car, an old Holden or an old Falcon, and a bit of gear together and they undercut and probably lived in a tent for a month or so. The farmers thought, 'Oh yeah, this is all right. So we'll get the Aussies to do it.' But the Aussies wouldn't do it. Once the Kiwis got themselves established they thought, 'Oh no, we'll shear for the Aussie rate now.'

His father, Lindsay, had had enough: 'I give shearin' away when the wide combs come in. Square-mouthed shovels I called 'em. I give 'er away. I was never real sure of sheep with the wide comb. I did have a bit of a go one day, picked the handpiece up but . . . it was all right but you know, it didn't attract me.'

Many shearers at the time believed wide combs were harder on the body. Some shearers left the industry and took other jobs. Thomas Flood thought sheep were harder to shear after wide combs came in, but not necessarily because of the combs:

> Because you push more. Over ten or twelve years it got easier because you start to use the whole comb and ra-ra-ra. Less second cuts and all that sort of stuff. It was harder on me body because the sheep was changin'. The wool was gettin' denser. More on 'em. Bigger frame. Bigger wrinkles.
>
> What it was. There was half a dozen of these so-called big gun shearers went down and shore sheep back of Ross there somewhere. 'Oh yeah. No we'll use these, these are right.' That was it. 'And you blokes use 'em.' You were mad not to.

Brother Winston was still using narrow gear, trying to wear out all the equipment given to him when he made his shearing comeback, when he found that wide combs didn't necessarily make you faster:

> I rocked up in a shed south of Broken Hill. Oh yeah, it was 46 in the waterbag and I drew number two stand and I'd me waterbag there and me old handpiece in it and these narra combs and narra cutters and these young fellas there they had wide combs and cutters, and their dungarees, holes ripped and torn. I thought 'Jeez these fellas can shear.' This is back in the '80s. Anyway, I'd been drivin' a truck for about three months and I was green. I started shearin'. I think I done 29 or 30 the first run and I thought, 'These blokes only doin' 32, 33.' So I think I done 35 the second run, thinkin', 'When these fellas gonna let go.' They're doing 32, 33. Took me all day to find out there was no guns, there was just loud-mouthed shearers. Then I started doin' 40, 45 a run and I'm usin' these little narra combs. 'Gee, can't this fella shear. Look, he's

usin' narra combs.' And they're usin' these big wide things, they was only doin' 30, 32, 33 a run. And I'm doin' 45, 46, 47.

The events of the 1980s neatly bookend those of the 1890s. In the 1890s shearers were in the vanguard in building worker unity to protect their interests. In the 1980s shearers led the way in dismantling worker unity when it worked against their interests.

Meanwhile, there were worse things for shearers than wide combs. The mid-1980s also saw the realisation of attempts to develop robots that could shear sheep. Archival footage shows the result of some 40 million dollars' worth of research in Western Australia and South Australia into making shearers redundant: a sheep is secured on the high-tech equivalent of a medieval rack, then a complex assembly of wires and metal arms wields a handpiece that slowly goes about the process of shearing the pinioned animal. Later models encased much of the operating mechanism in a rubber sleeve.

A production prototype of one robotic shearer, the Automated Wool Harvesting System, was developed between 1987 and 1990 but a further $6 million was needed to commercialise it. When funding couldn't be raised (the cost of each unit and animal-rights issues may have been a consideration), the company that developed the system went into liquidation.

However, there were benefits. As James Trevelyan, one of the engineers who developed the Western Australian robotic-shearing system and now Winthrop Professor in the School of Mechanical and Chemical Engineering at the University of Western Australia, told me in 2014:

> The original motivation for developing robotic shearing, when viewed with the benefit of hindsight, and confirmed by informal interviews with some of the decision-makers involved, was to display a technological alternative to manual shearing in order

to moderate the behaviour of shearers' organisations such as the Australian Workers Union. Since the robot was demonstrated in 1989 shearing an entire fleece in one piece, shearers have displayed much more responsible behaviour when it comes to pay negotiations.

The robotic sheep-shearing research project came to an end around 1993 having demonstrated not only the capacity to shear sheep at a commercially realistic speed completely automatically (around three to four minutes shearing in a commercial configuration), but also sheep manipulation technology required to eliminate heavy lifting for shearers while still retaining manual shearing in a much more comfortable position.

Last year I met an AWU organiser who told me about the great respect which shearers still attribute to robotic shearing and particularly (I was quite surprised by this) my team of engineers who developed the technology.

Time and effort were also put into a technology that chemically shears sheep. Experiments with 'defleecing' were begun by the CSIRO in 1975 and eventually resulted in the commercial release of BioClip in 1997. BioClip involves protein injections that cause the wool to break off at the skin. A specially designed net is put over the sheep to catch the wool (a process that takes half a minute) and it remains there for a month until the sheep has grown enough new wool to keep it warm. The net and fleece is then removed in a process that takes about ten seconds.

Bioclipping costs more than shearing but its promoters note its other benefits: undamaged fleeces and unstressed sheep in particular. However, as of 2015 sales of BioClip had been suspended while its cost issues were addressed.

Of course, considering American mass-production pioneer Henry Ford's comment that the Australian shearer is the most efficient machine on earth, it's perhaps understandable when alternatives struggle to compete.

***

In the aftermath of the wide-comb dispute, the culture of shearing changed once more. With union control severely weakened, suburban shearing became increasingly common as the most capable shearers rose to the top. If you were talented and motivated, there were no limits to what you could do. If you were mediocre or lazy, there were fewer places to hide.

Not every area reaped the benefits. Up in the north-west of Western Australia, for reasons unrelated to wide combs, the wool industry had all but ceased to exist. Marcus Synnot could only regret what was no more. In the late 1970s he told Patsy Adam-Smith:

> The big distances between the places there are being mined out of the ground. That place will end up a desolation. Even the men will go from it – the sheep have already gone. Wild dogs are taking over . . . Cattle men don't worry about wild dogs, but sheep men, that's different.
>
> It was the north that was the real shearing land. I can't tell you how exciting it was. You could hear the north calling each year when shearing time came around.

In 1987, one of the great shearers of the past, Henry Salter, saw a news item that said Australia's first shearing school was being conducted at Werribee. The first? Two decades had passed since Salter and Ron Arnold had run their schools and been shut down by the AWU. The events of those days had obviously been forgotten. They belonged to a different era.

Now shearers worked longer hours if they needed to catch up, or if they could cut out a shed on a Friday and move on to the next shed ready to start Monday. Wet sheep had to be really wet to hold up work.

In 1990, shearers were being paid $1.30 a sheep and many were earning $250 a day. It would be good money now. It was great money back then, especially for young shearers unfettered by union rules. For some, the new culture seemed to be a golden opportunity to build solid financial foundations and get a good start in life.

12

WOOL IS DEAD. LONG LIVE WOOL.

(1991–2015)

The optimism of the late 1980s was short-lived. In 1991, Justice Dethridge was proved correct in his opinion, expressed in 1930, that no power in Australia could control wool prices.

Since its inception in the 1970s, the wool floor price had climbed steadily upwards. Even as markets for wool fell away, and wool production continued to climb, pressures to reduce the floor price were ignored. Only when there was virtually no market, a stockpile of over a million bales of wool, and debts in the billions of dollars was the scheme discontinued.

For woolgrowers, it was a catastrophe. Many were forced to shoot their flocks. Some lost their properties and went bankrupt. A few despaired and took their lives. Whole regions that were once bastions of the Australian industry went out of wool and into cattle or cotton. In 1990 there were 170 million sheep in the country. Since 1991 that number has fallen by 100 million.

For shearers, the reduction in sheep numbers led to widespread unemployment. The loss of income and reductions in the workforce meant many country towns struggled to survive at the time and have struggled ever since.

The reserve-price debacle accelerated the slow decline of the wool industry due to increasing competition from other natural fibres such as cotton and a variety of synthetic fibres. Wool was by far the most expensive and labour-intensive fibre to produce. Its market share gradually declined to the point where today it comprises as little as three per cent of the global market for textiles.

Some districts that were thriving before the collapse of the wool-price scheme have been hit particularly hard. The region where Jack Howe set his famous tally of 321 with the blades, Blackall, was once shearing close to 800 000 sheep within a 100-kilometre radius of the town. In 2004, it was estimated to be down to fewer than 200 000. Muttaburra, in Queensland, which had swelled with the influx of New Zealanders until it had eight shearing teams, shrank to the point where it only had two. It was estimated that in towns like this, the loss of each sheep was equivalent to five dollars, so the loss of up to 600 000 sheep could cost a town up to $3 million.

Just out from Ilfracombe, the immense circular Isis Downs woolshed used to shear 320 000 sheep and send off 3000 bales in good years. In 2004 it shore the last of its flock of only 15 000. The shed has since been heritage listed but the sights and sounds of shearing have long gone. Not that everyone mourned its closure. The 1914-built shed, one of the first to be electrified, was also one of the hottest places to shear sheep.

In 1983, there were estimated to be 30 000 shearers across Australia. Today, there are as few as 3000.

And yet, reports of the death of wool have turned out to be premature. The demand for wool hasn't completely disappeared and in recent years there have been signs of resurgence in the industry.

Despite the usual setbacks, in particular drought, wool has endured. There are still seventy million sheep in Australia. And while the glory days of wool may have passed, they haven't been forgotten.

In 2002, the Shear Outback Museum and Australian Shearers' Hall of Fame opened in Hay, New South Wales, to honour and celebrate the contribution of shearers to Australian life. It was established in part with $4 million in federal funding but is publicly owned.

The complex includes a genuine twelve-stand shearing shed that was originally at Murray Downs, near Swan Hill. The red-gum and Oregon-pine shed can hold 1200 sheep under cover with a further 600 underneath, and is still operational. Daily demonstrations are conducted there and it is also used for shearing schools.

Shearing schools are needed more than ever because now there really is a shortage of shearers. A generation of potential shearers has been lured into the mining sector by high wages, generally less punishing work and the certainty of a weekly wage that's absent in shearing.

To fill the gap, contractors are now turning to the internet and to backpackers. Potential recruits are given very short training courses as rousies or pressers, then they're thrown into the deep end. For the backpackers, it can be a once-in-a-lifetime opportunity, and they're further encouraged by a scheme that gives them an extra year on their visa if they work in certain areas or industries for at least eighty days. Many rural industries, woolgrowing among them, would be in serious difficulties without them.

South Australian shearer Noel 'Grub' Johnson, who now has a business producing and selling shearers' clothing and equipment, told me in 2014: 'Shearing in Australia would be stuck without New Zealanders. Some Europeans come out just to prove themselves. We really would be stuck without imports. There is now a better class of New Zealanders and they come and stay.'

Noel started shearing when he was sixteen and shore for thirty years, but had to give it up when he found he couldn't shear and run his business. While wide combs were supposed to be the ruination of shearers, Noel reckons the opposite is true: 'A lot of good things have happened in my time. The technology has improved a lot. A lot of things inside the handpieces have changed. They might look the same but today they are very different. The tools are a lot better.'

The same can't be said for some of the conditions: 'In some of the remote places it's still a bit agricultural – the huts are pretty rough and the generators aren't up to the job. But most guys won't put up with it so they've had to improve.'

Another area of improvement is technique. Shearers didn't stop learning after the Bowen technique and Kevin Sarre's Tally-Hi were developed. There have been continual refinements in the patterns used to shear today's larger-framed sheep, and the latest can now be downloaded from websites such as that operated by Australian Wool Innovation. Not that shearing isn't still hard work. Said Noel:

> You still use as many calories every day as a marathon runner and when it's 47 or 48 degrees you're still working at full steam. I look at some of these guys today and think 'you crazy bastards' but not long ago I was one of them. When the New Zealanders started coming in I thought they wouldn't last but they were super fit.

Modern sports science has investigated just how fit shearers have to be and has found that they're in the same league as elite athletes. For example, shearers doing a tally of 160 sheep a day each move the equivalent of 9 tonnes a total distance of 2 kilometres. They push a 2-kilogram handpiece through fleeces at least 5440 times. In doing so they burn 25 000 kilojoules a day (an average adult burns 8700). Incredibly, they'll sweat as much as 9 litres of moisture during each two-hour shearing run, or 36 litres in a day's shearing. Considering an average male's entire body comprises about 40 litres of water, a shearer who doesn't replace fluids and electrolytes is in serious danger of lethal dehydration. As for gun shearers, shearing 200 sheep a day, their energy consumption matches that of cyclists in the Tour de France.

This for shearers who are generally growing older, in an industry that doesn't have enough fresh blood coming through. Many are in their thirties and forties. Some are in their sixties.

In 2004, shearer Wayne Bowden told ABC *Landline* reporter Tim Lee:

> You don't see any learners anymore. Well, have a look at the team here, there's no young blokes. They start off rouseabouting, then they get offered a job on the council or offered a job somewhere else and they're mad not to take it. You get no holiday pay, nothin' and the price of fuel, it's $1.10 a litre in Longreach now.

It's a similar story in Tasmania, where Winston Flood's son Shane has hung up his shears to go and work in the mining industry. If he did return to shearing, he might find it hard to find work. When Winston first started shearing there was plenty of shearing around Tasmania. Now, even in the heartland of some of the finest wool-producing country in the world, things are changing:

> This is what we used to do. First Monday in September we did Nareen, then Mona Vale and Tallagoram, down south and up here on the coast. It used to take us three months. So we'd go to Queensland then. Today, them sheds, well Nareen used to shear 28, 30 000 sheep. Now they've only got about 2500 sheep there. Mona Vale's got about 10 000 and Tallagoram's got about 5000. So all them numbers are gone.

Winston cited a couple of reasons for the change: the downturn in the wool and meat industry (as most sheep are now cross-bred for both products); and centre-pivot irrigation systems that have turned former grazing country over to crops.

When we spoke, in April 2014, Winston had just returned from the Masterton Golden Shears, where he'd been part of the judging panel. He was about to depart for Ireland, to represent Australia as a judge at the World Shearing Championships:

> I've got the world shears to do at Gorey, south of Dublin. Judging all sections of shearing – crossbreds, merinos, everything. Novice, intermediate, seniors and the open. Also the tests. There's a test between every country. I've never done one before. First time. And I'll have a green blazer with a gold logo on it so that'll be good.
>
> It took me twenty-five years to get there. I've been doin' it [judging] for that long. Not only that, what put the icing on it was two top shows in one year. And I was the first to go from here to there to do anything like that. I do 'em here. I do Perth, WA, Adelaide, and I do the nationals, we have nationals here every year. October, November.
>
> We judge the quality of the shearing, which is a component of the overall score. Wool left on, second cuts, that sort of thing. Scratches, if you nick one, the way they handle the sheep. Fleece, the way they leave the wool, stuff like that.

Given the AWU's reluctance to sanction competition in years gone by, the stranglehold the union exerted, and the criticism that the competitions it organised were designed for old men, I wondered what the attitude was to shearing competitions now. Said Winston:

> Sports Shear [an independent, voluntary association founded in 1995 and affiliated with the Golden Shears World Council] is better or a benefit to the shearer themselves. Today it's not only

speed. Back in the old days they used to set the pace, they had a timer on the pace and you had to shear them sheep in that time. You could shear them before, which is fine, but if you go over … Today, it's more or less the fastest shearer sets the time then all the rest have gotta be up there with him. To me that's a better way of picking out the better shearer of the day. And nine times out of ten it's only of the day. I've seen blokes practise for twelve months and they just, it just takes one blow or one second and that's it. They lose the plot.

His brother, Thomas, spoke about his own experience: 'When I was shearin', I went from narra gear to wide gear, I was rough as guts. Second cuts, third cuts, only use that much comb and everything. Then he [Winston] got me into show shearing. I learned a terrible lot. It made me a better shearer. You take note. You take more notice of everything.'

These days, you can forget about the best shearers only coming from Australia or even New Zealand. They come from everywhere: America, Sweden, Norway, Wales and Scotland.

'The bloke who won Masterton, he come from Scotland,' said Winston. 'A bloke about twenty-five, twenty-six, 6 foot 8 or whatever there was of him. There's no beer guts or anything, none of that. They all pump iron and they're fit as fiddles. No long hair. They're all a bit like Dad.'

'Wore it all off,' said the balding Lindsay.

Who were the shearers who impressed? The boys named several Tasmanians from days gone by but they also pointed to qualities of good shearers, rather than names. Said Winston, 'They're about. Magic to watch. They just, day in, day out. They're like machines. No effort.'

Thomas added, 'These shearers, they walk around and help everyone else and they still get their tallies out. And they're good blokes with it, too.'

They weren't so effusive when it came to their relationship with woolgrowers.

Said Winston: 'Pleased to see you come and pleased to see you go. Not only that, they'd pray for rain to wash our tracks away. Tasmania hasn't got a real good reputation for that. You get on that Eyre Peninsula in South Australia, they're different farmers. Talk to you in the pub, have a beer, buy you a beer.'

Thomas added:

End of the day there's a couple of cartons on the table. Over here [he grimaces] . . . it's an honour to go and shear for them people. They paid cash. They look after you. They feed you. Here, nah. Don't even get a beer. There's a shed on the way back to Launceston, up the top of the hill, near the old stone bridge on the old road, I shore there for eight, nine years in a row a few years ago and they'd feed ya, but you'd sit out on the balcony, freezin' cold, wind, rain.

Lindsay cited a different experience:

This bloke here. This Valley Field. When you're finished and shearin' cut out there he'd get the Caledonian Pipe Band to come out and put 'em away off up the road and march down to the woolshed and he'd send the truck to get the beer. The truck got to Campbell Town and no beer, couldn't get a barrel of beer. We'll go down to Tunbridge, they've got plenty of beer down there. So they sent a 7-ton truck to Tunbridge to get a 9-gallon keg of beer. When the bagpipes got there they nearly lift the roof off the woolshed.

**

Up in the Riverina, many of the stud properties that spread over the Old Man Plain north of the famous one-pub town of Conargo still shear their rams with blade shears. The practice continues at the famed studs of Wanganella and Boonoke, owned by the company F.S. Falkiner & Sons and birthplace of the Peppin merino bloodline. There I met operations manager Justin Campbell. He was also a blade shearer and one of a breed whose demise has long been predicted but hasn't yet eventuated.

Justin, who was forty-four in 2014, was raised on his parents' sheep and wheat property near Lightning Ridge, New South Wales.

'Mum always tells me when I was just about to be born she whipped over to Toowoomba and had me while Dad was out ploughing the paddock,' he said. 'Next-door neighbour brought over a big bottle, said, "Have a beer, you've had a boy."'

At Longreach Pastoral College he majored in stud sheep, then got work on the Webb family's Weewondilla Station near Muttaburra: 'I did two years there and absolutely loved it. Just jackarooing, learning and mustering big paddocks, and they mustered by aeroplane actually while I was the only jackaroo on the motorbike.'

Weewondilla's stud rams came from Uardry Stud, near Hay, so in 1992, when Justin heard of a job going there, he applied for it and got it. It was then that he started blade shearing. As he recalled: 'They did a course, I think it was run by Phil Venning from South Australia, that was a week's course over at Pooginook with the blades, setting your blades up and sharpening. It's like any tool; if it's not sharp it's not going to do a good job. Setting up your blade shears, how to work them, carving all your wood out.

'I've actually got my shears in the toolbox,' he said, pulling out an immaculate pair of shears that looked brand new, rather than twenty or more years old. 'That's my original pair that did the week's course.'

> They showed you how you made the wood up [to cover the metal handle where the shearer grips it] and you had to shape it and then it's just a matter of getting your cork from wine bottles and

making little grooves for them and setting the glue, a matter of grinding and cutting steel out of here so you can close your blade up to that distance from the tip. If that closed right up you'd end up without a smooth finish on the wool when you're blade shearing. And it's just a matter of keeping them sharp. I just used them two weeks ago when we did all the sheep in the shed.

We learned to blade-shear all in that week. The teachers taught us how to hold a sheep, which way to blade-shear a sheep, and you sort of went through that. You just grabbed a sheep out of the chute, practised with your fingers, worked out your positions, your angles, where you are going to go, then once you've got your shears right, they're sharp, then off you went. Eventually you get better and better and better. It's sort of like anything really, isn't it?

The reason rams are blade-shorn is because it allows for extremely accurate shearing. By law, rams that are going to be put on show are only allowed to have a maximum of 12.5 millimetres of wool on them on 1 March each year. That means that if you go to any show and one ram has grown more wool than another, you can assume it's better as a wool producer. In addition, due to the fact that inspectors can't get out to every stud on the first day of March, studs are allowed another 1 millimetre for every three days after 1 March. So if the sheep are inspected on 21 March, you're allowed another 7 millimetres on top of the 12.5. A blade shearer like Justin can shear exactly to whatever length is required:

> I find that it's not too bad once you're used to it and good at it. If I'm told shear at 22 millimetres, I'm 22. In some spots you might be 24 but the best thing about it, when you stand a sheep up, you can trim a bit off. Now if you went 20 you can't glue it back on. When the sheep stands up you've got your little ruler that you

actually check it all over with and if you do have some high spots where you might be 23 or 24 mill, well that's where you can trim it.

Such precise shearing is almost impossible with machine shears, which work best when right against the skin. The wool on blade-shorn rams also looks better. Justin likens the difference between machine shearing and blade shearing to the difference between using a lawnmower and a pair of clippers. Blade shears don't shatter the tip of the wool, so the finished ram (which everyone is looking at, rather than the fleece) looks nice and clean. At least, that's the idea:

> One time at Uardry I blade-shore a ram and it was worth about $8000. And I was just coming around and thinking, 'Oh, the ear is hanging down', and the next minute 'snip'. I cut his ear off. So you've got to take a bit more time and take a bit more precaution. In my younger days I had managers watching but now I'm in charge so no one sort of watches.

He has since shorn some of the most valuable sheep in the country:

> Rams at Uardry, we did $20 000 rams. Then there's been our $50 000 rams from Wanganella stud. I'm pretty sure he left in the wool [left the property unshorn], it was a beautiful long staple wool. I would say a couple of $20 000 rams we did at Uardry would have been probably the most expensive ones off the top of my head. We don't really approach the animal differently. Just have your shears sharp and make sure you do a beautiful neat job. The main thing is you don't go low over the shoulders. You try and get a good even back line.

Shearing the rams at Boonoke and Wanganella usually involves about 100 animals. In 2014 it took four shearers – Justin, Forbes Murdoch,

Angus Munro and John Deller – a couple of days to do them. It's obviously not about speed. It's also worth noting that three of the shearers were managers with the F. S. Falkiner & Sons company. Angus Munro is the stud manager; Forbes Murdoch is the stud classer. At the time, Forbes Murdoch was aged seventy-three. John Deller's family also owns a stud sheep property.

Justin noted that there's a big difference between his kind of blade shearing and commercial sheep shearing with machine shears.

> The shearers always look at the blade shearers and say, 'How do you do that?' It's a different culture, a different type of people. When I blade shear up in the shearing shed, when the shearers are going, they aren't shearing the sheep, they're all watching me blade shear because they find it interesting.
>
> I find the blades you get a bit more out of it. There is something special about shearing stud rams. Well, they're worth a few dollars. You spend a bit more time with it and at the end of your job, once your sheep stands up, it actually looks immaculate, it looks like a beautiful job well done. It's a matter of that evenness that's the tricky part.

From time to time, blade-shearing schools, such as at Shear Outback in Hay, are still conducted. When Justin was working at Uardry, he used to teach most of his jackaroos. They'd get their killers (sheep destined for consumption on the property) and practise on them. There's no training on Wanganella and Boonoke as they no longer employ jackaroos.

The days of managers issuing orders from the station verandah are also a thing of the past. It's all very hands-on now. Said Justin:

> My title is operations manager, so running the commercial and stud. So it's Boonoke, Wanganella, you've got your Boonoke

commercial sheep and then Wanganella stud, poll Boonoke stud, plus we've got properties like Warriston property, Peppinella property. Two studs and the commercial flock. It's about 190 000 acres [77 000 hectares] to look after so you clock up a few kilometres each day.

When I asked what it was like to run two of the most famous stud properties in the world, ones that have made such a large contribution to the financial wellbeing of generations of Australians, Justin turned out to be the kind of woolgrower who spends more time looking forward than looking back:

Wanganella turned 150 years old two years ago and the poll Boonoke stud was registered as number one poll stud when it first started. Today, we're doing very well. Our ram sales are on the way up, our semen sales are just unbelievable at the moment. In the last few years, we've changed our type of sheep and we're getting the benefits. Things died down there before I came here, ram numbers were dropping off, just little things, and I think the old heads here didn't change when everyone else was changing and some clients wanted change. They thought they were that big. So we can say we've turned it around and things are on the way up.

In his opinion, it's not just his studs that are doing well: 'I think the industry has turned around. The market is very good. It's been very good the last few years. If you are getting $1300 to $1600 a bale, you can't complain. I think Australian Wool Innovation is doing a good job promoting our wool and all that. It was only ten or fifteen years ago it was only $500 a bale or $600.'

According to the Australian Bureau of Agricultural and Resource Economics, overall sheep flock numbers across Australia grew strongly between 2010 and 2012, before stabilising in 2013. That didn't stop the renowned Uardry stud, home of the ram that once graced the Australian shilling, from going over to cattle and cropping in 2012. While others mourned the loss of one of the jewels in the stud-sheep crown, the new owners, the Brinkworth family, told *The Australian* that they considered the stud-merino breeding days of the squattocracy as over.

Meanwhile, according to surveys conducted by the Australian Bureau of Statistics and Statistics New Zealand, in 2012 there were no difficulties for contractors or farmers in finding shearers. Many positions were advertised on the internet, particularly on shearingworld.com. However, as some shearers have noted previously, many positions were filled by New Zealanders travelling to Australia for seasonal work.

The 2011 Australian Census also revealed that there were 3200 people who gave their occupation as shearer. This was down forty-one per cent, or 2270, on the numbers for 2001. Apprenticeships and training schemes were turning out 150 to 250 shearers each year, although not all of them remained in the industry. These figures don't include those shearers who still get their training in the time-honoured way, on the job, with supplementary training from TAFE institutions and registered training organisations.

Even shearing competitions are having mixed fortunes. One of Australia's biggest competitions, the Diamond Shears, held at Longreach, once had the highest prize money in the state with over 100 competitors. In 2013 it had only thirty entrants. The main event in Queensland is now the Jackie Howe invitational competition, held on the last weekend in August, at the historic Jondaryan woolshed, the scene of pivotal events during the strikes of the 1890s.

***

While many shearers in Australia now come from New Zealand and other countries, we're still able to produce those who can stand tall among the greats. One of those was a Queensland shearer named Steve Handley.

A large man, with a powerful physique and vivid red hair, Steve was known as the Chinchilla Killer, after the Queensland town where he grew up and his ability to shear around anyone who came near him.

Noel Dawson, long-time friend of Steve and principal with shearing contractor NGS, rated Steve the fastest shearer in Australia and recalled seeing him doing sit-ups, with weights on his chest, after a day's shearing.

He was able to shear merinos in less than two minutes from pen to chute and from the first bell at 7.30 to the last bell at 5.30 he set a furious pace. His best tally was 400 in a day, with daily tallies when he was in his thirties of 250 to 300 sheep. As a result he was also one of the best-paid shearers in the country, capable of earning more than $100 000 a year. Although, as he said himself, you could only do that if you had a strong work ethic. He told ABC *Landline* reporter Tim Lee in 2004: 'You're paid for what you shear but a good shearer can make up to $100 000, you know, if they want to apply themselves. There's a lot of work, to make $100 000. You've got to shear hard day in day out. It sounds a lot of money, but you've got a lot of work there too.'

Steve left school at fifteen and started shearing at age seventeen. He seldom entered competitions but when he did, he'd win. He eventually built a reputation in sheds from the Gulf of Carpentaria all the way down to Tasmania. Steve took pride in the fact that he was invited back to a number of properties to shear year after year, including Barcaldine Downs, Bimerah, Bunginderry, Goodberry Hills, Lansdowne, Mayvale, Moble, Powella, Ray, Teviot, Vellum Downs, Wallen and Whynot.

He was known for being intensely competitive, with a piercing gaze that intimidated any challengers. He once reduced a young rouseabout who got in his way to tears with just a look. Off the board, though, he was quiet, reserved and well mannered. As one colleague put it, on the board he had a scorching focus; off it, he was sincere, gentle and genuinely concerned for others. Another recalled saying to him, 'Steve, you've got so much class.' *[Social networking references reproduced by kind permission of* queenslandcountrylife.com.au*]*

His actions often spoke louder than words. One shearer, using the social networking pseudonym Bunginderry, recalled how it was hard to complain about tough sheep when Steve was shearing 350 of them, smiling and chatting with the owner at smoko. Bunginderry regarded him as both a good bloke and a leader.

He married wife Monica in 2007, and when they had a child, daughter Rhianna, the family travelled from shed to shed, living in a caravan bristling with antennas. When Rhianna reached school age, they settled in Charleville.

In 2013, Steve suffered a back injury that prevented him from shearing. Unable to work at the profession that defined him, he sank into depression. In early 2014, at age forty-nine, he died from a self-inflicted gunshot wound at Charleville.

Such was Steve Handley's reputation that the ABC's *Landline* ran an obituary in February 2014. In it he was described as 'a giant of the Australian shearing world'. Those who eulogised him described him as humble, gentle and well read, qualities not normally associated with a shearer.

Station cook Justine Fish recalled working at Kapunda, South Australia, when Steve was shearing. The station owner told her to forget smoko and come help in the shed. Steve and Paki Te Whata were pushing each other so hard that they needed a rousie each to keep up with them. That left one rousie for the other six shearers. Justine noted that Paki was 25 years younger than Steve. Steve's extraordinary intensity, athleticism and skill can still be seen in footage on YouTube.

It isn't easy to dismiss someone like Steve Handley as just a shearer. His contribution and that of so many others have helped form the

Australian character and done a great deal to lay the foundations of our economy, standard of living and institutions.

There is something about shearers that still grabs our attention. This was evident when a machine-shearing handpiece presented to Jack Howe in 1893 by the Wolseley company was put up for auction in October 2013. The handpiece hadn't been used during Jack's recording-breaking machine-shearing feat of 1892, but he did use it for many years afterwards. The auctioneers expected the handpiece to sell for between $15 000 and $25 000. It ended up going for $38 000, purchased by the National Museum of Australia, in Canberra, where it can now be seen on display.

Such is the value put on a heritage that extends back to the earliest days of the European presence in Australia. The country may no longer ride on the sheep's back but from the tennis courts of the Australian Open to the favourite pure-wool vest I'm wearing as I write these lines, it remains integral to our way of life. Without shearers, our history would have been very different: not only have they provided us with the means of keeping warm, they've also enriched us culturally, economically, politically and much more. We would all be poorer for a future without them.

Glossary

Bag boots
Moccasin-like footwear favoured by shearers, so named because they originated from jute woolpacks.

Blades
Shearers' term for hand shears.

Blow
A stroke of the shears across some part of the sheep. The common usage is the long blow.

Board
The floor of the woolshed, upon which sheep are shorn.

Classing
The process carried out by a trained wool-classer to identify the quality and characteristics of each fleece.

Clip
Total amount of wool shorn in a season from one property, a region, or a whole country. In both world wars, for example, the British government bought the entire Australian wool clip.

GLOSSARY

Cobbler or snob
A sheep that is difficult to shear, commonly the last sheep left in a pen.

Cut out
Completion of shearing at a particular shed.

Ducks on the pond
The traditional cry used by shearers to warn of women approaching the shearing shed.

Expert
The individual who grinds the combs and cutters and ensures the shearing-shed machinery is running smoothly.

Flock
Total of all sheep run on a property.

Fly-blown
Sheep that have been infested with the maggots of fly eggs. When applied to shearers it means having no money.

Gun
An extremely fast, competent shearer. At times it has referred to a shearer capable of shearing 100 or 200 sheep a day. A dreadnought is a shearer who can shear 300 a day.

Jackie Howe
A sleeveless singlet favoured by many shearers. Whether Jack Howe wore these shirts, or indeed any like them, is debatable.

Lambing down
The process whereby publicans separated a shearer from his cheque.

Lanolin
The natural lubricant of wool, of significance to the cosmetics industry.

Locks
Short pieces of wool, including second cuts, that are swept up from the shearing floor.

Merino
A breed of fine-woolled sheep that originated in Spain and has attained pre-eminence in Australia.

Mob
A collection of sheep.

Muster
A round-up or gathering of sheep.

Pen
Enclosure for holding sheep in woolshed environs. There are sweating pens, holding pens, catching pens and counting-out pens. A newly hired shearer obtains a pen.

Picker-up
Shed hand who picks up freshly shorn fleece and throws it onto the classing table.

Pinking
Very close, high-quality shearing. Owners always hope the shearers pink 'em.

Poll
A sheep without horns.

Pressing
Process by which the presser packs the wool into bales ready for transporting. Many pressers from the old days had flat noses, caused when the pressing handle slipped from their hand and swung back, breaking their nose.

Raddle
Coloured chalk used to mark sheep. Historically, sheep were raddled by squatters to mark poor-quality shearing.

Rep
Short for representative; the shearers' elected or delegated nominee in any union–management discussion.

Ringer
The fastest shearer in any shearing shed.

Rouseabout
General shed hand, anything from the board boy to a wool roller, often shortened to 'rousie'. Sometimes considered to be religious because after two weeks of constantly running to pick up fleeces or sweep up locks, they can be seen praying, for rain.

Run
The official shearing time period, a run is an unbroken two hours. There are four runs per working day. A run can also refer to a sheep property.

Scour
To wash wool, removing impurities from the fibres. Also the shed where this occurs.

Second cuts
Short pieces of wool that result when a shearer does not cut close enough, thus having to go over the sheep a second time.

Shed hand
See 'rouseabout'.

Sheep-o
Call given by a shearer when more sheep are needed in the pens.

Smoko
The thirty-minute tea-break between the two morning and two afternoon runs.

Snob
A rough, untalented shearer. See also 'cobbler'.

Staple
A natural cluster of wool fibres grouped together.

Tally
Number of sheep shorn during a period, anywhere from a run to a day to the duration of a shed; recorded in a tally book.

Tomahawking
Rough, careless shearing.

Wet sheep
Sheep that cannot be shorn because their fleece is too damp. Shearers vote on whether sheep can be shorn (a dry vote) or whether they will have a day off (a wet vote).

Wether
A castrated male sheep.

Yolk
The yellowish greasy matter in unprocessed wool; when heavy it tends to plug up shearers' combs. Lanolin is a by-product of yolk.

Primary source: Shear Outback Museum

Shearing Hall of Fame Citations

† *indicates shearer who appears in the text*

John Bray Allan OAM (1935–)
John Allan grew up in Gippsland, Victoria, and began shearing about 1953, encouraged and taught by his father. In 1955 he signed on with Grazcos, at The Yanko, Jerilderie, New South Wales. He met the Australian team in New Zealand at the first Golden Shears in 1961 and won the intermediate event; in 1962, he was a member of the team. Also in 1962, Sir Percy Lister invited John to work in England, where he stayed until 1971, before moving on to Australia, New Zealand, Peru, Ecuador, Colombia, Argentina, Chile, Uruguay, India, Norway, Sweden, Mexico and the United States.

John joined Sunbeam Corporation Ltd in 1973 as rural manager and over ten years built the rural division up to a turnover of more than $20 million. Keen to export to China, he joined an Australian trade mission in 1974 and demonstrated Sunbeam gear to 40 000 people a day for twenty-one days. After leaving Sunbeam to concentrate on his own business, Botany Bay Imports, John was approached by the Heiniger company to go to Switzerland, where he became director of production, using Botany Bay as the Australian distributor.

In 1974, with the help of the Euroa Apex Club, he was instrumental in establishing the Golden Shears in Australia, changing competition shearing in Australia forever. John was a member of the Australian Wool Board's wool-harvesting research and development committee from 1972 until 1991 and was awarded the Order of Australia in 1988 for services to the shearing industry. His biography, *Shear Magic*, was published in 2007.

Gordon Cahill (1898–1981)
Gordon Cahill was born in 1898, at Tunbridge in the Tasmanian Midlands. He was one of eleven children raised on the family farm. As a young man Gordon learned to shear with the blades, but eventually became one of about thirty Tunbridge men who travelled all over Australia from March to October each year before the Tasmanian season began in the spring. Gordon is credited with having shorn 750 000 sheep over a 49-year career, with the high point being 326 at Woodbury Estate in 1960 at the age of sixty-two. He was recognised and respected as both a gun shearer and a quiet, unassuming man who got along very well with property owners. Younger shearers looked to him for advice and guidance while trying to beat him on the board. On the day before he retired in 1968 he shore 258 in the Warringa woolshed, where he had shorn for twenty-three consecutive years. This great old shearer passed away in 1981.

John Ernest (Jack) Cameron (1933–)
Known as 'the Bald Eagle', Jack Cameron's shearing career lasted more than fifty-four years, during which time he shore over 1.8 million sheep. Born in Dalgety, New South Wales, in 1933, Jack started professional shearing when he was fifteen, although he could shear well prior to this. At seventeen, Jack joined a team of four shearers. He then left Dalgety at the age of twenty-three and moved to Dubbo, into 'the big shearing business'.

Of his time shearing at Bendemar [sic], Jack said: 'In the old shed I was the first one to shear 200 using narrow gear. I did hold the

Australian record for about three days. It wasn't officially proclaimed that I held the record. I shore 332 sheep in seven and a half hours, and Kevin Sarre shore 346 on the following Monday in seven hours and 46 minutes.' Jack's biggest shed was Toorale near Bourke, where he earned his nickname: 'There was an American lady there and I heard her as plain as English. "My God, isn't that old bald-headed chap a good shearer for such an old man."' Jack was twenty-seven at the time! During his career, Jack won ninety open shearing competitions and has been placed in many state and Australian titles. Jack also participated in competitions as a judge for over ten years.

Raymond Edward Gordon Congdon (1906–1990)
Ray Congdon was born at Gunbar, New South Wales, in 1906 and left school at fourteen to work on Sunrise Station as a station hand. He began his shearing career at Ravensworth in 1925. For the next twenty-two years Ray was known as a very well-respected and accomplished shearer through the Hay–Booligal area and parts of Victoria. In 1947 Ray began contracting and gave many men the opportunity to become part of the industry as shearers and wool-handlers. He always did his best to ensure that both his men and the sheep owners were well looked after. His two sons, Bruce and Tony, both became good shearers in charge of shearing teams. As a contractor for twenty-eight years, Ray put a wealth of knowledge into the industry and his men enjoyed the use of expertly serviced handpieces and expertly ground combs and cutters. Excellence was his benchmark. Ray passed away in 1990, but his foresight in training for the future left an undisputed legacy to the Hay district.

Mark Conlan (1953–2012)
Mark Conlan had an outstanding professional shearing career. A notable speed shearer, he set a record shearing 852 in one day with his brother John, using narrow combs. As a champion show shearer

he was four times Golden Shears Open Champion, competed in seven Trans-Tasman Tests and was Australia's first World Shearing Champion in 1986. Mark first started shearing in competitions in Kyneton, which were the basis for the development of Sports Shear Australia. Mark ran a successful shearing business that employed up to fifty at its peak.

† **James (Jim) Davidson** (1865–1936)
Born at Woolsthorpe in Victoria, Jim Davidson started 'picking up' at Quamby Station at age twelve and got his first pen blade-shearing at Caramut Station before he was sixteen. In 1888 Jim was impressed by the Wolseley shearing-machine demonstration in Melbourne and was one of forty shearers to draw a pen when James Wilson of Dunlop Station wanted to shear entirely with machines. Davidson made several record tallies and spent many years 'preaching the gospel of mechanical shearing'.

Frederick York Wolseley employed Jim to demonstrate the Howard Geddes shearing machines throughout eastern Australia with creator and chief mechanic John Howard. When the 1890s' depression inspired Howard to devise and patent a portable shearing plant, transported and powered by bicycle, Jim was given the job of promotion, pushing his bicycle and 32 kilograms of gear around Queensland. In 1908 Howard was incapacitated by paralysis and Davidson took his place as workshop manager. In the same year he also blade-shore sheep in the stage melodrama *The Squatter's Daughter* at the Criterion Theatre during its 29-week run. In 1909, he travelled to England to develop an improved shearing machine for R. A. Lister and Co., which had taken over Frederick Wolseley's company. Until his death, Jim supervised the Sydney workshop and pursued ongoing development and experimentation. 'Kindliness, genuine sympathy and a fine capacity to help lame dogs over stiles' were his marked characteristics. He was modest about his charitable acts, which included supporting fifteen fatherless boys through apprenticeships at the Sydney workshop. Colleagues acknowledged his loyalty to Lister, his patience and good temper, and his 'great mechanical skill and inventive faculty'.

John Edward (Ted) Dean (1882–1959)

Ted Dean is credited with shearing 1584 sheep in one week at Alice Downs in Queensland, the best day's tally being 284, and in the early part of the last century was recognised as being Australia's greatest shearer after Jackie Howe. The son of a wool-classer who came to Australia from England in the 1860s, Ted was born in Tenterfield, New South Wales, in 1882, and went to school in Deepwater before starting his working life learning to blade-shear in the New England district. Ted travelled to Queensland in 1906 and was based at Blackall for the next twenty-five years, shearing on properties in Queensland from Julia Creek to the New South Wales border. By 1908 Ted's working team was known as Queensland's best, making record tallies that year. In the same year, Ted was featured in the poem 'The Western Shearer'.

Ted remained a respected shearer; on his sixty-fifth birthday, it is claimed, he shore 225 sheep. He continued to work until he was seventy-one and then spent his retirement in Brisbane with his wife and family until he passed away in October 1959, aged seventy-seven.

One hundred years after this 'forgotten hero' commenced his shearing career, he was honoured by a recital of 'The Western Shearer' before an international audience at the 2005 world shearing championships in Toowoomba, Queensland.

Maurice Doyle (1935–1993)

Maurice had a professional shearing career in Albany, Western Australia. With an exemplary physical performance he shore 3286 over three weeks at De Grey Station. A successful show shearer, he represented Australia in 1962 and was Australian Cross-bred (meaning merino and other breeds) Champion in 1963. Maurice became a coach with the Australian Wool Board, developing shearing techniques with Viv Parkes, Kevin Sarre, Bimby Martin, Fred Jarvis and John Harris. As an instructor in Western Australia he then introduced the Tally-Hi method to that state. He subsequently ran a contracting business at Perillup before retiring.

Dick Duggan (1935-)

Dick, 'The King', is known as a quality show and shed shearer, and for his noted 'Blindfold' demonstrations. First shearing 200 at age 18, he was then 'ringer' for many years. Competing in shows from 1952 – 2010, Dick won over one hundred open, state and national titles, representing Australia in three countries. As a product consultant and sales rep, he contributed to product design, actively supported competitions in many country towns, and has mentored many. Dick leaves a legacy with nineteen family members, spanning three generations, working in the industry, five of whom are shearers. With a lifetime in the industry, he has filled all roles including contractor, cook and wool-classer.

Ian Elkins (1963-)

A professional shearer, particularly in the fine-wool sector, Ian has represented and promoted the industry at the highest levels. He competed as a successful show shearer from 1992–2000, winning over 120 open competitions. Ian provided product development expertise for Sunbeam, Tru-Test and Heiniger, before representing Australian Wool Innovation in R&D, promotion and innovation services. Ian has a continuing role in shearer training with AWI and TAFE, and in advancement of shearing in the community.

Kevin Gellatly (1948–)

Born at Perenjori, Western Australia, Kevin shore and contracted throughout the wheat belt and station sheds for 34 years. As Heiniger representative from 1995, he advocated for shed and equipment improvement in Australia and New Zealand. Since then, Kevin has been active in training with TAFE, Western Australian Colleges of Agriculture, Muresk University and the disabled, including training and development of shearing technique for the alpaca industry. Kevin has also been shearers' representative, judge and advisor for competition shearing in Western Australia.

John Thomas Harris (1940–)

John Harris began shearing with his father at age sixteen, working through Queensland, New South Wales and Victoria. In 1957 he won his first competition, a learners' event at the Euroa Show. He won the 1963 Victorian open title followed by four Australian strong-wool (now generally defined as non-merino) championships. The Australian open title eluded him until 1980, when he also won Shearer of the Year in Canberra. In 1965 the Australian Wool Board set up the Tally-Hi shearer-training scheme and John became the youngest of the original six instructors. He was one of four top-line shearers invited to contest the 1973 Forlonge invitation event at Euroa, which led to the establishment of the Golden Shears in Australia in 1974. John won the Forlonge in that year. He was a member of the Australian team in 1976–77, 1977–78 and 1980–81, competing at the Golden Shears in Euroa and at Masterton, New Zealand. Following his 1980 Shearer of the Year win, John and his wife travelled to England as guests of R. A. Lister and Co., where John did a number of demonstrations.

John began contracting in 1974, with up to three teams in the Riverina, central and western Victoria. Many of these shearers were top-level New Zealanders. John also became one of the first contractors to employ women as shed hands, shearers and cooks.

† John Robert (Jackie) Howe (1861–1920)

Jackie Howe was born near Warwick in south-east Queensland, and was probably taught by Chinese shearing teams working in the district. He set the (still unbroken) blade-shearing record of 321 sheep in seven hours and forty minutes at Alice Downs near Blackall, Queensland, on 10 October 1892. His legendary speed, skill and grace were rewarded with competition medals and cash prizes. With hands the size of 'small tennis rackets' and a physique to match, Jack found that short-sleeved flannel shearing shirts restricted his biceps and this was the inspiration for the famous 'Jackie Howe' blue singlet that was the shearer's uniform for the next 100 years.

Like most other shearers of the time Jack was a dedicated unionist, but unlike others who walked or cycled between sheds, he could afford to arrive on horseback trailing a packhorse. He was active during the shearers' strikes of 1891 and 1894 and remained a loyal member of the Australian Labor Party. As president of the Blackall Workers Political Organisation in 1909, he took the lead in arranging for T. J. Ryan to stand for election to the Legislative Assembly. In 1900, he hung up his shears and bought a pub in Blackall. In 1919 he retired to his own sheep station, Sumnervale, but died the following year at Blackall. After Jack's death, Queensland Premier T. J. Ryan said, in a telegram to Jack's widow, 'I have lost a true and trusted friend and Labour has lost a champion.'

Herbert James (Herb) Hutchins (1934–2006)

Herb Hutchins was born in 1934 at Hamilton, Victoria, and began shearing in 1951, starting a career spanning fifty-five years. Having established his own run around Hamilton, Herb claimed to have handled well in excess of one million sheep. He commenced competition shearing in the late 1960s, winning over forty open events. He naturally progressed into judging, highlights being the 2005 world championships in Toowoomba and the world fine-wool (now generally defined as merino) titles in Alexandra, New Zealand, in 1993. Herb also organised the Hamilton P&C society competitions from their inception.

Herb began as the shearing instructor with the Australian Wool Corporation in 1985, continuing until 2005. He also ran the shearing courses at Longerenong College for over twenty years. He taught himself to blade-shear in 1990 and was able to use this new skill to help stud breeders and to teach others. To better assist left-handed learners, he taught himself to shear this way. Herb really enjoyed helping young people succeed and always advised them to look after their money.

A member of the group that established the Big Wool Bales in Hamilton in 1989, Herb later bought the struggling tourist attraction and developed a shearing-supplies business. He was also secretary/treasurer of Sports Shear Victoria from 1995 until his death in January 2006.

John Williss Hutchinson OAM (1943–)

Fascinated by shearing from childhood, John Hutchinson practised 'shearing' his brothers. One day he even used his father's seed potatoes as sheep – and peeled them all! His career as a third-generation shearer began at the age of thirteen, shearing sheep bellies on a spare stand in the shearing shed. John learned to shear cleanly from his father and, at age fourteen, learned speed from 'Lino the Magnificent' (Keith Lyons), working in a neighbour's shed. In 1969 he won the first of six Australian championships and demonstrated shearing at the Osaka World Expo.

Despite fame as the 'quiet gun from South Australia', and success in competition well into the 1980s, John found greater satisfaction in teaching. His first trainees were boys from remand homes, to whom he gave a vocation, and a way out of strife. At one point he even taught shearing to the Bedouin of Jordan. In 1999 John was awarded the Order of Australia medal for his work as a trainer and teacher.

Henry Ferdinand (Fred) Jarvis (1914–2001)

Fred Jarvis was born at Benambra, Victoria, in 1914. He left school aged fourteen and learned to shear in 1929. At eighteen, Fred began his shearing career in the Riverina, New South Wales, shearing at Bundy out of Deniliquin and Toogimbie near Hay. Life was hard at that time, with plenty of shearers looking for employment.

Fred went on to become an excellent shearer. In a four-stand shed at Wondabar, in the Western District of Victoria, Fred's team shore 942 sheep in a day. At Ned's Corner, near Mildura, Fred and Mick Nixon, a two-stand team, shore 480 sheep in seven and a half hours. Fred participated with varied success in many shearing competitions and in 1960 he won the Australian shearing championship. He captained the Australian team that competed in the Golden Shears championships in New Zealand in 1961.

From 1964, Fred worked with the Australian Wool Board as a shearing instructor and in fifteen years he taught more than 800 young shearers. Fred judged at shearing competitions throughout Australia and in 1974 he was the first international judge to be invited to New Zealand for the Golden Shears. Fred passed away in December 2001. He will be remembered for the patience and guidance he supplied to a great many young shearers throughout his career.

Melville Earl (Mel) Johnston (1938–)

Mel Johnston was born at Carcoar, New South Wales, in 1938. He began shearing in 1955 and shore throughout New South Wales and southern Queensland for the next thirty-three years. In 1960 he began competing at shows and scored his first win at Quandialla the next year. His first major win was the 1977 New South Wales state title at Bombala. Mel then won the 1978 Australian Shearer of the Year in Canberra. Part of his prize was a trip to England where he gave many demonstrations and shore for the Queen on the royal farm at Windsor Castle. In 1980 Mel won the inaugural Diamond Shears in

Longreach, and in 1984 he won the Jackie Howe championship, an invitation event at the Royal Canberra Show. The prize was a trip to Denver, Colorado, to compete in the international professional sheep-shearing contest at the 1985 National Western Stock Show, which Mel won. Just a month after returning from the US, he won another Jackie Howe event at Howe's birthplace, Warwick in Queensland, during the Woolaway Festival. Mel believes he won about 100 open-class competitions during his career but is not sure of the exact number.

Mel was also employed by the Australian Wool Corporation as a part-time shearing instructor. He did many demonstrations: throughout New South Wales at venues including the Sydney Royal Easter Show and the seventh floor of the Grace Brothers store; at the Royal Bath and West Show in England; and the State Bank in Denver. Mel retired from shearing in 1988. He became a publican in Canowindra for seven years before retiring to Orange, where he now lives.

Bert Lowrey (1917–)

Bert Lowrey's capacity as a champion shearer and contribution as a shearing contractor sets him apart. A gun shearer, he was knocking wool off 320 sheep in one day at Edgeroi (New South Wales) in August 1944. In 1945, he shore 1200 sheep per 44-hour week; when the forty-hour week was introduced, he shore 1100 per week.

Bert learned to shear in the late 1930s following a stint working as a builder. In 1949 he became a shearing contractor, employing up to 100 men, and he had to hire an aeroplane to fly around to his sheds in the west of the state. In 1960 Bert produced a transportable air-conditioner to suit a nine-stand shed, cooling it down from 117°F to 75°F (47°C to 24°C). It is said that he never had a sick shearer after that! Bert worked as a shearer and contractor for thirty-one years and retired when wide combs were introduced in the 1980s. At the age of eighty-five, Bert was still shearing at events around the northern parts of New South Wales and was immortalised in a poem written by former shed hand and friend James Elliott.

> I was just a lad from Sydney
> When my working life begun
> They sent me out to Midkin
> Where Bert Lowrey was the gun!
> And his tally on the board began to tell
> All their stealth and cutting
> And the champ just up from Gunning
> Could not match the fleece that flowed
> From Lowrey's pen

Bimby John Martin (1938–)

Bimby Martin was born at Queanbeyan, New South Wales, in 1938. The son of a sheep dealer and drover, much of his life has been associated with sheep, from full-time shearing in Queensland and New South Wales to research and development work with Sunbeam's rural division. His easy, distinctive shearing style, developed as he recovered from tetanus in Queensland, caught the eye of the late Les Batten at the Australian Wool Board, which led to Bimby becoming one of the original six instructors who introduced the Tally-Hi method to the industry. Throughout Bimby's time with the Wool Board he spent regular two-week stints in sheds to maintain his skills and fitness.

In 1973 he was seconded to the International Wool Secretariat to introduce shearer training in Uruguay, South America. He joined Sunbeam in 1974 to assist Euroa Apex Club introduce the Golden Shears to Australia, and acted as Australian team manager in New Zealand in 1975. He also travelled the country trialling and promoting the Sunbeam range, including the revolutionary ergonomic Supergrip handpiece. In 1976 Bimby became general manager of the Sydney

Agrodome and selected and trained the rams and dogs for the show. He also provided commentary.

Bimby and his wife of fifty-five years, Gwen, went into business in 1980. In 1990 they bought a large motel in Bega, New South Wales, which they ran for thirteen years before retiring to Cootamundra, where they now live. Bimby still maintains contact with the many friends he made in the shearing industry, when the name Bimby Martin was synonymous with all that is good in shearing.

Ronald James 'Jumbuck' Niven (1952–)

Ronald Niven was born in 1952 and raised on the family farm at Rocky Gully in the south-west of Western Australia. He became an outstanding machine shearer, but was fascinated by blade shearing. When he moved to Kojonup in 1979, he set about learning and developing the necessary skills to shear with the blades. From 1982, he established and built up the Jumbuck shearing business, which specialises in blade shearing stud rams as well as conventional machine shearing of commercial flocks. Today, Ron and three other blade specialists shear some 3000 merino rams from up to 100 studs, including some in the eastern states. Ron also owns Jumbuck Shearing Supplies, a shearing gear repair and maintenance business at Manjimup, where he now lives and where each year he presents the Jumbuck Award to the stud breeder who best presents his sheep for shearing.

For seven years Ron was employed part-time by the Australian Wool Corporation as a shearing instructor working in most woolgrowing areas of the state. He is in demand to demonstrate both his blade- and machine-shearing skill at shows, schools and industry promotions. He has also judged shearing competitions at many agricultural shows. Ron is always ready to share his knowledge with others; he is passionate about the shearing industry and sets a very high standard. He says you have to love sheep to have a feel for them, and you need patience and an artist's touch to shear them well.

Donald Francis Orgill OAM (1929–2005)

Donald Orgill was born in Rockdale, New South Wales, in 1929 and took up shearing in the Cootamundra district in 1953. In 1967 he shore 236 sheep in one day at Hillside, Cootamundra. He was twice judged the best shearer at the Cootamundra Show. He later helped Kevin Sarre promote the Tally-Hi method of shearing. Donald went on to become a shearing instructor for the New South Wales Department of Technical Education, and decided the best way to promote quality shearing was through shearing competitions. This led him into the field of competition-shearing judging from 1964. Donald judged shearing competitions for thirty years, including the Melbourne, Sydney and Adelaide royal shows, the Diamond Shears competition at Longreach, and most major country shows in New South Wales and Victoria. Donald was a life member of the Shearing Competition Federation of Australia and the Australian Workers Union. In September 1994 he was awarded the Order of Australia medal for 'services to the wool industry as a judge of sheep shearing competitions'. Donald passed away in 2005.

Andrew Vivian (Viv) Parkes (1907–1993)

Born at Benambra, Victoria, in 1907, Viv Parkes left home at fourteen years of age and at nineteen started his fifty-year shearing career, working in South Australia, Victoria, New South Wales, Queensland and New Zealand. He was a well-respected ringer in many major sheds and had a reputation for great physical endurance. His greatest performance was in the summer of 1938, when he shore 1100 merino wethers a week for eleven consecutive weeks at Commonwealth Hill Station in South Australia. Vivian won the Victorian shearing championships in 1954 and the Australian shearing championships in 1958, aged fifty-one. In 1956 the organising committee for the Melbourne Olympic Games asked the Australian Wool Board to stage a sheep and wool display, with Viv Parkes' shearing demonstration a highlight.

In 1961, the Australian Wool Board invited Viv to commence a study to improve the quality of the Australian shearer. With fellow Hall of Fame inductee Kevin Sarre, he developed the revolutionary Tally-Hi shearing method and the national shearing training scheme. The streamlined shearing technique was smooth and quick, meaning high tallies with less effort, and made it easier to teach beginners the art of shearing. In 1970 woolgrowers in Uruguay invited Viv to visit their country and set up a shearer-training scheme.

Viv was a member of the Australian Workers Union for more than fifty years and passed away in August 1993. Friends remember him as a quiet, retiring man, with a dry sense of humour, known as a 'gentleman shearer'. His daughter recalled: 'It never ceases to amaze me that a man with such strength who could control big rams could also nurse a baby so gently, do delicate carvings on an emu egg, mend grandchildren's broken bikes or mend shoes.'

Stephen Claude Amos (Steve) Pittaway (1932–2002)
Born at Wirrabara, South Australia, Stephen Pittaway left school at thirteen to become a mechanic, but joined his father, a noted blade shearer, to become a third-generation shearer when he was fifteen. He won his first competition at Kalangadoo in 1959 and was soon recognised for his ability to rise to the occasion and for never giving in, no matter how hot the opposition. He enjoyed a very long and successful competition career, winning the Millicent Show competition in 1960, 1961 and 1962, the Victorian title in 1963 and 1978, and the South Australian championship six times. He won the Australian open championship in 1964 and in 1978, and Shearer of the Year in Canberra in 1977. This win took him to the Golden Shears world championship at the Royal Bath and West Show in England with fellow South Australian John Hutchinson, where Steve finished fifth. He was a member of the first Australian team to contest the Golden Shears test match at Euroa in 1974. The team won and Steve

took out the gold medal for best individual score. He was also best of the Australians in the return match at Masterton, New Zealand, and a member of the 1977–78 team. Steve won the 1975 Forlonge invitation, defeating fellow South Australian Gil Wenke by .09 of a point. He had a remarkably long career in a physically tough industry and was known far and wide for his clean, quality shearing. He was not noted as a big-tally shearer, with a top narrow-gear tally of 240, but as he once said, 'that's the only job I know, so I stick to it'.

Vincent Rainbird (1897–1991)
Vincent Rainbird was born in 1897 and raised on a farm on the Macquarie Plains in Tasmania's Derwent Valley. After leaving school Vincent became a champion hop-picker before learning to shear. Moving to the mainland, he became a genuine gun, living in Footscray, Victoria, while shearing mainly in Victoria and South Australia. About 1930, he was credited with shearing over 300 sheep a day for five consecutive days. He was a strong union man, well respected by both his teammates and station owners and managers for his ability to negotiate an amicable resolution to any dispute. Vincent won the 1936 Cooper Gun competition for highest daily average when he shore an average of 186 per day for seven months. He became known as the 'Bradman of the board' for his big tallies. After he retired from shearing he kept contact with the wool industry, working as a wool-handler at the Australian Estates Company wool store in Sunshine, Victoria. Vincent passed away in 1991, aged ninety-four.

Anthony Joseph (Tony) Ryan OAM (1923–2011)
Born in Burra, South Australia, in 1923, Tony Ryan began shearing at Middlebank Station near Broken Hill in 1943. His tallies include 243 merino ewes with a narrow comb at Mt Victor, near Yunta, in 1950. Tony established himself as a contractor operating in South Australia's north-east, mid-north and south-east, earning a

reputation for reliability, integrity and the great rapport he had with his employees.

Tony was a senior instructor and coach with the South Australian Department of Agriculture and the Australian Wool Corporation, where he placed emphasis on training being provided in an environment as close as possible to industry conditions. He contributed to fitness research and training, and expanded the shearing-training curriculum to include handpiece maintenance; grinding, shearing judging, the role of the Australian Workers Union, and legal, industrial-relations and occupational health-and-safety issues. Tony helped devise and conduct a short residential course for part-time shearing instructors in South Australia, ensuring training methodology was consistent and of a high standard. He was also a member of the South Australian wool-producing industry training committee.

Tony was largely responsible for the revival of shearing competitions in South Australia, ensuring they were organised and fairly run, and conducting training courses for shearing judges over a period of forty years. He demonstrated the Tally-Hi shearing technique throughout Australia, in Jakarta and Taiwan and at Commonwealth heads of government meetings in Zambia and New Zealand. Tony received an Order of Australia medal in 1990 for services to the shearing industry. He was a life member of the AWU and the Shearing Competition Federation of Australia.

† Henry Salter MBE (1907–1997)

At sixteen years of age, Henry Salter learned to shear at Allambee Estate near Kerang in Victoria, finishing off sheep for a 68-year-old 'old timer' with a bad back. At eighteen, he had his first job as a shearer. He managed a tally of only forty-one sheep the first day; three days later it was down to thirty because as he said, 'I was that sore I could hardly move.' Despite his reputation for being 'not the fastest in the shed, but the cleanest', Henry won one of the first-ever organised shearing contests at Pyramid Hill in 1934. He was Australian machine-shearing champion in 1953, and was in demand as a blade shearer well into his eighties. Henry set up the first Australian shearing school at Kerang in Victoria in 1946 and kept a list of all 6557 students he taught over the next twenty-six years. In 1968 he was made a Member of the Order of the British Empire for his contribution to the wool industry.

† **Kevin Francis Sarre** (1933–1995)
Runner-up to Henry Salter at the Australian championships in 1953, Kevin Sarre's natural competitiveness would reward him with sixty-seven shearing titles by 1963. He was Australian champion in 1954, 1955, 1956 and 1961, and represented the country internationally from 1961 to 1963. His style was deceptive: he didn't seem to be working any faster than anyone else on the board, yet he was always ahead. It's even said that he shore 200 sheep left-handed one day, just to prove he could.

In 1963 the Australian Wool Corporation asked Kevin to develop a standard method of shearing. His Tally-Hi technique reduced shearing times by up to thirty seconds a sheep and still influences shearing today. Tally-Hi was popularised in synchronised-shearing shows performed around the country by a group of elite shearers. At Batesworth Station near Penshurst, Victoria, Kevin set an Australian record tally of 346 sheep on 26 October 1965. His skill lives on in his son Rick, also a shearer, and daughter Deanne, who set an Australian women's record tally of 392 in 1990 (using a wide comb).

James Leslie (Les) Seary (1880–1955)
Les Seary was born in 1880 at Crookwell, New South Wales, the youngest, with his twin brother, Frank, in a large family. Later based at Winton, Queensland, he became one of the greatest left-

handers the industry has known, and was credited with shearing over 1300 in a week. The five Seary brothers claimed a world record in 1903 when they shore over 1200 in a day. Les shore for years at the Winton wool scour depot shed, where thirty shearers in some years shore over one million sheep. Gun shearers came from everywhere to shear against Les, but he outshore them all. He later drew a grazing block at Richmond, Queensland, and remained there until 1936. He then retired to Brisbane, where he passed away in 1955, aged seventy-four. He is buried in the Lutwyche cemetery. Asked if he knew a man named Les Seary, one western Queensland station owner said, 'Where I come from, he's more than a man – he's a legend.'

Anthony (Tony) Smith (1935–)
Tony Smith was born at Charlton, Victoria, in 1935. The family subsequently moved to Werribee where, after leaving school, Tony became a rouseabout in the depot shed owned by H. L. Baden Powell, later shearing there for 28 years.

Tony began shearing in 1952 at Manfred Station in the Riverina and his best tally was 248 at Darlington Point. His first competition, a learners' event at Deniliquin, created an interest in competitions that has lasted his whole life. A foundation member of the Shearing Competition Federation of Australia, Tony had a very successful competition career, winning the Victorian fine-wool title three times and the Australian fine-wool twice. He was a member of four Australian teams between 1974 and 1980, contesting the Golden Shears trans-Tasman test matches in Euroa and Masterton, New Zealand.

Tony retired from full-time shearing in 1980 to take a position as an instructor at the Melbourne College of Textiles, teaching students wool-classing and shearing as part of their course. He also helped to organise competitions and demonstrations at the Royal Melbourne Show and commenced judging, later conducting seminars for judges and becoming chief judge for the SCFA. Tony also provided the commentary at the Royal Melbourne and Geelong shows and many country competitions. When he finally retired in 1996 he was able to look back with pride over his life as a shearer, and his involvement with the wool industry.

William 'Deucem' Smith (1896–1947)

William Smith was an Aboriginal man from the Muruwari tribe of the Bourke area and first shore at Dunlop Station in 1912. Writer D'Arcy Niland told the story of his entry into the shearing world: 'While roustabouting, a dark, good-looking, curly-headed lad, Deucem, determined to turn shearer and cut 200 a day, declaring that he would deuce all the back-bent, bag-booted jumbuck-barbers of the shed. They referred good-naturedly to him as "two-em" then "Deucem" and the name stuck.'

Deucem shore in New South Wales and southern Queensland between 1912 and 1947. In 1936 he shore 290 stud merino two-tooth hoggets in one day at Mirrool Park, Griffith, New South Wales. One week he shore 1430 sheep with a broken right thumb. Deucem said his speed came from his 'knack of holding the sheep in position'. In a 1943 *Walkabout* article, D'Arcy Niland noted that he was 'rated as one of the greatest shearers in the world, who time out of number has eclipsed records and cleaned up the best of his natural competitors'. The Leonard brothers, who ran a contracting company in Yass, listed him in their register as one of the best in Australia. Deucem was such a valuable member of a shearing team that one of the brothers would drive up to Bass Hill in Sydney and bring him back to Yass when the Hume Highway was not sealed.

Deucem's reputation for quality- and quantity-work meant he was offered a lucrative contract to do demonstration shearing in England but he turned it down as it required shearers to refrain from drinking. Deucem was regarded as more than a champion – he was a phenomenon.

† Julian Alexander Salmon Stuart (1866–1929)

The formation of the shearing unions in 1886–87 heralded a time of turmoil and hatred between woolgrowers and shearers. The conflict came to a head in January 1891 when wool prices were falling. In a bid to reduce costs, growers resolved to break the power of the unions and introduced a new contract that would cut wages, force shearers to supply their own cutters and combs, and ration food. It was rejected. Shearers stopped work throughout Queensland, New South Wales and Victoria and set up strike camps. The largest camp of 4500 men, headed by poet and labour activist Julian Stuart, was near Barcaldine in Queensland. Non-union labour, including the officially despised Chinese, was brought in, inflaming the strikers, who resorted to vandalism, bullying and arson. In March, Julian was arrested. He and twelve other unionists were tried at Rockhampton, found guilty of conspiracy and jailed for three years with hard labour. Without leaders, and running out of money, the unions ended the strike on 14 June 1891. As a result woolgrowers agreed to seek arbitration on wages and conditions. Although Julian never again worked as a shearer, one of his finest moments was fighting for their rights.

William Robert (Mick) Thomas (1923–1998)

Mick Thomas shore from Queensland right down to Tasmania in his early years, and became known as 'the Big Whirly' and 'the Moree Idol'. He worked for various contractors including Grazcos and fellow Hall of Fame inductee Bert Lowrey, shearing across a wide area of northern New South Wales, from Wanaaring and Bourke in the west to Glen Innes and Walcha in New England, as well as down south in the Monaro region. Mick earned a reputation as the best quality- and quantity-shearer of his time and is still held in the highest regard as a legend of the Australian shearing industry. In 1963, he retired from shearing to become a representative for R. A. Lister. At this time the

Golden Lister overhead gear and handpiece and Olympic comb were the most popular combination in Australian shearing.

Mick was considered a freakish shearer by his peers. It was said that the rougher and tougher the sheep were, the more superior he was. Mick died on 15 August 1998 at Moree, and was posthumously inducted to the Hall of Fame by his family.

Shannon James Warnest OAM (1974–)

Shannon Warnest has established himself as the best fine-wool shearer of the current era, winning the Golden Shears world shearing championship in 2000 and 2005.

Shannon was taught the basics of shearing by his father, a good shearer himself. Such was Shannon's ability that he became keenly sought after by contractors, and spent several seasons in the heat and dust of South Australia's north, shearing up to 50 000 sheep per year. His first competition win was the intermediate event at the 1993 Royal Adelaide Show, and in 1996 he organised the first shearing competition at the Angaston Show. By 2009 he had won 154 open competitions with a best sequence of forty-four consecutive wins, and had won the South Australian championship nine times. He has best tallies of 325 lambs in eight hours in Australia, and 405 ewes and 421 lambs in nine hours in New Zealand.

Shannon has been a member of an Australian team at sixteen major competitions and has travelled extensively overseas. He won his first world title, and the world team championship with Ross Thompson from Inverell, New South Wales, in Bloemfontein, South Africa, and his second at Toowoomba, Queensland, where he and Daniel McIntyre from Glen Innes, New South Wales, also won the world team championship. Since the inception of Sports Shear Australia in 1995, Shannon has won the Australian national championship on seven occasions, the last six consecutively. Prior to this, he won ten Australian title events under the old Shearing

Competition Federation rules. In 2001 Shannon was invited to shear at the Commonwealth Heads of Government Meeting in Brisbane, and in September 2002 he received the Order of Australia medal for services to the wool industry.

Shearing Records

Details of latest records can be found at shearingworld.com (click on World Records), including records for teams of two or more shearers, 24-hour records and more.

1835   Tom Merely establishes the first authenticated daily record tally of thirty sheep shorn with blade shears in Western Australia.

1892   Jack Howe sets the world record of 321 merinos shorn with blade shears in seven hours and forty minutes at Alice Downs, Queensland. The record has stood for over 120 years.

1900   Jimmy Power machine-shears 315 sheep at Barenya Station. He was on track to eclipse Jack Howe's blade-shearing record but ran out of sheep before the end of the day.

1925   The 'mad eight' shear 2000 sheep in eight hours in Western Australia.

1949   Dan Cooper is the first to break Jackie Howe's record by machine-shearing 325 Corriedales at Glenara in Victoria.

1950   Ted Reick machine-shears 326 merinos at Brinard, Julia Creek, Queensland.

1965   Kevin Sarre machine-shears 346 merinos at Penshurst, Victoria.

1972   Brian Morrison, who had given up a career as an AFL footballer, shears 410 sheep in seven hours and forty-eight minutes, averaging 68.5 seconds per sheep. His fastest sheep was forty-three seconds, a world record.

1972   Bill Robertson shears 421 sheep at Glenaroua Homestead, Broadford, Victoria.

1979   David Ryan shears 501 merino lambs at Penshurst, Victoria.

1996   All records now verified by the World Sheep Shearing Records Society.

1999   Grant Smith sets the world record of 418 merino wethers in nine hours at Lake Coleridge, South Island, New Zealand.

2002   Dwayne Black sets the world record of 570 merino lambs in eight hours at Yeeramulla, Badgingarra, Western Australia.

2003   Cartwright Terry sets the world record of 466 merino ewes in eight hours at Westerndale Station, Western Australia.

2004   Dwayne Black sets the world record of 664 merino lambs in nine hours at Yeeramulla Park, Badgingarra, Western Australia.

2005   Dwayne Black sets the world record of 513 merino ewes in nine hours at Duck Farm, Kojonup, Western Australia.

2005   Dwayne Black sets the world record of 519 crossbred lambs in eight hours at Bendigo Showgrounds, Victoria.

2006   Samuel Juba sets the world record of 245 merino lambs shorn with blade shears in eight hours at Victoria West, South Africa.

2007   Emily Welch sets the world women's record of 648 lambs in nine hours at Waikaretu, New Zealand.

2007   Rod Sutton sets the world record of 721 strong-wool ewes in nine hours at Moketenui Station, Benneydale, New Zealand.

2007   Dion King sets the world record of 866 strong-wool lambs in nine hours at Moketenui Station, Benneydale, New Zealand.

2007   Dave Grant sets the world record of 356 merino wethers in eight hours at Hughenden, Queensland.

2010   Stacey Te Huia sets the world record of 603 strong-wool ewes in eight hours at Moketenui Station, Benneydale, New Zealand.

2010   Hilton Barrett sets the record for the fastest time to shear a single mature sheep – 39.31 seconds – at the Wellington Show in New South Wales.

2012   Ivan Scott sets the world record of 744 strong-wool lambs in eight hours at Opepe Trust Farm, Hawke's Bay, New Zealand.

2012   Kerri-Jo Te Huia sets the women's world record of 507 strong-wool lambs in eight hours at Te Hape Station, Benneydale, New Zealand.

References

Chapter 1 – Click Go the Shears

Bean, C.E.W., *On the Wool Track*, Angus & Robertson, Sydney, 1910.

Bonwick, James, *Romance of the Wool Trade*, Griffith, Farran, Okeden & Welsh, London, 1887.

Bossence, Willliam Henry, *Numurkah*, Hawthorn Press, Melbourne, 1979.

Brown, P.L. (ed.), *Clyde Company Papers*, Oxford University Press, London, 1941–71.

Bucolic, 'A North West Station', *The West Australian*, 6 December 1889, p. 3.

Drysdale, Anne, 'Diary', in *Clyde Company Papers*, ed. P.L. Brown, Oxford University Press, London, 1941–71.

Giles, Alfred, *Exploring in the Seventies*, W.K. Thomas, Adelaide, 1926.

Gill, Merri, *Weilmoringle: A Unique Bi-cultural Community*, Development & Advisory Publications of Australia, Dubbo, NSW, 1998.

Historical Records of Australia, vol. 1, pp. 45–51. Governor Phillip to Under-Secretary Nepean, 9 July 1788.

Mills, A.R., *Sheep-O!*, Reed, Wellington, New Zealand, 1960.

Ranken, G., *The Squatting System of Australia*, Bell & Bradfute, Edinburgh, 1875.

Spence, William, *History of the AWU*, Worker Trustees, Sydney, 1911.

Stuart, Julian, *Part of the Glory*, Australasian Book Society, Sydney, 1967, p. 104.

'To Shearers', *The Australasian*, 3 April 1886, p. 5.

Chapter 2 – The Rise of the Machines

Brown, P.L. (ed.), *Clyde Company Papers*, Oxford University Press, London, 1941–71.

Mills, A.R., *Sheep-O!*, Reed, Wellington, New Zealand, 1960.

'Wolseley's Sheep Shearing Machine', *The Sydney Mail*, 30 April 1887.

Chapter 3 – Shearers Unite!

'Bread or Blood', *National Advocate*, 24 April 1891, p. 2.

Canney, E.H., *The Land of the Dawning*, Remington, London, 1894.

Colonial Secretary's Files, 1891, Public Records Office, Brisbane.

Eynesbury, C.C., 'The Bare Belled Ewe', *The Bacchus Marsh Express*, 5 December 1891, p. 7.

'The Labour Difficulty', *The Queenslander*, 10 May 1890, p. 897.

'Prosecution for Seditious Libel', *The Brisbane Courier*, 12 March 1891, p. 5.

'The Queensland Shearers' Manifesto', *The Brisbane Courier*, 28 February 1891, p. 5.

'The Shearers' Dispute', *The Brisbane Courier*, 23 February 1891, p. 5 and 21 March 1891, p. 5.

'The Shearing Difficulty', *Riverine Herald*, 17 August 1888, p. 2.

'The Shearing Dispute', *The Brisbane Courier*, 3 February 1891, p. 5.

Chapter 4 – The Year of Living Dangerously

Gough, William, *Droving in the Early Days*, Riverina Press Office, Hay, New South Wales.

Lonsdale, Thomas, 'The Last of the Blade Men', *The Brisbane Courier*, 14 July 1923, p. 18.

Merrii, Wulla, *The Fire Stick*, Brisbane, 1893, pp. 80–1.

Pastoral Employers Association minutes 13 and 14 January 1891, John Oxley Library, AD5/1.

Queensland Legislative Assembly Debate, The Recent Labour Troubles, in *The Queenslander*, 11 July 1891, p. 1.

Supreme Court Conspiracy Trial, Smith-Barry to Blackwell, in *The Morning Bulletin*, 5 May 1891, p. 5.
United Pastoralists Association report 10–13 May 1892, opinion of S.W. Griffith, 12 May 1892, John Oxley Library.

Chapter 5 – The Rise of a Legend
'Australia's Champion Shearer', *The Richmond River Herald and Northern Districts Advertiser*, 11 July 1924, p. 3, reprinted from *The Barcoo Independent*.
Mills, A.R., *Sheep-O!*, Reed, Wellington, New Zealand, 1960.
'Queensland's Champion Shearer', *Warwick Examiner and Times*, 29 September 1894, p. 2.

Chapter 6 – Fire and Blood
'Attack on Dagworth', *The Brisbane Courier*, 22 September 1894, p. 2.
Paterson, A.B., *Three Elephant Power and Other Stories*, Angus & Robertson, Sydney, 1917
Paterson, A.B., 'Golden Water', ABC Radio Talk, 1938.
'Poisoning at Bowen Downs', *The Brisbane Courier*, 22 July 1895, p. 5.
Robertshaw, Charles, *Wirragoona: Tales of Australian Station Life*, Tytherleigh Press, Melbourne, 1928.
Spence, William, *History of the AWU*, Worker Trustees, Sydney, 1911.

Chapter 7 – Rise of the Middlemen
'Anarchists of the Bush', *The Bulletin*, 1 September 1894.
Commonwealth Arbitration Reports, 1907.
Spence, W.G., *Australia's Awakening*, Worker Trustees, Sydney, 1909.
Svensen, Stuart, *The Shearers' War*, Hesperian Press, Victoria Park, 2008.
The Worker, 13 May 1905, p. 7 and 12 March 1908, p. 29.

Chapter 8 – The Golden Fleece

Adam-Smith, Patsy, *The Shearers*, Nelson, Melbourne, 1982.
Archives of Business and Labour, ANU, Shearing Company Minutes, 11 August 1919 and 1 March 1920.
Barker, H.M., *Droving Days*, Pitman, Melbourne, 1966.
Bean, C.E.W., *On the Wool Track*, Angus & Robertson, Sydney, 1910.
The Brisbane Courier, 11 August 1917, p. 6.
Commonwealth Arbitration Reports, 1911 and 1926.
Munday, Don, *Tin Dog, Damper & Dust*, UWA Press, Nedlands, 1991.
Smith, G.A.W., *Once a Green Jackeroo*, Hale, London, 1975.
'The Wool Industry – Looking Back and Forward', *Year Book Australia*, ABS, Canberra, 2003.
The Worker, 9 September 1915; 17 February 1916, p. 20 and 16 October 1924, p. 10.

Chapter 9 – A Matter of Survival

The Brisbane Courier, 30 January 1931, p. 11.
Commonwealth Arbitration Reports, 1930.
Denning, Warren, *Caucus Crisis*, Cumberland Argus, Parramatta, 1937.
Gresser, Percy John, '1963 Weilmoringle and the Aborigine Cemetery', manuscript held by AIATSIS, Canberra.
Munday, Don, *Tin Dog, Damper & Dust*, UWA Press, Nedlands, 1991.
O'Malley, Rory, *Mateship and Moneymaking*, XLibris, Sydney, 2013.
Report of the Wool Advisory Commission, Queensland Parliamentary Papers, 1939.

Chapter 10 – Sunday Too Far Away

Adam-Smith, Patsy, *The Shearers*, Nelson, Melbourne, 1982.
Australian Financial Review, 23 August 1951, p. 1.
Barnes, Ern, *Easier Shearing*, Whitcombe & Tombs, Melbourne, 1955.
Day, Ian, 'Quick Go the Shears', *The Northern Times*, 1993.
Hardie, Jenny, *Nor'westers of the Pilbara Breed*, Hesperian Press, Victoria Park, 2001.

Hobson, Valerie, *Across the Board: Stories of WA Shearing*, Back Track Books, Lisbon, 2003.
Mills, A. R., *Sheep-O!*, Reed, Wellington, New Zealand, 1960.
The Worker, 24 August 1966, p. 49.

Chapter 11 – Whatever Makes it Easier
Adam-Smith, Patsy, *The Shearers*, Nelson, Melbourne, 1982.
The Advertiser, 13 June 1984.
AWU Conference Papers, 1985.
Commonwealth Arbitration Reports, Print F2060, p. 8–9; Print F5655, p. 85–6.

Chapter 12 – Wool Is Dead. Long Live Wool.
The Australian, 8 December 2012.
Lee, Tim, 'End of an Era', *Landline*, 26 September 2004, www.abc.net.au/landline/content/2004/s1206251.htm.
Lee, Tim, 'Final Bell Sounds for Giant of the Shearing World', ABC News Online, 16 February 2014, www.abc.net.au/news/2014-02-15/steve-handley-final-bell-sounds-for-shearing-giant/5261396.
Cripps, Sally, 'Loss of a Shearing Legend', *Queensland Country Life*, 13 February 2014.
Reader comments, 'Loss of a Shearing Legend', queenslandcountrylife.com.au, 13 February–25 April 2014.

Acknowledgements

This book would not have been possible without the assistance of a number of people, to whom I am sincerely grateful, including: photographer Andrew Chapman, for his generosity in sharing the impeccable contacts he's developed over a lifetime photographing the shearers and sheds of Australia (and for the use of some of his work); Rory McIlroy for his meticulous research into many aspects of shearing, in particular the wide-comb dispute; and the Shear Outback Museum for access to their extensive resource material built up over many years. Thanks also to the Flood family, Justin Campbell, Noel Johnson and Greg Charles for being so generous with their time and memories, photographers Scott Bridle and Chantel McAlister for use of their superb material, and journalists Tim Lee at the ABC and Sally Cripps at *Queensland Country Life* for use of their recent features. A special note of thanks to Peter Bridge at Hesperian Press for his many years of dedication to preserving the stories of WA's pioneers and for access to the publications that are the fruits of his labours. As always, I'm indebted to the team of professionals at Penguin, who can find diamonds in the rough and make them sparkle.

Every effort has been made to identify copyright holders for material used in this book but the publishers welcome any additional information.